ALSO BY SALLY HAYDEN

My Fourth Time, We Drowned

This Is Also a Love Story

A Reporter's Search for Goodness in a Cruel World

SALLY HAYDEN

SCRIBNER

New York Amsterdam/Antwerp London
Toronto Sydney/Melbourne New Delhi

Scribner
An Imprint of Simon & Schuster, LLC
1230 Avenue of the Americas
New York, NY 10020

For more than 100 years, Simon & Schuster has championed authors and the stories they create. By respecting the copyright of an author's intellectual property, you enable Simon & Schuster and the author to continue publishing exceptional books for years to come. We thank you for supporting the author's copyright by purchasing an authorized edition of this book.

First Scribner hardcover edition June 2026

SCRIBNER and design are registered trademarks of Simon & Schuster, LLC

Simon & Schuster strongly believes in freedom of expression and stands against censorship in all its forms. For more information, visit BooksBelong.com.

For information about special discounts for bulk purchases, please contact Simon & Schuster Special Sales at 1-866-506-1949 or business@simonandschuster.com.

The Simon & Schuster Speakers Bureau can bring authors to your live event. For more information, or to book an event, contact the Simon & Schuster Speakers Bureau at 1-866-248-3049 or visit our website at www.simonspeakers.com.

Manufactured in the United States of America

10 9 8 7 6 5 4 3 2 1

Library of Congress Cataloging-in-Publication Data has been applied for.

ISBN 978-1-6680-3462-0
ISBN 978-1-6680-3464-4 (ebook)

Scan here to get book recommendations, exclusive offers, and more delivered to your inbox.

To everyone who dares to love, and to my family.

*'It is love ... that is the true explanation of this world,
whatever may be the explanation of the next.'*

– Oscar Wilde[1]

Contents

Prologue

'*Whoever gives nothing, has nothing. The greatest misfortune is not to be unloved, but not to love.*'

– Albert Camus[1]

'*The fundamental weakness of Western civilisation is empathy.*'

– Elon Musk[2]

I write this with the hum of drones above me. In the past fortnight, Israel has killed more than one thousand people in Lebanon, where I currently live. The speed and force of this bombardment means it has been labelled one of the most intense aerial campaigns in contemporary warfare.[3] Everyone I meet is anxious: their words come in a rush before they stop talking mid-sentence; their bodies move a little too quickly and their minds too slowly. Like me, they have given up making plans, because no one knows what might happen in the next day or even the next hour. Many people have left the country, especially the relatively wealthy and those with other citizenships.

Regardless of anyone's views on the politics of what is taking place, it is frightening to live in a war zone. We, who remain, discuss the latest news in oblique terms and staccato voices. We make dark jokes that friends laugh too readily at, while leaving the impression that they might rather cry. Underpinning every-thing are varying levels of pain and privilege – some, including me, could still get away if they chose to and others will always be stuck here.

There is already a staggering division in terms of who and what has been lost; which communities are being targeted and which people most affected. Despite those inequalities, when we talk about our problems, one big anxiety is the same: how to respond to the incessant messages from loved ones, both inside the country and abroad, who are concerned about our wellbe-ing. We have suddenly become receptors for their worries, their conflicting advice and pointed reminders that what happens to us affects them too. No man, nor woman, is an island.

Shortly after I graduated from university in 2013, I began reporting internationally on human rights abuses. Much of my work since then has focused on tragedy – wars, upheaval, migration, separation – with an undercurrent of corruption and exploitation. I have witnessed the impact of airstrikes on buildings; seen bodies scarred from torture; heard testimonies about the countless cruelties which people inflict on each other. One aspect has never altered: the way the powerful seem able to disregard the humanity of those they deem to be beneath them. The levels of greed and self-interest can feel fathomless.

When I started out in journalism, I wanted to under-stand every aspect of the human condition. I did not know that, even while standing at a remove and striving to be an objective observer, you will be damaged by the violence and impunity that you witness. It is hard to explain the cumula-tive effect. It makes you angry but it also dulls you, the result being a blunting ennui that hardens into cynicism and a sense of futility.

Yet there has been another theme which I have observed regularly in situations I reported on, though I did not always stop to appreciate it: love. In the eye of war in Lebanon, in 2024, I saw it again in those distressed messages from abroad, and in my Lebanese friends' efforts to care and make provisions for their relatives still inside the country.

I was first drawn to writing more extensively about love because I had become profoundly sad, both as a result of the state of the planet, where inequality and ruthlessness seem ever on an upwards trajectory, and also because of the limitations and failures I perceived in my profession. My mind was struggling to process all that I had witnessed and how little impact came from exposing it. I felt desperate to be reminded that humanity has positive aspects to it, that we can be good to each other.

'I want to write a book of real-life love stories! They're going to be really happy and from all over the world,' I messaged a colleague through Facebook in early 2018. He had worked as my translator. Together we travelled through rural Gambia interviewing victims of the eccentric and brutal former president. Yahya Jammeh carried out literal witch hunts, commanding his soldiers to force elderly people to drink hallucinogenic liquids that in some cases killed them. We were investigating his dictatorship's legacy quite soon after its fall, when it still felt risky. Some Gambians assumed we were spies, and we spent one fretful night in a confined room listening as the family outside discussed what to do with us.

Our interviewees included a widower whose wife died after being targeted. Years later, the man remained too scared to say what had happened outright, relying on neighbours to explain it instead. His, and the other accounts we heard on that trip, sucked the air from my lungs. I found them difficult to write up afterwards, not knowing how to convey the raw sentiment visible in his face when his words were unforthcoming. It is not lost on me that there is an irony inherent in how reporters are expected to quickly grasp and convey the emotions of others, even as most of us methodically and deliberately shut off our own.

I have often worried that news reporting is dehumanising, reducing people, and the dense complexity of their lives, to basic facts and figures or overly simplistic and reductive headlines. That is inherent to the job: journalists are under time pressure to publish quickly, and space pressure to keep reports digestible, fitting them into radio bulletins, newspaper pages or television segments with limited space. Media summations of global issues are selective, highlighting only a few key threads, but life is more complicated than that.

Journalists undoubtedly have a role to play in restoring humanity to the public understanding of events – such as when we hear politicians making statements which ignore or obfuscate the direct lived experiences of vulnerable people. Yet we quote data and press releases more than personal testimonies; we move on to the next crisis before the last one has found any resolution.

Reportage can be cold and exacting. Journalism is the first draft of history, but it only offers fragments of a wider truth. What can go missing in that initial retelling is a much fuller tapestry of human behaviour, interactions, and the connections that drive them. Statistics do not tell us about someone's hopes and dreams, their skills and weaknesses, or who and what they live for. People are much more than the worst thing that has ever happened to them.

As a counterpoint to all of this, I wanted to look at crisis situations with reference to the role love has played in them.

Frequently, while listening to an account of something horrific, there will be a moment when I think to myself: 'this is also a love story.' I encounter love daily – more than fury, revenge, greed or abuses of power. This book is an attempt to honour that: charting romantic love, but also love for family and community, and the search for love and connection amid disaster. I looked back over reporting I have done in a number of historically fractured places, like Rwanda, Iraq and Syria, combining those accounts with new ones from countries including Ukraine, Japan and Ghana. Throughout, I have been moved by love's persistence in the direst of circumstances, and the ways I have seen it influence and guide people who are going through some of the most intense situations imaginable.

Those encounters pushed me to consider what crises reveal about love and the quest for it, whether the love is explicitly named or not. Love can be goodness, I determined. It can mean kindness, care or consideration, and can encourage bravery or hard work. It can propel demands of accountability for gross wrongdoing, and can be directed towards a group or community, rather than an individual. While it is clear that love does not conquer all, and that its presence does not override other sins, I discovered that love plays a crucial role in forgiveness and what follows after tragedy. I was reminded that people living through crises tend to be erudite about love's challenges because their love is being tested every day.

The result is probably not the happy book I had imagined. While that says something about my choices, it says more about the age we live in. Today, it feels like the world is burning. We are witnessing, in real time, the weight of agony inflicted on fellow humans; the collapse of global orders that at least paid lip service to lofty ideals of humanitarian law and basic freedoms; disregard for the health of the planet we all share. The dead rack up and the trauma mounts. Injustices have cut deeply.

Access to the internet, and specifically social media, means we should feel closer to people living far away from us than before. Instead, we see increasing levels of dehumanisation. Global systems become ever more unequal, shutting out the poor, oppressed and marginalised. We view livestreams as children are bombed, their faces coated the grey colour of concrete and their limbs torn off; their cries disregarded by politicians as the unavoidable collateral of combat. People in need risk everything to travel global migration routes towards safer or more prosperous countries, and when they drown in the sea, or die of thirst in the desert, western officials blame them for their own demise. We are watching a wholesale gutting of basic universal rights and dignities, foreign aid and international cooperation.

One inevitable reaction to this barrage of pain is to feel hopeless and lost, to close in on ourselves and tune out of frequencies that carry and amplify suffering. A 2024 study by the Oxford-based Reuters Institute found that almost four in ten people globally now selectively avoid the news, for example.[4] Reporters themselves are not immune from this phenomenon. But shutting ourselves off – for those who have that privilege – is not the right answer.

I have asked myself the same questions repeatedly. How can anyone live a comfortable life in this cruel world? How can there be such a disconnect between human experiences?

Most of the crises described in this book were manmade, including war, economic collapse and state-sanctioned repression. They took place amid a period of increased loneliness and atomisation in western society, and at a political moment when even the idea of having empathy for our fellow humans is under attack.

Might the world be a different place if we more regularly told news stories through the prism of love?

I believe you can read these accounts as love stories and this book as a meditation on love itself. When faced with abuse and barbarity, love feels like a form of resistance. Its existence can offer hope and inspiration, something to fight for and a goodness to hold on to.

Perhaps highlighting love amid crisis is also a plea for empathy. This is not a book about the powerful, but the grassroots: regular people getting by as their lives are shaped and jolted by forces outside of their control. I hope it will give readers some cause for reflection on the links that bind us all together, near and far.

A note on interviews:

Some names have been changed at the request of interviewees, or to protect their privacy and security.

Chapter 1

Ukraine: A wartime Christmas

> *'I'll wait.*
> *I'll wait both day and night.*
> *I'll wait forever, for your return.'*
>
> – Words written beside a mural of an embracing soldier and young woman, on a wall in Lviv, western Ukraine

> *'There is no romance in war . . . nothing like that. Only patience, understanding and support can save relationships.'*
>
> – A thirty-five-year-old IT worker and mother of two, whose husband is fighting on Ukraine's frontlines

Irina was attracted to Sergei, the man who would become her husband, as soon as she saw him: he was 'very handsome', with a 'tremendous moustache like Salvador Dalí'.

On their first date, she cooked him ham garnished with herbs and mustard. As Sergei ate it, Irina recalled, he began to moan 'in an indecent manner'. This was the first home-cooked meal Sergei had eaten in six months, though he did not disclose that at the time. 'I was so surprised,' Irina told me later. 'Until then, I was doing everything myself. I was very tough and I was lonely. When I was looking at him something melted in my heart, something female was coming back to me. I couldn't understand it, it was just so surprising that someone loved a usual ham in an unusual way.' She grinned. 'I took the occasion to lasso him.'

Irina and Sergei first met in September 2018, when he turned up at her workplace with a friend. They had much in common. Both had been married three times. Both had two children: a girl and boy. They liked 'silly films', spending time at the same beach, and, maybe most importantly, they were part of a community of former volunteers and veterans from the war in eastern Ukraine. Sergei and Irina had both been heavily involved there – Sergei as a fighter, while Irina was active in efforts to help the troops.

Within a month of meeting, they took a trip to Germany, marking Sergei's first time outside of Ukraine. It was a big milestone for him and Irina saw it as an early example of her positive influence, expanding his horizons. By November, they had registered a publishing company together. They named it 'Bilka', which means 'squirrel' and is a play on Irina's surname, Belotserkovskaya. It was part of a vision they had to publish books about the conflict in the east – particularly literature written by veterans.

I met Irina for the first time in Veterano Pizza, in central Kyiv. It was December 2023. Irina, curly haired and in her fifties, wore a white turtleneck and bright blue trousers, and greeted me with a radiant smile. At her suggestion, we ordered a 'Ukrainian pizza' ('Totally Ukrainian: lots of onion, lots of meat . . . a lot of cheese and a lot of cream'). She drank ginger tea.

Veterano Pizza was set up by veterans of the fighting in Ukraine's east. That conflict had begun in 2014, with Ukrainian forces battling Russia-backed separatists. It fluctuated in intensity, though never stopped completely. By early 2022, when Russia launched its full-scale invasion of Ukraine, more than fourteen thousand people had already died and more than one million were displaced.[1]

The restaurant's decor and drinks menu referenced those events. Table glass lay on top of bullet casings. Customers drank F-16 cocktails (bourbon, Amaro tincture, lemon and sugar syrup), Brothers in Arms (Irish whiskey, ginger ale and rosemary), or Sisterhood (Aperol, elderberry, lime and brut). There was the Crimea (gin, blueberry liqueur, elderberry, lavender and lemon) and the Donetsk Sour (bourbon, sugar syrup, lemon and smoky Scottish whisky). On the walls were framed medals, badges and photographs of soldiers posing on the battlefield, sometimes astride armoured personnel vehicles or tanks.

In years gone by, Irina had smuggled supplies to troops in eastern Ukraine – everything from towels, medication and bottled water to sniper rifles. *Daughter*, a book published by their publishing house Bilka, provides a fictionalised version of this experience: it was written by Tamara Duda, another former volunteer. It is surprisingly funny as well as desperately sad, and was celebrated as the BBC Ukrainian Book of the Year in 2019. 'This book is about love,' reads the introduction. It is also 'about magic, not the cheap kind you see on TV screens, but the real kind'.

Sergei fought in eastern Ukraine from 2015 to 2016. In the aftermath, decommissioned soldiers were supported in acquiring a new skill. He was naturally talented at drawing, and learnt how to apply permanent makeup: eyeliner, brows and lipliner. 'He was a marine, you can imagine, women loved him, he was doing very well in his business,' Irina said with pride. When the COVID-19 pandemic brought the world to a halt, they locked down together and focused on their publishing company. 'At least people were buying books. We didn't get so much money but we paid for the apartment and we even got a new cat.'

At the same time, the pair were becoming increasingly anxious. The 2019 election of Volodymyr Zelensky was a bad omen, in their minds, and it accelerated their decision to marry. Zelensky had begun his career as a comedian. On the Ukrainian TV show *Servant of the People*, he played a fictional Kyiv history teacher who unexpectedly becomes Ukraine's president when his surreptitiously filmed rant about corruption goes viral online. Zelensky was also the voice of the Ukrainian Paddington Bear and won Ukraine's version of *Dancing with the Stars*. Then stunningly – aged forty-one – he was elected as the actual president of Ukraine, with more than 73 per cent of the vote, while leading a party named after his television show.

In his early years in power, Irina and Sergei believe that Zelensky appeased Russia, through a misguided conviction that he could pacify strongman president Vladimir Putin and stop him from seizing more Ukrainian territory by force. Any lack of a firm stance against Putin put veterans from the east at elevated risk, the couple determined. So they decided that they should either leave the country or ready themselves for adversity, 'and one of the ways you prepare is to take care of your partner', Irina told me. 'We understood with Russia you can never achieve peace, and so we understood we had to prepare for war.'

In June 2021, they got married without fanfare or photographs. 'We just needed this document,' Irina said, pulling her marriage certificate out of her fluffy handbag. 'This document is always with me, I always carry it in my bag because I never know at which moment I will have to go to rescue him.'

The full-scale invasion began in the early hours of 24 February 2022. In Putin's words, it was a 'special military operation' with the goal of 'demilitaris[ing] and denazify[ing] Ukraine'. As civilians panicked, Ukrainian authorities made a strategic determination to preserve their stock of potential soldiers. From that day on, martial law was in force. The country's borders closed to the passage of Ukrainian males between the ages of eighteen and sixty, in anticipation that any of them could be called upon to fight. Only a limited number of men – those too old or with medical exemptions; fathers with three or more children; people who paid hefty bribes to corrupt officials or used illegal crossings – were among the two million Ukrainian refugees who streamed out of Ukraine over the next fortnight. In such a short period, the conflict was already forcing agonising, impossible choices and altering the course of everyone's lives. When days turned into months, then years, the consequences of those choices grew into widened chasms or strengthened bonds between Ukrainian couples, families, neighbours and communities.

As I spent time thinking about different types of love amid crisis, my attention turned towards the war on my birth continent. I had never been to Ukraine before and knew little about what life was like for the partners of people on the frontlines. I learnt that many of them were keen to speak, to chronicle how their lives had been upended and to explain how they were adapting to a new, never-wished-for reality. Some suggested their experiences and insights might be helpful for couples facing upheaval elsewhere. They were keen to find commonalities, to share wisdom and, through that process, to feel less alone.

By the time I arrived in Ukraine, in the run-up to Christmas 2023, the conflict was almost a stalemate, a war of attrition. It involved trench combat that felt remarkably akin to the world wars of the twentieth century, albeit with greater surveillance capabilities and the use of drones. The scale of the battlefield was almost incomprehensible: Ukraine's frontlines extended about 1,000 kilometres. Russia's fortified frontlines wrapped around Ukraine's north, east and south, at a length of roughly double that.[2] This distance would take around a month to cover by a person walking twelve hours a day – though anyone who attempted it would certainly be killed before they reached the finish line.

The longer the war went on, the more it appeared to benefit Russia, which had greater reserves of manpower and resources. There was a feeling that Russia was waiting it out; a sense, as more than one Ukrainian told me, that the countries supporting them would get tired and move on. Even at the peak of a much-hyped offensive on the southern front earlier that year, Ukrainian forces had only advanced around ninety yards each day.[3] As they withdrew, Russian forces planted explosives, leading some analysts to label Ukraine the most heavily mined country in the world.

Getting to Ukraine was no simple task. Due to airspace restrictions and the risk of being shot down from the sky, commercial airlines no longer served Ukraine, so I first travelled to Warsaw, in neighbouring Poland. There was a lot going on the day I arrived. After eight years of right-wing, populist leadership, Poland had a new government that would be led by Donald Tusk. On small screens in a central bus station, I watched his first speech to lawmakers. 'Only a united West can help Ukraine win in the fight for democratic values,' said Tusk, a former president of the European Council. 'The attack on Ukraine is an attack on all of us . . . I will demand help for Ukraine from day one.'

European ministers were arriving for a summit in Brussels, where right-wing populist Hungarian prime minister Viktor Orbán had threatened to halt a €50 billion support package meant for Ukraine and to block the beginning of formal talks related to Ukraine joining the EU. In Washington, DC, Zelensky was scheduled to meet US president Joe Biden, in an effort to shore up support. Overall, I read, there had been an 87 per cent fall in new aid commitments from the international community towards Ukraine compared to the previous year.[4] If more military aid was not approved, analysts suggested, Ukraine would lose the war. Russia already occupied nearly 20 per cent of Ukrainian territory. Ben Hodges, the former head of US forces in Europe, told CNN's chief international anchor Christiane Amanpour that the conflict was at a 'tipping point' and the Kremlin had a 'long war strategy'.

That week, as Kyiv faced the most intense missile bombardment in months, a video of Putin drinking champagne at a Moscow award ceremony spread online.[5] In it, he said Ukraine had no future. 'When the free world hesitates, that's when dictatorships celebrate,' Zelensky proclaimed in his own speech in the US.[6]

Hours before I boarded a bus to Lviv, a city in western Ukraine, the country's top phone network Kyivstar was hacked and its infrastructure partially destroyed, with around twenty-four million users affected. Ukraine's intelligence agency said it could have been a Russian operation. 'This is a war, it takes place not only on the battlefield, it also takes place in virtual space,' said Kyivstar boss Oleksandr Komarov. It was a reminder that the perimeters of modern fighting were ever shifting. I wondered whether my phone would continue working and warned my family that I might be out of contact for a while.

Everyone on the bus was female. In the early hours of Wednesday, 13 December I disembarked with these women of all ages, groggy from sleep, arms pulling coats closer to their sides as protection against the frigid air. We showed our passports to a gruff Polish border guard, then lumbered back onto the vehicle to drive a while further. At the next stop a young, blonde, khaki-clad Ukrainian border guard stepped on board and peered at me curiously. 'You know Ukraine is at war? You not afraid?' she asked.

'The bomb shelter is in the basement,' declared the receptionist, hours later, when I finally checked into a hotel in Lviv. Only then did I use Wifi to download the recommended app, 'Air Alert', onto my phone. It would act as my own personal alarm if an air raid warning was issued for the city, and was surreally voiced by Mark Hamill, the actor who became famous in the late 1970s for playing Luke Skywalker in the *Star Wars* films. A siren sounded at the beginning of a raid, and when it ended – anything from thirty minutes to three or more hours later – Hamill's voice announced: 'Attention, the air alert is over. May the force be with you.'

That night, Kyiv – hundreds of kilometres away – was hit by a series of ballistic missiles. While the air defence systems intercepted them, debris landed on the city, injuring at least fifty-three people, including six children.[7] The following evening, I boarded the night train to Kyiv, falling asleep to the sound of the engine propelling us along the tracks and my unseen cabinmate's snoring, and waking up to the sight of snowy trees rushing by.

I was to stay in a friend's apartment. It was located behind Buena Vista, a cocktail bar known for its live music and dance parties. In March 2022, Buena Vista also became famous as the last and only bar open in Kyiv – a place where visiting journalists wore flak jackets as they gathered for a hot meal and most likely an alcoholic beverage. Half of the city's population had fled, not certain whether the capital would soon fall into Russian hands. Yet Kyiv stood strong. By the time I arrived there, in December 2023, its population had returned to the pre-invasion figure of 3.6 million people.[8] Around 300,000 were Ukrainians displaced from other parts of the country, replacing those among Kyiv's original inhabitants who had left the city or the country altogether.

Sergei volunteered to fight the very day that Russia launched its full-scale invasion. Like many former soldiers, he showed up for duty in his military uniform; other volunteers, less experienced, were wearing tracksuits and sneakers. City commanders handed each of them a submachine gun and four magazines, Irina told me. In the pizzeria, she took out her phone to show me photographs from that time. 'This is the volunteer centre, the uniform Sergei had. This is the missile attack on Kyiv on the twenty-fifth of February 2022 . . . These are my first friends who died. This man and woman, a husband and wife, they died near Kyiv when both of them tried to stop a convoy of tanks.'

In those initial days, people assembled whatever they could find for the fighters. Volunteers, who had originally mobilised during the war in the east, gathered tourniquets, sleeping mats, food and crutches, and extracted bulletproof vests from storage. Civilians rushed to evacuate. Irina helped her friend's daughter board a train in Kyiv's main station. It was a desperate scene, she said. Tickets became redundant with crowds crushing together, standing for hours in a bid to make it to safety. Sergei suggested Irina leave Ukraine completely. 'I will ask you only once, and maybe I know the answer,' she remembered him saying. Irina brushed this proposition away. Her choice to stay was a pivotal moment for their relationship, she would say later: a mark of her unwavering dedication to her husband and their country.

Early on, Irina grew tired of being inside bomb shelters. She turned off the air raid alerts on her phone. Out of her handbag she now pulled a penknife, torch and tourniquet, a slim device of cloth and plastic used to staunch catastrophic bleeding.

'Since the twenty-fourth of February, I always carry these three items with me,' she said. 'I know exactly how long someone can stay without food: one month. If the rescue comes within a month they'll take me out of the wreckage for sure.'

Her role in her relationship morphed: she became an 'anchor' for her husband. 'Normally people, they're very simple beings. But with such a difficult situation, difficult conditions, comes a time when they really decide whether they need each other or not,' she told me. 'Maybe in Ukraine, now, people know much better than anywhere else what a couple is.' Ukraine, she clarified, is 'like anywhere, a man can leave a woman or a woman leave a man, they can divorce. But those that stay together, they keep this connection based on pure love. That's all it is. For me it's so easy to understand.'

Strictly, Sergei should get thirty days away from the army annually, Irina said – but soldiers and their leave is an inexact science. Often, he was suddenly allowed home with no notice. Scheduled holidays could be cancelled at the last minute. It was the same for everyone fighting – managers in Ukrainian businesses told me they made allowances for staff needing unexpected, immediate breaks to spend with partners given time off from duty. How could they say no?

In October 2023, Irina travelled for hours just to see Sergei for twenty minutes at a petrol station, where he stopped en route to a new base. That November, they spent seven days together: the break a reward for his completion of officer training. Irina was hoping to visit Sergei again the week we met. She planned to travel to a town sixty kilometres from the frontlines, where they would spend two days together. But he ended up in hospital instead – he had headaches, high blood pressure, and had already suffered five concussions from shelling, she said. Any further leave had to be postponed.

Sergei was well respected in the army, where he progressed from private to lieutenant. 'He has a company of soldiers and he is responsible for many lives,' Irina said. An unexpected consequence was that his desire to take breaks declined: he argued that being with Irina put him in the wrong mindset for leading a battalion. It made him too 'relaxed'.

Transitioning between fighting and civilian life was difficult. Irina compared soldiers coming back from the frontlines to 'a wild animal' when it is put into a cage and retreats into one corner. 'Their reaction,' she said, 'is to control their perimeters, to be alert all the time. They don't want to go out of their apartment, they stay at home for two or three days. When they go out they are afraid to look at people, they feel discomforted to stay in masses of people. Only on the fourth day they can go to see their mother or anyone else.'

Even for soldiers on leave, the lament of war underlaid everything. During Sergei's last break, the couple felt compelled to pay their respects to fallen fighters in a Kyiv cemetery. Afterwards, they visited the children and wife of a commander Sergei knew who had died of a heart attack. These courtesies were simultaneously imperative and heartbreaking.

In 2023, Ukraine was facing its second Christmas since the war began. It was also, notably, the first one that Ukraine would celebrate on 25 December in more than a century. The government passed legislation officially moving Christmas Day from the traditional Orthodox date of 7 January, in what was seen as another break from Russia and Russian influence. The majority of churches endorsed the move.

Martial law meant employers were not required to give staff a holiday and overt celebrations did not feel appropriate. Everyone I spoke to seemed uncertain how cheerful they could or should be. Many people did not feel like celebrating anyway. But there were several huge, decorated Christmas trees around Kyiv city centre, and various iterations of Santa Claus. The frequent repetitions of 'Carol of the Bells' by buskers injected an affecting soundtrack into the fraught atmosphere. The carol is based on the song 'Shchedryk' by Ukrainian composer Mykola Dmytrovych Leontovych, which was first performed at Christmastime in Kyiv in 1916. In 1921, Leontovych was shot dead by a Soviet state security agent.

Bars, restaurants and coffee shops were open as normal, with mild adjustments from pre-war times. A Moscow Mule was now a Kyiv Mule. I could order a coffee, but also a 'patriotic cappuccino', made with what a waiter advised me was anchan, to turn it blue, and a yellow spice, which I believe was turmeric, marking out the Ukrainian coat of arms on top. A shop selling Christmas tree decorations included among them miniature plastic soldiers holding rifles or cats, their arm patches painted in Ukraine's blue and yellow.

My kind translator was a middle-aged man who usually interpreted for UN conferences and people negotiating military contracts, so interviewing people was a welcome change in topic, he said. It was an appreciated distraction as well, given that he, too, would be separated from his wife for Christmas.

I was surprised that, despite constant news updates and the presence of ubiquitous khaki-clad soldiers, the war could feel far away in Kyiv. This rankled with some Ukrainians. Several times during that visit, I passed a Christmas tree outside a bakery. It was made of spent ammunition shells collected at the frontlines. Beside it was a QR code, which linked to a site taking donations for military drones. Text written on an information label to one side read 'Live, work, celebrate. But remember reality. This

A Christmas tree made of spent ammunition shells, pictured in Kyiv in December 2023.

Christmas tree is our window into reality. The war in Ukraine continues and it should become the business of the whole society.'

In Suite13 bistro bar, one lunchtime, I met thirty-five-year-old brand designer Olha and her husband Andrii, who was one year older. A series of Christmas songs played in the background: The Pogues' 'Fairytale of New York'; Shakin' Stevens' 'Merry Christmas Everyone'; The Eagles' 'Please Come Home For Christmas'.

Olha had short red hair and delicate features. Andrii, who was home for a medical checkup, was slim, still wearing his soldier's uniform. He had joined the military just over a year before, marking the first time the couple had spent a day apart since meeting, they said. Both came from the port city of Kherson, but they moved to Kyiv to study and were introduced through a mutual friend. They had been married for eleven years, and together for thirteen.

'Could you tell me a bit about your experience since the war started?' I suggested.

'When the Great War started,' Andrii interjected. 'Sometimes we call it a Great War. Because of the conflict [in the east] since 2014, though that was in a smaller area.'

A systems administrator by profession, Andrii joined the military with a friend's encouragement – the troops needed radio, digital mobile connections and IT support. 'Focus', the brand of his favourite bicycle, became his 'call sign': the name other soldiers referred to him by. Deciding to sign up was 'terrifying', he said, crediting the other 'guys' in the military for helping him. Their vow to stand together reassured him, though, 'as it turns out, there are a lot of things to be scared of. Constant artillery, fighting, constant aerial fighting, a lot of artillery from the Russian side. It was a total nightmare.'

Andrii asked why I was writing about love in the midst of all this, and nodded approval when I tried to explain how I felt news reporting can be reductive, that human relationships are stripped out. 'You're doing great work because the world needs to know what's going on here from all sides, all spheres of our lives,' he said. He knew soldiers who had been fighting for eighteen months without rest. In four days, Andrii too would return to the frontline and likely stay for months. 'There are no easy places on the combat line now,' he said, but where he was headed for – Klishchiivka, near Bakhmut – was possibly the 'most difficult'.

Olha rested her hand on Andrii's arm or leg while he spoke. At other times, their elbows touched on the table. Both had tattoos extending up their arms and big silver rings on their fingers. I am not sure whether I believe in this concept, but looking at them I saw souls entwined. They seemed to be soothing each other simply through their presence.

'The first time, when I got back home, it was very difficult to adapt to civil life,' Andrii explained. 'When you realise that there are no dangers, this is a quiet place, but your brain, your mind cannot get back. It's a difficult process. For example, the loud sounds of transport and the streets, even in your flat. You become aware in one moment, you're trying to find where the danger is coming from.'

'We have a tram line near our house and it's quite loud,' said Olha. 'The first days after Andrii came home from the frontline . . .'

'I was very nervous,' recalled Andrii. 'I woke up, I started to get nervous because the sound is similar to artillery. There was some difficulty with socialising, I felt uncomfortable in crowded places. The main problem was that I thought that if artillery was shot there would be a lot of dead people, a lot of wounded, injured, and a lot of death, and that scared me.' During his medical checkups, he found the sight of young men missing limbs in the hospital unbearably upsetting. 'They just got their lives broken. They can't return to their life before the invasion, I don't know how to explain it.'

When they were on the frontlines or close to them, I knew, Ukrainian soldiers commonly lived in bunkers together, or moved between fox holes and trench networks. On just one seven-week mission, ninety-nine soldiers went to defend one strategic patch of forest, close to Kupyansk – a frontline around five hundred metres wide. Sixty-six were seriously wounded by the end of the mission, and ten were killed.[9]

'It's the price we're paying for staying free,' said Olha. 'A few of my female friends have joined the army and I think it might be the way for me. Maybe, why not?'

'Honestly, I don't want Olha to go there,' said Andrii. 'I think it's enough, there's one crazy person in our family, and it's me.'

'It depends on the situation in our country,' interjected Olha.

I suggested that it might become even harder to see each other if she joined up.

'I don't think it could get worse,' responded Olha. 'I feel like I live my life but at the same time I, for example, have no left arm . . . I don't know how to explain it another way but I must learn how to live without a part of my body.'

Andrii said he was continually impressed by her strength. 'Anything can happen. This is life, this is war, unpredictable. So every moment, every hour, every day that we're together has become priceless. And as I always say to Olha, she is the best thing in my life, the best thing that's happened to me. I'm grateful to, I don't know, this God, some higher thing that I met Olha and we became a couple.'

Olha worried about her husband, but 'you cannot be frightened all of the time. You need to function.' She is a talented artist, and sold drawings to raise money for the military: designs which incorporated both animals and weaponry. Cycling long distances used to help her support what she called her *kukuha* or 'cuckoo' – her mental health – but she was diagnosed with an autoimmune disease and could not manage that any more. Her latest tactic was working long hours to distract herself.

The war affected Olha's other relationships. She stopped communicating with friends who moved abroad. 'When we try to talk I don't know what to say. We see the same things in very different ways.' Experiences she grew accustomed to were 'awful' to them. She spent her time trying to forget, while they seemed intent on remembering. 'Sometimes it makes me angry. I just want to talk about their children, about my cats, and they

Olha and Andrii in a restaurant in Kyiv, in December 2023.

want to talk about war, about death, about the situation, about occupation. I don't want to talk about it . . . I'm here now. I don't want to talk about it because I'm in the middle of it.'

In any conflict zone, there are always frontlines and safer spaces. In Kyiv, some lives continued with a semblance of normality. And maybe that was necessary. The income tax money raised from Ukrainian employees doing ordinary jobs funded the war effort. Businesses kept the economy, and therefore the military, ticking over.

The language people used could feel distancing too. Ukrainians, I realised quickly, often avoided saying 'Russia' at all. Some said this was done for self-protection, or, more commonly, that it was a gesture to deny legitimacy and respect. 'Our northern neighbour', 'the enemy', 'our crazy neighbour' and 'the bad people' were terms I heard in Kyiv, along with the *Lord of the*

Rings-derived 'Orcs' for Russians, and 'Mordor' for Russia itself. 'We need to protect ourselves psychologically from thinking about them,' one man explained.

For civilians, war is heard more often than seen. The air raid sirens regularly dashed attempts at mental self-preservation. They sounded that Christmas Day I was there, as they had on other days. The following happened when they went off:

First, the air alarm app sounded on my phone. If alone in my apartment in Kyiv, I felt drawn towards the window – against all advice to avoid glass – as if seeking confirmation that it was to be believed. Over a landscape veiled and softened by snow, I would listen to the wailing start up across the city.

Next, I checked specific channels on messaging app Telegram, where well-informed experts shared what they knew. What was the risk, exactly? A MiG-31K could potentially be carrying hypersonic Kinzhal missiles. Did it sound like a unmanned aerial vehicle – a drone? What I thought was a car revving one night turned out to be a Shahed, the specific type of drone nicknamed 'moped'.

Were there particulars about where exactly it was heading? That might influence any decision about whether to ignore the warning completely or to follow the 'two wall rule', putting two walls between myself and the outside. Many people hid in bathrooms; I retreated to an inner hall, though this could mean sitting or lying on a cold floor for hours. It made more sense than going to a bomb shelter. Not all shelters were open, and walking on the streets could prove more dangerous than staying put. Several people told me the story of the two women and a nine-year-old girl who were killed trying to enter a locked bomb shelter earlier that year.[10]

By then, Kyiv had a good (if noisy) air defence system. So an explosion might be a positive sign that armaments were being shot out of the sky, prevented from damaging key infra-structure. Without adequate air defence, the previous winter had been bleak. There were electricity blackouts and stretches without running water (one friend even advised me to fill the bathtub so I had stocks in case it happened again). Despite the improvement, falling shrapnel, from when an attack was halted, still posed a significant risk.

Lessons on survival were being adopted across the country. People learnt that, if there was bombing, opening their mouth could reduce damage to their organs. Keeping windows ajar, or covering them with criss-crossed tape, could prevent a rush of pressure from shattering the glass or hold back shards which might otherwise slice through a body.

In Kyiv, the air raid sirens went off so frequently that it was difficult to adhere to them all. They often sounded at night, right as I was about to sleep. I tried to imagine how Ukrainians had put up with nearly two years of this: work and rest interrupted; businesses opening and closing; buildings being evacuated. I wondered how children matured in this febrile environment and what would be the long-term impacts on them.

After the terror of each night, the sun rose. Through my window, I would watch the winter sky get lighter beyond the swirling clouds. Anxiety was replaced by the hope of a new day, even as I checked a summation online:

On the night of December 21, #Ukraine's air defense shot down 34 out of 35 Russian #Shahed kamikaze drones, according to the Ukrainian Air Force.

Irina wanted me to properly understand the history of the war, so she took me on a tour of central Kyiv. It was a city where she could trace her own family back six generations through the cemeteries. Our first stop was Independence Square, also known as the Maidan. Snow fell gently. Red and white tape marked patches where the pathways were slippery or there was danger from tumbling icicles, which hung like daggers from the edges of many buildings.

Both Irina and Sergei had been involved in the 2014 Euromaidan protests, which were prompted by President Viktor Yanukovych's decision not to sign an association agreement with the European Union. It was a turning point for the country. A violent police reaction only bolstered widespread support for change, propelling growing numbers of Ukrainians to join in. Back then, Irina would go to work, then stay on the square all night. 'When you came to the Maidan you did everything. You built a new wall with your own hands,' she recalled. 'People will tell you "do this, this, this". You will say "I can boil tea, I can bring sandwiches", and you do what they tell you.'

Now dusk was falling. The street lights made the snow-filled sky glow orange. We walked to the golden-domed St Michael's monastery – St Michael the archangel is the guardian of military personnel, among others. During the Euromaidan protests, wounded people – driven or carried from Independence Square – slept inside. Emergency surgeries were performed in an outer building; the injured were afraid of being arrested if they presented at state-run hospitals. After the full-scale invasion began, ceremonies for soldiers killed in action took place there.

Another square, close by, had become a kind of living museum. Crowds gathered beside a blue and yellow train. A sign said the train had saved ten thousand lives by providing the last available evacuation route from the city of Irpin, as the Russians took over in March 2022. It was eventually hit by a missile, derailing two wagons. Behind, also on display, were burnt-up armoured personnel carriers. To the left were marble statues. Among them was tenth-century ruler Princess Olga, with the contemporary addition of a bullet-proof vest.

Nearby was a 'memory wall' lined with photographs: hundreds of faces of the dead, mostly men and some women. 'When my husband comes we always come here,' Irina said. 'We have a tradition to come see friends and tell them "I found you" to pay tribute'. The exact casualty figures among Ukraine's soldiers were being kept secret, though a Reuters report had recently put the number of Russia's dead and injured troops at roughly 315,000 – an incomprehensibly high figure.[11] 'Ukrainian propaganda is very good,' a foreign volunteer told me, right after I arrived in the country. 'We obviously don't want to be telling everyone all the time about how many guys are dying every day. It's incredibly demoralising. [But] everyone knows

Photographs on the 'memory wall' in Kyiv showing Ukrainians killed during the war.

because everyone has family or friends on the ground. So they understand the level of losses.'

The monastery's bells began to ring. 'Aren't they handsome?' Irina asked me, still gazing at pictures of the deceased. 'I want to find my friend but they are so numerous it is hard.'

We trekked further, through dark streets now, to a park that overlooked the city, then down through an area once popular with tourists who bought trinkets and souvenirs from stalls. Music emanated from St Andrew's Church, where, inside, a woman in a black puffy coat was approaching a nun in a black habit to request prayers for her soldier husband. We withdrew and entered a restaurant.

A doorman took our coats, now sodden from melting snow. The lampshades were traditional, white and embroidered with flowers. We were served *pashtet*, or chicken liver pâté, and borscht, the soup – mine arrived inside a cabbage, a special treat for the foreigner.

When Sergei came home, he made borscht, Irina told me. He ate just one serving and the rest lasted her two weeks, its flavour improving with time. 'That is the best borscht for me,' she extolled, before asking if I wanted to hear what it is like to be lonely.

Around a year into the full-scale invasion was when Irina realised she was struggling. She described it as a severance: an interval when she stopped paying attention to her body because of the thoughts swirling around her head. She gained twelve kilograms. Her joints began to hurt.

'I understood that if I wanted to help my husband and support my husband I needed to take care of myself too,' she said, about the aftermath. 'I stopped crying because I couldn't understand how I could cry when the men were living in terrible conditions . . . It would be better to be strong. That's why I smile, especially when I'm in front of the cameras.'

With her husband, Irina developed a code: 'red lipstick'. It meant putting on a brave face, gleaning some enjoyment and not succumbing to misery, even though there was so much to be miserable about. It symbolised the fact that, while circumstances were abject, it was better not to complain or wallow. Life goes on: life was what the soldiers were fighting for, after all.

On the phone, Sergei would ask her: 'When will you buy your red lipstick?' If Irina was sad, he would tell her to put on red lipstick 'and go on the street, let other men see you and look at you so you feel well dressed and you feel comfortable and I don't stay here in vain'.

Irina confessed that she now had a saved 'database' of photographs of her smiling with red lips, to send to Sergei when he requested a selfie of her. 'When you talk to the other ladies, ask everyone what they do to keep afloat, because everyone has a different answer,' she advised me. 'Unfortunately each of us has to develop their own method to fight their depression . . . This is an open situation and no psychotherapy can end it . . . We have our husbands who risk their lives every day in dangerous conditions . . . we needed to get accustomed and there is no other way out. The majority of women waiting for someone, they're taking antidepressant pills. I'm proud of myself because I don't take them or drink much either. I can drink a bit of white wine but otherwise it's too tempting.'

The day before we met, Irina found herself crying at an episode of the television adaptation of Agatha Christie's Miss Marple detective stories: 'It was a happy ending, everyone was kissing.' Sergei called her at that moment and she told him she was lonely. 'He replied: "you're not alone, you're not alone".'

Nearly every day, Irina managed to speak to Sergei through WhatsApp calls. 'The most difficult is when he goes away, sometimes he says he won't be online for four days, it means he's gone somewhere with no connection.' She constantly checked his 'last seen' setting, and messaged asking how things were going, or sent him photographs of their cats and good news about their publishing company. Sometimes he was so busy or exhausted that he simply replied with a plus sign: '+'. Irina clung to her phone in Sergei's absence: she slept beside it and took it to the toilet. 'It's terrible when I miss a call. He wants me to talk to him, to help him, and if I miss it I never know what could happen.'

Like everyone else, Sergei and Irina had aspirations for their life after the war. Theirs were all related to travel. She hoped to go to London, he wished for Paris; they both envisaged flying to the US 'to take a big American car and drive along big American roads'. Before the full-scale invasion, they visited Italy, on a trip related to their publishing business. Now they fantasised about buying a small house on the coast and retiring there.

'You always have to dream about something. People who are dreaming in Ukraine, they are very tough optimists,' Irina told me. But though a conclusion to this war had once seemed inevitable, 'the end is feeling further and further away. The longer we continue, the less we can imagine the end.'

The following day was Sergei's birthday. Irina posted on Facebook, alongside a photo of the couple face to face and holding hands, a mural of wings behind them.

Today my beloved Sergei was born.

I told a journalist from Ireland about him all day yesterday and barely covered a small part of our stories and my feelings.

Love, as it turns out, is a pretty tricky thing . . .

Now that we are so far apart, there are so many things that are important.

To be strong, to carry on, in spite of doing their own thing, each in their own place (you know, my happiness, how I would like to exchange places with you so that you can rest a little bit), to think about each other, to wish, to protect from despair, to keep in touch, to enjoy every photo you share and to dream of growing old together.

Be proud of each other.

This is what it means to love.

To be the best version of ourselves.

Thank you my love for my wings!

Come back to me alive and well, as far as possible, and with Victory!

Thank you because under tension, constant fear for you, under fatigue, loneliness, somewhere deep inside me lives happiness – my source of strength and inspiration!

I'm happy because I have someone to wait for.

In an office in central Kyiv I sat with Artem Denysov, the board head of Veteran Hub, in a room usually used for public events. The organisation was set up to support former soldiers and their families. Community is vital and networks are essential, Artem emphasised. People need to know they are not alone.

Veteran Hub provided a range of services, including running peer-to-peer support groups and groups for family members. They also produced guidance documents[12] and recorded podcasts, including *Kohany*, or 'The Loved Ones', detailing the stories of spouses affected by the war. Through it, Artem said, they tried not to dispense advice, but to highlight diverse experiences incorporating both suffering and brightness.

A common mistake was to treat families just as caregivers, Artem said. 'They also have their own experience and it's hard to say . . . it could be more traumatising.' While a soldier could be wounded or killed on the frontline, Artem posited, at least they have some agency. 'When you're sitting at home with the phone in your hands, you cannot influence anything, you don't have any information.'

When men and women volunteered in the early days of the conflict, they were motivated by the conviction that it was the correct thing to do. They may not have realised the length of that commitment. By late 2023, the average age of Ukrainian soldiers was estimated at around forty-three – making it a notably older fighting force than existed elsewhere.[13] Changing skilled personnel is difficult to do without damaging the war effort, military experts say. The 'one hundred per cent thing' soldiers lose is 'time', especially with their families, said Artem – who volunteered with a medical battalion when the full-scale invasion started.

Preparation needs to begin early for demobilised soldiers to be supported once the war ends, when attention will likely turn to rebuilding and infrastructure, he argued. There are a host of risks associated with inadequate mental health provisions, including an increase in domestic violence rates, and failure to identify and protect victims. 'With soldiers seen as heroes defending the country, there is a reluctance to criticise those who are also abusers,' noted a March 2023 article in *TIME* magazine.[14]

In a separate but related concern, the war had forced a new gender distinction. While women signed up, they were in the minority. Others, whose husbands were fighting, worried that their relationship dynamic had permanently shifted and potentially become regressive. They cared for children alone and performed other traditional gender roles more than before, including tasks like cooking and clothes buying, which some would not have been willing to do completely solo before. They felt they could not always speak their minds, because there was no space for negativity or disagreement when a struggle was under way for their country's very existence.

'I understand that during the war my life is devoted towards helping him and maintaining our family,' said forty-six-year-old culture manager Liudmyla Fit, who had resolutely refused to take her husband's name when they married twenty-three years before. The couple previously maintained a healthy relationship dynamic because 'we both love freedom,' she told me, toying with her wedding ring as we spoke. Yet she worried that her husband would expect her to continue behaving in a more traditional, conservative way when peace returned, whereas she was longing to feel unconstrained again.

In the run-up to Christmas in Kyiv, I attended various performances. One was an end-of-year concert at Kyiv's Opera House. Ballerinas pirouetted across the stage. Singers emoted in front of colourful backdrops, their voices containing a level of passion which words often fail at. It was transcendent and surreal, odd and yet meaningful, to see art continuing amid war.

The following day I went to a different kind of show: a Vogue battle. For the uninitiated, this is a competition which sees two people at a time face off in categories including dance, fashion, and the striking of poses. A disco ball spun above us as an MC urged on contestants dressed in sequins, feathers, leather or lingerie. They twisted and contorted as the judges deliberated and the crowd roared. This event, like many taking place across Kyiv, was a fundraiser for the Ukrainian military.

After the competition ended, the dance floor was democratised, the audience spreading exuberantly across it. One of the most striking dancers was tall and long haired, his movements crisp and purposeful, glowing lights strung around his neck. Maxim Potapovych was a communications manager with the organisation Ukraine LGBT+ Militaries for Equal Rights. We had spent an hour, earlier that week, sitting in a bustling bar discussing love and relationships. In Ukraine, same-sex marriage was not allowed. That meant the partners of those who died fighting, or who were captured by Russia, lacked the right to be informed about their loved ones' fate. They would not receive state compensation, or even have a say in where those they loved were buried. So the war had fuelled calls for equal rights for LGBTQI+ couples.

For non-heterosexual Ukrainians, Maxim said, 'it's still difficult to hold hands in the streets.' Maybe attitudes were shifting. More than twenty-eight thousand people signed a petition, months after the full-scale invasion began, calling on the government to legalise same-sex marriage. President Zelensky responded saying that the constitution – which specifies that marriage is between a man and a woman – could not be changed during wartime. Might civil partnerships be an alternative? A draft civil union law was introduced in March 2023 and the government vowed to approve it. Ukrainian TV stations even changed their logos to rainbow colours. The war offered a 'window of opportunity' for reforms, even amid heartbreak, Maxim suggested.

Anti-LGBTQI+ rhetoric was being weaponised by Russia, along with everything else, he told me. If Russia managed to occupy the whole of Ukraine, the outlook was not good for his community. 'Not a lot of our society understand that a lot of the roots of homophobic attitudes, especially among the elderly population, came from the Soviet Union and Russia,' said Maxim. Ukraine only became independent in 1991 but the country now had forty-four LGBTQI+ organisations, he said. Equality marches had been taking place since 2015, with thousands attending.

The activist organisation Maxim worked for was set up by Viktor Pylypenko, an east Ukraine veteran, who called their stance a patriotic one. Pylypenko also established private communications groups for LGBTQI+ soldiers and veterans, including the Achilles Brotherhood, for gay men and bisexuals, and Sisters-in-Arms for lesbians.[15] Around twenty of their members had died since the full-scale invasion began, according to Maxim. Only one was openly gay: twenty-one-year-old Roman Tkachenko, who was killed by shelling in May 2022, near Kharkiv. Maxim showed me a joyous picture of a khaki-clad young man hugging and kissing his boyfriend at a Kyiv equality march.

'Queer soldiers is one of the biggest arguments for the whole community to be supported,' said Maxim. 'We say that we can't wait, our soldiers can't wait, they are dying now. They need this right now.' LGBTQI+ people would be more willing to fight if they knew that their rights were protected, he argued.

Within Ukraine's Department of Defence, Maxim said, there had been denials around how many LGBTQI+ soldiers there actually were. 'There was a lot of narrative of "we don't see you, you are not fighting, you are not here, [so] you don't deserve rights or respect"'. To counter that, activists began posting coming-out stories from soldiers online, which received a notably positive reaction. 'It's quite fulfilling for us because we see, despite this huge tragedy, [that] people who face frontlines, trenches, missiles every day, see blood and death, also have it in their power to be open, to fight for queer rights.'

But the armed forces in Ukraine, as in other countries, had a 'conservative structure'. He said some LGBTQI+ soldiers faced discrimination or nasty jokes, though others had been supported. 'War is the thing that props up the terrible and beautiful things and shows the people who they really are,' said Maxim. 'It's really changed attitudes because you can die tomorrow. It pushes our members to come out, even though they can be judged.'

The Christmas Eve Vogue battle started early, so those attending could dance for hours without defying the midnight curfew – the same curfew putting a stop to the conventional night-time Christmas masses. I did not stay late. Instead, that evening found me standing on platform 11 at the main Kyiv train station. The service I was waiting for was nicknamed the 'love train'. In the afternoon it left Kramatorsk, in the Donbas region of eastern Ukraine, arriving back in the capital seven hours later. On board were soldiers on temporary leave from the frontlines on leave, or their partners, fresh from precious hours spent with them nearby.

Arriving early, I noticed a woman standing alone, holding a heart-shaped balloon decorated with a teddy bear and the words: 'I love you this much'. Over the next twenty-five minutes, a smattering of eager individuals multiplied into an expectant crowd, before the train finally pulled in. I saw that first woman scan each carriage, then catch sight of the man she was searching for. She was already running when he stretched out his arms. They kissed.

I didn't know it at the time, but somewhere along that same platform Irina was reuniting with Sergei. He had called her just six hours beforehand to announce that he had unexpectedly been granted time off. Amid a joyful panic, Irina scrambled to set up a white, artificial Christmas tree, adorned with multicoloured lights and blue baubles. She scoured their apartment, keen that it look welcoming for his return. It was a 'Christmas miracle', she would later tell me. 'I couldn't do a manicure but I got everyone out of the house,' she laughed.

On the platform, Irina waited until 'he got out of the train carriage and I saw him and I didn't see anything more at all.'

'I was almost fainting because she was hugging me so much,' beamed Sergei.

I met them both together, in their apartment, the day after Christmas. Tree lights glowed in one corner of the room we sat in, sipping herbal tea and eating biscuits. There was a rug with the Union Jack on it, and a shelf with books they worked on together. Irina wore a light blue dress, her nails painted red. Sergei was still dressed in his military fatigues.

Irina and Sergei in front of their Christmas tree on 26 December 2023.

He asked me what I had learnt in Ukraine. I tried to sum-marise the personal challenges narrated to me, the longing, the stoicism. I have heard the Corinthians Bible verse, 'love is patient / love is kind', read at many weddings in Ireland and the UK, but I knew most of those couples would never be tested in quite the same way as the couples I met in wartime Ukraine. During a crisis like this one, patience is a requisite if love is to survive at all, I had realised. Of course, Sergei knew this much better than I did.

'I would like to know if you know how many families, according to statistics, were broken after the invasion?' he asked. I told him I had not found exact figures. Sergei said he knew of numerous divorces, some initiated by soldiers with partners wait-ing for them, who decided they needed to start a new life anyway.

'Some of them even found new women and some of them married these women,' he said. 'But when they come back from war they will be different totally, psychologically they will never really be the same. They will have to reform themselves and even women, when they wait for their husbands, they change. To remake the family they will need to have psychological help as well.'

Sergei described his battalion to me. It encompassed dozens of men who previously had no experience of either fighting or following commands. Among them were former senior politi-cians, successful musicians and millionaire businessmen, he said. At the beginning, they were 'kind of a bunch of cowboys'; now they had adapted.

He explained how his last marriage had ended years before, when he first returned from war in the east. 'I passed all of these difficult times, when you come out of war you have this PTSD.' Ukrainian officials estimate that around one thou-sand soldiers took their own lives in the first four years of fighting in eastern Ukraine.[16] Sergei brought up the importance of seeking out psychological help, as he had. That 'should be obligatory but it is not in the culture for people to go and complain to a psychologist', he said. He wanted soldiers fighting under him to access psychological support, for the sake of their own futures and the lives of their loved ones. 'Everyone needs help,' he said he tells them. 'It's nothing bad, it's not that you are sick or you're mentally different but it's necessary, it's normal.'

Regardless of that, and alongside everything else he was going through, his relationship acted as a grounding force for him, he emphasised. 'I met Irina in 2018 and she supports me with everything. It makes you stronger when a person knows when he will come back he is supported and he has a home. It means a lot.'

It was, as Irina would later post on her Facebook page, a 'joke of the universe' that she had been granted 'not an easy life, but a man with whom you can endure all this Armageddon'.

Chapter 2

Rwanda: Forming new families

Abantu ntibava inda imwe bava inkono imwe
(Kinyarwanda)

– 'Real fraternity is not about blood, it is about sharing',
Rwandan proverb.[1]

*'Cultivate not only a solid love, but a tender, gentle, meek
love for those about you.'*[2]

– St. Francis de Sales, the patron saint of journalists (among others)

April 2014 marked the twentieth anniversary of the Rwandan
genocide. It was also the first year I called myself a journalist –
though perhaps I had not earned that title yet. I was twenty-four
years old: young and inexperienced, with no commitments.
Rwanda would be my first professional foreign assignment.

I had given up my sublet in London and funded my travel
with a reporting grant. I managed to stay in Rwanda a whole
month, stretching the money out by living in a Kigali hostel
which doubled as a bowling alley. Enrique Iglesias' 'Hero' was
playing when I arrived there, following a one-way flight. Everything I owned from the UK was stuffed into my inappropriately
bulky luggage.

My only previous trip to Africa had been to Malawi, in the continent's southeast, where I travelled on a student scheme. In Rwanda, I was surprised to find a green land of misty valleys and rolling hills – so many that the local film industry was known as 'Hillywood'. Kigali's streets were clean and ordered, with traffic police in neat, unwrinkled uniforms a regular sight. Single-use plastic bags had been banned nationwide since 2008, meaning they were not strewn across the pavements, or waving from tree branches, as I have since seen in other African countries. While I was aware of Rwanda's tumultuous past, I noticed little outward sense of chaos or strife upon arrival. But the longer I stayed, the more I detected the air of heaviness which never quite went away.

I was a young child in Ireland when the 1994 genocide happened, though, of course, I later learned about it. Rwandans had been formally identified by ethnic groups since colonial times, with Hutus making up the majority and Tutsis the biggest minority. These were more rigid designations than the actuality, given there had always been intermarriage, for example. Still, those deemed to be Tutsis were given a monopoly on political and administrative jobs, education and other coveted opportunities, while many Hutus were forced into onerous physical labour.

The power balance shifted long before the 1990s, but tensions remained. The genocide was triggered when the plane carrying Rwandan President Juvenal Habyarimana, a Hutu, was shot down above Kigali. From there, murder became methodical and swift. Hutu militias were known as 'Interahamwe', meaning 'those who stand together', and they labelled the Tutsis as *inyenzi*, or 'cockroaches'. Wielding machetes, grenades and nail-studded clubs, they killed Tutsis at roadblocks, alone at home or en masse inside churches, schools and sports stadiums. They offered some victims the chance to pay, with money, for the price of a bullet so they were granted a faster death. The media, particularly radio presenters, concurrently spewed hatred. 'Moderate Hutus', perceived as sympathisers, were murdered too. In total, as many as 800,000 Tutsis and moderate Hutus were killed over one hundred days.

It might sound like a misnomer, but the Rwandan genocide was one of the most intimate mass killings in modern history. The country is among the smallest geographically on the African continent. In 1994, it had a population of nearly eight million people, packed throughout cities, towns and villages. Almost all Rwandans were involved in agriculture, and the genocide that erupted was largely carried out with the same tools people used for everyday farming. Neighbours turned on neighbours; even husbands on wives. There were reports of pregnant women being raped before having their stomachs sliced open. Tens of thousands of corpses lined the streets and hundreds floated down the Kagera River each day to neighbouring Tanzania.[3]

That inaugural professional trip tested my understanding of what being a journalist meant in reality. It was the first time I received guidance on interviewing traumatised people. This includes giving them the chance to take breaks or stop at any point; offering water; making it clear that they do not have to answer any questions or do the interview if they do not want to; carefully explaining who I am and why I am interested in talking to them; having a discussion around how identifiable they are comfortable being; and not pushing for more information than they want to disclose. The guidance came from an organisation that worked with genocide survivors and I have referred back to it during interviews throughout my career.

The trip also made me consider love, family, sacrifice and renewal in a whole new way, most notably when thinking about support for survivors whose families had been killed.

At its best, a family acts as a backbone and a safety net: they are the people you contact if you are in trouble and celebrate with when you succeed; who remind you where you originated and give you courage to push further. The precision of your similarities, even when expected, can catch you off guard: from niche preferences and aversions to allergies, physical attributes and ways of laughing. If family members disagree or are unkind to each other, there is often an underlying assumption that they can recover because of an unbreakable bond between them. I wondered: if your family were forcibly taken from you, could they be replaced in any sense? Could there be compensation for the support they might have provided; the love, even?

I first met an 'artificial family' on a sunny afternoon at the University of Rwanda in Kigali. They were clustered on a knoll behind an office block, where the grass looked green in the way a photograph is when the contrast has been dialled up. It was one week before the start of their exams, and Paul Henri was giving his twenty-four children a talking to. 'Study hard everyone,' he said. 'If you work hard you can improve your life and make it better.' I smiled shyly, self-conscious as an intruder, aware of the distinctiveness of this scene.

Paul Henri – twenty-three years old – was slender and welcoming, with the air of someone bequeathed a mission. None of his 'children' shared his DNA: in fact, the only thing linking them was that they were genocide survivors who had lost their families in the 1994 violence. They huddled together in a circle to pray, each person's arms around the backs of the two beside them. Afterwards, they stopped to chat and take photographs with me – this unexpected foreigner expressing curiosity – before going on their way.

Creating 'artificial families' to help young genocide

survivors cope was an idea conceived by the Association of Student Genocide Survivors (AERG). The organisation was founded by twelve university students in 1996. By the time I came across its work, in April 2014, these numbers had expanded to more than forty-three thousand students across this tiny landlocked African country.

AERG initially arranged families based on the secondary school or university the survivors attended. In some cases, committees appointed a father and mother for each one, and in others newly formed families democratically elected parents from among their ranks. Each family might have dozens of members.

'You need someone to care about you,' explained the association's then-national coordinator Constantine Rukundo. That was a basic necessity, and the aim was that these families would stay together for life. Even if one person merely required

An 'artificial family' pray together at the University of Rwanda in Kigali in 2014.

soap, they now had 'so many who can share', Constantine said. 'When you get married your family will be there; they'll be the first to help you.'

Paul Henri was younger than several of his artificial off-spring. Though they did not live together, they helped each other out financially and attempted to pool their resources. Twenty-seven-year-old Augustin – one of Paul Henri's 'children' – told me he called up his artificial mother for all sorts of small things: 'For example if I don't have a pen, or I don't have soap. Or I call and say "oh Mommy, I'm not eating". They would praise and encourage each other, the mother and father congratulating the children on their latest achievements. On whether his father ever scolded him, Augustin answered diplomatically: 'We have general discussion and argument. We're used to negotiating.'

'I joined this organisation because it was very helpful,' Augustin continued. 'After the genocide a lot of people were alone around the country . . . During the genocide our fathers, our relatives, our friends were killed, so joining this organisation, the purpose is to help us to rebuild our life. When we meet together here it is to increase our knowledge. It is to share ideas, to share our feelings and our beliefs.' He said they were united in a desire to have a good future, to help those around them who were worse off and to confront challenges together. 'So, for us, a big family improves our life, and helps us to live together and move away from the problems caused by genocide.'

Another 'child', twenty-one-year-old Kevin, said being in a family-style environment helped young Rwandans deal with their emotions. 'Some people used to be very angry,' he said. Together they discussed their feelings and how to control them enough to live peacefully with their neighbours. Yet, he added, the long-standing consequences of what they had endured were still evident. 'We have kids who have been so shocked from genocide that they have a permanent shock. That is one of our big problems.'

Fatherhood was a lot of responsibility, but Paul Henri relished it, he told me. 'You have to know every situation that your children are in, if they're studying without any problem, if they're eating, everyday life. If one of them is sick, I have to be the first one to know it.' He had named their family Urumuri. 'Urumuri,' he said, 'means to light something up. It's when something was dark, and now it is bright again.'

As Rwanda marked the twentieth anniversary of the genocide, 'Kwibuka20' signs were hung prominently across Kigali, with the slogan: 'Remember – unite – renew' (Kwibuka translates from Kinyarwanda, Rwanda's national language, as 'remember'). The annual week of mourning meant many restaurants and businesses were closed. Wreaths were being laid and minutes of silence observed all over the country. During the period of remembrance, with daily life muted, it seemed easier to imagine what it must have been like with militias on the prowl, blood pooling on the streets and the bodies of those who could not get away piling up.

'That's where there'd usually be karaoke,' said a new friend as we sat inside a bar called Papyrus. 'The place would normally be packed; wall to wall.' The customary interjections of music notable in any urban area had been replaced with disclosures, admissions and apologies. Days earlier, I heard a former génocidaire named Dominic Mukeshimana tell a packed stadium never to listen to their parents, because his parents had advised him to become a murderer. A Belgian soldier testified that his colleagues had watched 'killers wielding machetes' through their rearview mirrors as they abandoned the Tutsis they had been protecting.

In my notes, I wrote that Rwanda was 'a country commonly described as "safe", "calm", "organised" . . . But to dig beneath the surface [was] to find wounds still raw, trauma untreated, survivors still suffering. Making choices about how to balance progression with remembrance, or the measure of forgiveness required for reconciliation, are issues that the citizens of this country are still grappling with.' Reminders of the genocide appeared frequently, such as moving to shake someone's hand, and realising their sleeve was empty – the ghost of a missing limb, a forced amputation. Through a scratched perspex-fronted helmet, whilst desperately clinging to the shoulders of a 'moto' motorcycle driver – a common means of transport around this city – I had my first glimpse of the famous Hôtel des Mille Collines: the setting for the Hollywood film *Hotel Rwanda*. Later I would sit in its grounds, listening to a soundtrack of tinkling piano music, as raindrops plopped into the pool in front of me.

Fresh flowers were everywhere in Kigali's Genocide Memorial Centre, which acts as a final resting place for around a quarter of a million victims. A ribbon read: 'We miss you Daddy', while a 'Wall of Names' was notably incomplete. Efforts to create a full record of those killed were far from being finished.

Francine
Age: 12
Favourite sport: Swimming
Favourite food: Eggs and chips
Favourite drink: Milk and Fanta Tropical
Best friend: Sister Claudette
Cause of death: Hacked by machete.

David
Age: 10
Favourite sport: Football
Dream: Becoming a doctor
Cause of death: Tortured to death

Fillette
Age: 2
Cause of death: Smashed against a wall

One afternoon, I gained access to a press meeting with then-United Nations Secretary General Ban Ki-moon. 'I am going to re-affirm the international community's commitment to "Never Again" . . . and this should never happen again in human history,' the diplomat said, journalists' microphones and recorders bunched together in front of him. Later, he would tell a crowd of Rwandans how he had heard and felt 'the silence of all those lost and the silence of the international community in your hours of greatest need'. Though bravery was shown by 'many UN personnel and others' while the genocide was taking place, he said, 'we could have done much more. We should have done much more.'

I was on the edge of the pitch in Rwanda's largest stadium, Amahoro, when the screaming began. It was 7 April 2014: twenty years exactly since the genocide started. Thirty thousand people had packed inside, most queueing for hours to get a seat. About ten minutes into the speeches, a single wail pierced the air. The atmosphere became tense. This lonely note was joined, in short succession, by many others, like a disturbing canon, as if each individual was suddenly reawakening to their history. Speeches by dignitaries continued, but, as the distress crescendoed, stewards in fluorescent yellow vests sprang up in the stands. They physically picked up and carried out dozens of distraught and collapsing men and women – at least five from the stalls where I was sitting. Reporters from across the world had flown in for the event, but I got the impression that few were expecting the scale of anguish apparent around us. The screams were the sound of a pain so pure that it felt physical: a puncturing of my insides. Later, reflecting on the impact this had on me, I wrote: 'I didn't know I had a soul until it started hurting.'

On the grass in the centre of the stadium, we were witnessing a genocide re-enactment. White colonialists in straw hats arrived in a jeep, before swapping their headgear for blue berets, to resemble UN peacekeepers, and striding away again uselessly. In the wake of their dramatised abandonment, Rwandans in flowing outfits fell to the grass, before khaki-clad men, meant to depict the rebel forces which eventually became the government, ran onto the pitch in pairs to bring those murdered back to life.[4]

'Twenty years ago, Rwanda had no future, only a past,' President Paul Kagame intoned in his keynote memorial speech. The man who had led Rwanda since the genocide's cessation spoke about 'bearing the burden of our history', and said it was choices, not feelings, that had enabled the country to move on from what it had been through. 'All genocides begin with an ideology. A system of ideas that says this group of people here, they are less than human and they deserve to be exterminated. If the genocide reveals humanity's shocking capacity for human cruelty, Rwanda's choices show its capacity for renewal,' he said. 'Rwanda was supposed to be a failed state . . . We could have allowed the country to become divided with groups deemed incompatible assigned to different corners. But we did not end up like that. What prevented these alternative scenarios was the choices of the Rwandan people. We made choices that guide us to this day. We chose to stay together.'

There were, of course, tensions underlying his words. I knew, both inside Rwanda and internationally, there was some discomfort around who held power, how the justice system had functioned, and numerous other specifics. But young Rwandan genocide survivors were completely innocent, and it was clear that they needed support. It was into this environment that the artificial families had become a lifeline for those who might flail. It was a contrived love, but it existed nonetheless.

I believe that love can be an action, directed towards anyone in need. When I think of this in practice, I sometimes picture Zula Karuhimbi, who perhaps temporarily created a different kind of artificial family through the dozens of lives she saved.

Zula was well known in Rwanda for using 'sorcery' to combat the Interahamwe – she was even referenced on the walls of the Genocide Memorial Centre in Kigali. One day, I set off in a car with two other journalists, on a quest to locate and interview her. Arriving in the southern Ruhango District, we stopped to ask if anyone could give us directions to the 'witch' who saved lives. When we found Zula, after ploughing by foot through waist-high shrubbery, she was snoozing on a straw mat outside her tiny home in Musamo Village, hugging a similarly sleeping child. I later discovered he was an orphaned boy she had recently adopted. Despite her wizened and frail appearance, Zula jumped to attention when she realised we were standing there and saying we had come to hear her story. 'Yes,' she confirmed. 'I'm the Zula who hid Tutsis.'

More than one hundred people took refuge in and around her two-room house at various points during the genocide, she

Zula Karuhimbi, when I visited her at her home in 2014.

said. 'I hid so many people that I don't know some of their names. I hid little babies I found on the backs of their dead mothers, and I brought them here.' Inside her compound, she covered them 'with dry leaves of beans and baskets'. Forty Tutsis hid in the bedroom, she said – both under her bed and above a false ceiling. The high, rectangular window only admitted a weak beam of light, and with no electricity – both in 1994, and when I visited two decades years later – I struggled to imagine these concealed inhabitants lying side by side, enduring pitch-black nights with little hope of salvation and no foresight as to when the killing would end.

As militias encircled her enclosure, Zula described covering her hands in herbs that caused skin irritation. She recalled touching the killers, who became fearful, convinced she was cursing them. Zula grabbed whatever she could find that could make a noise and shook or banged it, claiming that it was the sound of the spirits becoming angry. 'I hid those people seriously. I would prepare some magic, and when the killers came, I'd tell them I would kill them. I told them no Tutsis had come to my house, that no one comes in my house, while all the time they were all inside.'

When we visited, Zula's home still displayed markings from that period. Bullets, fired by the Interahamwe militias, left holes in the front wall. 'When they shot I told everyone in the compound to lie down so that the bullets would pass over them,' she recalled. 'They killed my first-born, my son Hanganimana; and my other daughter, Ugiriwabo, was poisoned and died. People would mock me, saying, "You hid people, but your own children were killed," and I replied to them, saying, "Our days to pass away are not the same. God is the only one who understands why these things happen."'

At one point, Zula pulled out printed photographs of people she had saved, which she kept among her most treasured possessions. Few came to visit her any more, due to sickness, forgetfulness or death. She spoke wistfully about one child in particular: a baby when she found him. 'I don't know where he is now,' she said.

Zula grew up at a remove from conventional society, in a family of traditional healers. She had also lived through much more of her country's history than any other Rwandan I met. Though she told me she was older, her identity card said she was born in 1925. That meant she could have been five or six when the Belgian administration – which controlled Rwanda from the early 1920s until 1962 – deposed Rwandan king Yuhi Musinga, partially because of his refusal to be baptised a Roman Catholic. During this period, Zula said, her mother too would regularly hide people. Young Zula was responsible for delivering their food and she was sworn to strict secrecy.

'Whenever I spoke out, I'd be beaten by my mother, who eventually brought a fiery leaf of a plant and slid it over my lips and told me, "If you say anything I will kill you".'

When Zula was at least eight, the Belgians conducted a countrywide census to issue 'ethnic' identity cards, classifying every Rwandan as either Hutu (85 per cent), Tutsi (14 per cent), or Twa (1 per cent). The seeds had been planted for the genocide that was to come.

Maybe all true magic involves an element of both fakery and self-conviction. Though part of her narrative involved pretence, Zula did actually describe herself as a witch at least once while I was with her. With pride, she listed her potions, which she claimed could fix unemployment or 'ugliness'. Herbs dried in the sun in front of her home, and the remnants of a fire occupied one corner of her bedroom's stone floor. Ushering me in, she reached under the mattress for yellow powder which she encouraged me to snort, saying it would fix 'head problems'. She then sieved ash into a brown envelope. The mixture would rid me of my many mosquito bite scars and freckles, Zula said encouragingly.

Yet it was Zula's love for humanity which was her real magic. She was an iconoclast, and it was clear, amid a violent frenzy where so many murdered their countryfolk simply because they were told to, that living on society's margins may have kept her conscience engaged and enabled her to step forward as a saviour. But she also had great empathy. In a time of mob domination, Zula's actions were courageous and remarkable.

She told me that she had acted selflessly during the genocide because it was the only behaviour that made sense to her. She held my hands in hers as she spoke. 'We are one. Our forefathers and foremothers are one for all of us. We are siblings to each other.'

Zula would die just four years later, still in her dark and crumbling, bullet-scarred home, in that same village. When I heard about her death, I thought back to her response when we asked how she felt about the future of her country. 'Love is the most important thing,' she said. 'Find someone to love, and the future will always be bright.'

Ten years passed. Ten years of other interviewees and assignments, yet I found myself thinking back to the artificial family I had met on that bright April afternoon. I was curious about what had happened to them and whether the scheme still had any role in their lives. In January 2024, I got back in contact with Paul Henri, the 'father'. By that time, he was living in the US.

Paul Henri told me that he still communicated with his family members, 'and they are doing fine. A lot managed to get jobs for themselves and others have their own families now, and they're now OK and able to support themselves.' His pride was evident. 'They've become [the] men and women we wanted them to be.' As for him, he had 'a wife and two amazing children, a boy and a girl'.

Paul Henri and I were almost exactly the same age, only a year apart. When we first met, in the way of the young, it had not occurred to me that time passes so quickly, and, in the near future, these student survivors might reach a new life phase: falling in love, having children, generating their own nuclear families. I had not understood how much of family love is about choice anyway, rather than the coincidence of where a person is born and to whom. Though Paul Henri had left Rwanda, I decided to go back. The thirtieth anniversary of the genocide was approaching and I hoped to track down the others whom Paul Henri had parented, to understand how they were living now and what their relationships to each other were.

In late March 2024, I flew overnight from Paris to Addis Ababa in Ethiopia, an airport I regularly passed through, where I had a layover of six hours before the final connection to Kigali. Exhausted after an hour's sleep slumped upright on a seat, I waited to join the line of passengers at the gate. At the top of the queue, I handed over my passport as usual. It took me a few moments to realise that something was wrong. Four staff members checked my documents in turn, alternatively peering and scrunching up their faces, before one told me that I was not permitted to board the plane. The Rwandan authorities, the airline employee said, had emailed two hours before with my name and those instructions. Someone in Kigali must have examined the flight logs and decided to send that email, I deduced.

It seemed that my barring was related to some reporting I had done in 2019, for a British newspaper, on the challenges faced by refugees Rwanda was hosting. It was a sensitive topic at a time when the UK Conservative Party sought to push through a plan to deport asylum seekers there. (This controversial and expensive scheme was shelved months later, following a change of government in London.) Even the airline employees seemed confused about my predicament, until I told one that I was a journalist and he said everything made sense to him now. A decade after my first visit to Rwanda – a country where I discovered courage and love and an extraordinary capacity for renewal – I had become persona non grata.

My travel ban was inseparable from political developments over the period since the genocide took place. President Kagame steered Rwanda's transformation. The former rebel leader, once described by the *New York Times* as the 'global elite's favourite strongman', also faced ongoing accusations of overseeing repression, quashing critical voices, ordering assassinations abroad and playing a role in destabilising and plundering the eastern area of neighbouring Democratic Republic of the Congo (DRC).[5]

In 2015, the year after my first visit, Rwanda's constitution was amended to lift a two-term limit, allowing Kagame to remain president. In 2024, he was elected to a fourth term, with more than 99 per cent of the vote. Critics and analysts have argued that Rwanda's peace remains fragile as long as real democracy does not exist. Through the decades of colonial rule, instability and eventual dictatorship, citizens never learnt to exercise free speech and practise peaceful dissent, they determine. What could happen when Kagame dies or leaves power, they wonder.

I had assumed that my mission investigating love amid crisis, and highlighting the work done to help young Rwandan genocide survivors in its aftermath, might avoid some of the censorship barriers I had come up against with other journalistic expeditions. My barring was a reminder that politics is unavoidable, no matter what you are reporting on – in the same way that the personal and the political can never be completely separate, despite any walls humans may build in their minds between the two.

I could no longer enter the country, but the internet enabled me to still speak to people inside it, and migration meant I could meet Rwandans outside. The effects of Rwanda's genocide – as well as the impact of the artificial families formed afterwards – stretched far beyond that country's borders.

I received messages from two Rwandans in their forties who were keen to tell me what being in an artificial family meant to them. Uwase Devotha, a forty-three-year-old from Rusizi district, said she had been welcomed into her family as a child and remained a member 'up until now' – in 2025. When she gave birth her artificial family visited her. 'We celebrate our achievements, which gives us positive feelings.'

Forty-two-year-old Damas had fond memories of trading proverbs, dancing and praying every week with his family members. At a vulnerable age, they supported and accompanied each other. It gave him a sense of protection, rescuing him, and others, from 'isolation'. It was also realistically a subtle form of counselling, he said, coming at a time when 'there was no hope of life for some of them.'

Damas has a WhatsApp group where his family share updates, despite having their own spouses and children now. When they meet up 'it's like we're brother and sister.' They trade stories, projects and progress, sometimes over coffee or lunch. They show up for each other when there are births, weddings or deaths.

In the closing closing days of 2024, I met Emmanuel in a coffee shop in a European capital. His mother and siblings had survived the genocide, but his father was murdered, he told me. His maternal grandfather was also killed, as well as around ten other relatives of his father's.

He pulled out his phone. 'It's always at the top,' said Emmanuel – by then in his late thirties – about his WhatsApp group, which was made up of members from the artificial families formed in his secondary school. He scrolled through their messages: a wedding invitation; people who had moved abroad announcing when they would next be in Rwanda; suggested contributions towards gifts for each other.

Emmanuel attended boarding school in southern Rwanda's Nyanza District. AERG ran a committee in his school. Members would keep an eye out for eligible students and do screenings, 'not necessarily on day one'. Some students formally requested to join; others were approached when word of their personal history spread.

Asking about students' backgrounds was not easy: this was a time when national reconciliation was prioritised, with children encouraged to see themselves as Rwandans, rather than Hutus or Tutsis. But Emmanuel says the organisers found a way. 'They would be gentle. Someone would come and talk to you . . . They would share information . . . ask you [questions], observe.' Who could join depended on 'how stringent' the committee was: one student was barred because he had grown up in neighbouring Burundi. Others might be welcomed if a parent had died fighting with Kagame's rebel forces, rather than being killed during the genocide itself.

Emmanuel was unusual in that his mother was still alive, though he remained eligible, given the scale of his personal tragedies. Most other members were orphans and people who did not have families to go back to when there were holidays: they needed 'that support, to try to create a family that is not there'. But members had to want to be involved: 'there was really no force.' He remembered one girl refusing to join until her final year. It took him a long time to understand why, he said. 'Maybe she wanted to move on, she didn't want to remember . . . Maybe she associated joining as reviving the trauma.'

Emmanuel was put in a family of between six and ten students, the number shifting each year. His parents were selected by the committee. Annually, the oldest would graduate and new students would arrive.

Members who could afford it were invited to make a voluntary contribution of cash. This money was used to operate a public phone, which all students in the school could pay to use. The income it generated helped AERG members in need.

During school holidays, the association might cover transport costs so students could go back to their home areas. That journey saw some of them morph from being children in their artificial families to the head of a household, parenting younger siblings. 'Having a family while they were at school was more like a relief,' Emmanuel said.

Emmanuel's artificial family met at least twice a week, for around an hour on the weekend and up to thirty minutes after dinner on a weekday. Attendance was optional and they tried to keep meetings interesting so people kept turning up. No one argued, he said. 'By default you have to get along, there was no opportunity for fights, it was more organised around supporting each other.' He said his artificial parents would ask questions like 'Is school going OK? Are you performing? Are your grades up? Are you struggling?' They focused on 'emotional support', limiting gossip and topics 'not related to school or the lives of the kids', though 'there were also moments of fun, we'd play games.'

The families promoted considerate and diligent behaviour, he said. Knowing they had a 'family member in the vicinity' gave students the sense that 'someone's watching, I need to behave. You did not want to make them ashamed or disappointed.'

His own artificial parents could be persistent. At one point, Emmanuel grew an afro. His 'mom' misinterpreted what was going on. She thought he was struggling to afford a haircut, so kept offering him money, finally slipping cash into his hand despite his protestations.

Emmanuel was sporty: at the weekend he travelled away from the school for games and championships. This meant he never became a 'father' himself: in his final year, his 'dad' was in the year below him. Later, in university, he would join another family, though a part-time job, on top of his studies, meant he missed most of the meetings.

It was his secondary school family that had the biggest impact on his life, creating a foundation for long-term support. More than 50 per cent of his Facebook friends, two decades later, were people from AERG and the families associated with it. Only a few were 'really good friends', but others got in touch when they needed help. One man, Emmanuel said, grew up as the 'head of his own family, four kids who survived the genocide. He didn't manage to be successful afterwards, but up until now, every time he's in need of something, he reaches out . . . he tells me the situation and I'm happy to send some money.'

The collective losses they dealt with as young people were unimaginable, he noted. There was an added strain, too, because of how highly Rwandan society prioritises maintaining control over one's emotions. Stoicism is respected. 'You're supposed to keep all your problems to yourself, you're supposed to endure,' said Emmanuel. 'One of the signs of being strong is to be able to manage your own feelings and that applies to both positive and negative.' He said for a sad person to cry would be regarded as socially unacceptable – others would 'be saying "calm down", they'd take you out of the crowds to a private space'. Contrastingly, even if a Rwandan had won the lottery, he said, 'you can celebrate when you're at home or with your close friends. You wouldn't want the neighbourhood to know.' Emmanuel smiled at me then, saying that, sitting so near to him, I might realise that he was in a good mood, but no one else in this coffee shop would have any idea.

I had seen pain in Rwanda, a country now physically closed off to me. But now, as Emmanuel explained it, I also re-envisaged it as a place where feelings were bottled up, pushed down, even in the wake of some of the most grievous crimes against humanity ever known. When Emmanuel was a school student, he recalled, 'there was also a lot of trauma, people were trying maybe to prevent it destroying the next generation.' Having the artificial families in place 'helped with ensuring that those problems would not be for the whole school to know'. Those efforts were partly about maintaining the children's dignity, he said. For example, 'if my family member did not have school equipment, they didn't need to go to anyone, they could come to the family who could figure out how to help them.' Decades later, Emmanuel said artificial families were no longer necessary for Rwanda's young people, but 'it was needed back then and it was one of the best solutions.'

We sat for longer, talking about current events: the bombardment of Gaza, the devastating conflict tearing Sudan apart. In other countries, grappling with wars or genocides, 'an exact replica or duplication' of the artificial families programme probably would not work, Emmanuel mused: you might 'have to adjust it to take into consideration the culture', but 'the idea is possible'.

By the time we met in that coffee shop, Emmanuel was married and the father of a lively little boy. I guessed that, like Paul Henri, this was where the weight of his love was directed now. Still, he considered it likely that being part of an artificial family had shaped him, including in ways that positively influenced his parenting. As a teenager, it made him realise, 'You can find family outside your family. And you can learn to trust others, to trust strangers, and to open up. There can be people who can care for you to the same extent as your family, who are not necessarily your family by blood, and you can also similarly take care of them.'

Chapter 3

Iraq: Secret weddings

'You will not enter Paradise until you believe, and you will not believe until you love one another.'

– Hadith attributed to the Prophet Muhammad

For Saif Muhammad, a man of gentle demeanour and studious air, working with Iraq's electoral commission meant being in a pressured and risky position that made it hard to turn his mind towards marriage – any new responsibility felt like too much of a burden.

After militants from the self-proclaimed Islamic State – aka ISIS – took over his home city in 2014, he believed his life was in even greater danger. The extremist Islamist militant group strongly opposed democracy, among many other things. In the early months, as ISIS commandeered institutions, raising their black flags over Mosul and inviting in a flood of foreign fighters, Saif hid at home, afraid that he would be targeted and killed. Yet he was in his late twenties, an age – he supposed – when it would be good to start a family. Six months in, with little else to do, he decided to find a wife.

It had become almost impossible to meet women by then. The rules enforced by ISIS meant women were generally forbidden from interacting with men they were not related to.

When women went outdoors, they wore long black abayas and niqabs, their eyes only visible through slits. Saif decided to marry in the traditional way: by asking his mother to search for a match. At her suggestion, he visited some women in the privacy of their homes, where he was able to see their unveiled faces in the presence of their families. Until Marwa, he 'hadn't found the right girl'. His eyes fell on her and he accepted her. 'She should be beautiful first and then from a respectful family, and I found these things in my wife and that's why I chose her,' recalled Saif, the thick wedding ring on his left hand attesting to what came next.

However it comes about, falling in love is an extraordinary feeling: the thrill of discovering someone you truly care about, of reorienting yourself towards them and sensing them doing the same; realising that you may even build the rest of your lives around each other. During their engagement, Marwa and Saif met once a week, but they also began conversing through secret phone calls.

Marwa waved her hands recalling the numbing chill in the air when she phoned Saif from her roof at night – it was the only place she could get reception. Wrapped in darkness, together but apart, the couple spoke from midnight until four in the morning. Marwa remembers Saif begging her to let him hang up because he was so cold. 'The biggest challenge we faced was that if ISIS knew we were calling on the phone they would kill us, because they would believe we were spying,' Saif recalled. The militants had forbidden phones and disabled cell towers. But the calls felt crucial enough to take the risk and both credit those early conversations as setting them up for a durable relationship. Marwa estimated that 70 per cent of couples she knew who wed during the ISIS occupation divorced afterwards. 'They didn't have enough connection with their wives in that period. They didn't know each other,' said Saif.

Less than two months passed between Saif and Marwa's initial meeting and their marriage in 2015. The occupation made everything uncertain and it felt necessary to progress speedily. 'We did it quickly because ISIS were in the city. No one knew what would happen in the future,' Saif recalled.

Almost a decade later, I sat in their living room. It was elegantly decorated with russet orange-coloured furnishings – armchairs, couches and pouffes – and a glittery table centrepiece of flowers, the vases adorned with a flora and fauna design. Saif, in glasses with black frames, a moss-green sweater and dark jeans, was beside Marwa, whose beige sequinned headscarf matched her fluffy slippers.

I first visited Mosul's outskirts in late 2016, the year after Saif and Marwa were married. ISIS had controlled Iraq's second largest city for more than two years and an offensive to oust them was under way. Even then, alongside decimated buildings in recently reclaimed territory, I remember spotting elaborate dresses for sale, and interviewing a beautician who spoke joyfully about preparing brides for marriage in her newly refurbished salon. Between 2016 and 2018, as fighting raged and subsided, aid agencies funded mass weddings in refugee camps. Other displaced people – the beneficiaries of donor-funded skills training programmes – prepared cakes and finessed the brides' hair and makeup.[1]

At its purest, a marriage can be a traditional expression of both love and hope. Marriages have always taken place both in times of tranquillity and under fraught circumstances, and it seemed to me that the chequered history of Mosul could be re-examined through their lens. Multiple wars, economic sanctions under Saddam Hussein, the American invasion, and the rise and fall of ISIS all impacted how these milestones were marked, how couples were united – including through pragmatism, family pressure or desire – and whether love blossomed or was thwarted forever.

Mosul's Arabic name is Al-Mawsiil, meaning 'the linking point'. Historically, the city was known for its position along trade routes and its diversity of religions, with Christians and Yazidis living alongside Sunni and Shia Muslims. In Mosul, marriages can be seen as a union of families, a prerequisite for producing children, a way to consolidate wealth and to keep young people in check. As elsewhere, they also provide an excuse to celebrate.

Rasha Al Aqeedi, a writer and analyst now living in the American state of Virginia, was born in Mosul in 1984. Weddings are woven through her childhood memories, though getting married was far from guaranteed. She grew up aware of what she described as a lost generation: people born in the 1950s and 1960s who came of age during the Iraq–Iran War, which lasted from 1980 to 1988. Hundreds of thousands of men are thought to have been killed then, while others fled the country, were held as prisoners or developed major psychological issues. A significant number of Iraqis never wed as a result – including three of Rasha's aunts, she said. 'This generation of women didn't have the same opportunity to marry as the generation before or after them.'

Following Saddam Hussein's invasion of Kuwait in 1990, the UN, pushed by the US, imposed crippling economic sanctions on Iraq, banning almost all imports and exports. The country's GDP sank to less than 10 per cent of what it was before: the poverty was a mocking irony for citizens with one of the world's largest known reserves of oil under their feet.

While aimed at punishing those in power, the sanctions proved ruinous to every aspect of civilian life. Chronic malnutrition increased while the health sector was decimated. Essentials like water purification treatments, hospital equipment and certain medications were banned, because of a determination that they could be used to create weapons of mass destruction. By the mid-1990s, scientists working with the UN estimated that more than half a million children may have died as a result of their impact.[2]

Marriages, of course, were affected too. The scale of a wedding party had always been dependent on how wealthy each family was, but now many Muslim families were unable to buy the traditional gold for the *mahr*, a financial payment supposed to provide a bride with security should something go wrong in the future. People wed in their houses, or had no celebration at all, with the groom simply collecting the bride to bring her to his home. If there was food, it might only be cake.

Rasha said she would not historically describe Mosul as a racist or sectarian city, but it was a 'classist city', which had been home to some of Iraq's richest families throughout the centuries. Those families acted concurrently as the leaders and foundations of society, with marriage both expanding and consolidating their control. Mosul's traditional wedding songs boast of wealth: one references bringing a bride gifts from the Syrian city of Aleppo, hundreds of kilometres away; another mentions the cool water served in her home, an indication that the family had a fridge when that was rare. 'Extravagant' weddings have always been a way for people to show off, Rasha said. 'These families, when they have an opportunity to showcase their money they do.' During sanctions, she remembered the anticipation around elite weddings, when an invite would mean servings of meat and fruit, which most people were deprived of.

The US-led invasion, which began on 20 March 2003, was launched largely under the false pretext that Iraq had biological, chemical and nuclear weapons – claims repeated and not adequately challenged by the media.[3] Saddam Hussein's regime toppled in weeks. Though many Iraqis initially celebrated, there was a spiral into sectarian war. Around 200,000 are thought to have died violent deaths in the subsequent years.[4] More than four and a half million people were forced out of the country or displaced inside it by 2007.

The number of weddings decreased. 'People weren't going to school. They weren't going to work as much. It was constant violence on a daily basis,' said Rasha. There were regular suicide attacks and kidnappings, prompting fears that weddings could become a target. Those of Rasha's friends who married then had small, family-only parties. No one wanted to be the reason someone else was in the wrong place at the wrong time, she said. There were surprising moments of bravery too. Rasha was part of a procession for her cousin's wedding. The groom left on his way to pick up his bride, only to find the road blocked with US Humvees. One of his relatives risked approaching the American soldiers, waving a white flag. In response, fully armed soldiers emerged and began dancing with the wedding party. 'And then they opened the road for us. We were allowed to cross,' Rasha recalled. Their subsequent mood was triumphant.

Aside from conflict and economic circumstance, falling in love became harder in Mosul because of growing conservatism. Dating in Iraq had always been 'very different to dating in the West', Rasha said. It usually meant young men and women met at university and took walks together, keeping their interactions on campus. In the 1990s, even that started to be frowned upon, as Saddam Hussein's 'faith campaign', which put a greater emphasis on Islam nationwide, was implemented. Women were encouraged not to speak to men at all. Marriages were arranged through relatives instead, effectively by a 'scoring system': 'she's attractive, she's from a good family, she has good manners'. The couple might never speak to each other beforehand, said Rasha. 'Some people still broke those rules and still dated, they didn't seem to care,' but women who did could be gossiped about, their reputations damaged, and in some cases the man would leave her eventually to make a more conservative match. Before her own marriage, Rasha said 'suitors' – families she did not know – called at her home every weekend after hearing she was of 'marriage quality'. Almost all of her friends from university wed that way, she said. 'It's hard to tell if they were happy or not, honestly, I couldn't tell.'

The Muslim weddings Rasha attended growing up were segregated, meaning they were 'women-focused'. Women wore what they liked, 'show some skin perhaps, sleeveless dresses, short dresses, lots of makeup, do their hair very nicely, and they can also dance'. It was an opportunity to assess the evolution of fashion among women who, 'if you mostly see them in public, you've never seen their hair, you've never seen the shape of their bodies.' The groom would be outdoors or in another room or hall with friends and male relatives, having their own party. When he briefly entered, most women, apart from the bride and his direct family, would put on abayas and cover their heads.

There were other traditions: the night before the wedding, henna was painted on the bride's hands. At some point in the following week, there was a celebration of the consummation of the marriage, also just for women.

Divorce was less socially acceptable after the 1950s, Rasha said. While 'Islam fully gives the right to divorce in a way that's very progressive,' the social conservatism that gained traction was not in sync. 'I had not seen or heard about anyone divorced while I was in Mosul. I know that sounds very shocking,' said Rasha, who left the city in 2013. She was the first divorced woman in her entire family, and moved to the US in the aftermath. 'I told my family, "I'm old enough now to do this and I'm not inside Mosul, you will not be shamed for it".' In time, her cousin found the courage to end an unhappy marriage too, she said.

The year after Rasha left, Mosul would face a major new challenge. In interviews about her work as an analyst, she has talked about the 'fatalism' of people from her city: how they do not like to take a stand against whoever has power. 'Their way of approach is never resistance, it's just waiting it out,' she explained.[5] That attitude was about to be tested to its limit.

ISIS appeared on the international stage in increments, but there was a specific moment when I think most civilians in Europe and the US became aware of the threat the group posed. I was interning at the *Financial Times* in London the summer American journalist James Foley was murdered. I remember arriving at our office beside the River Thames, seeing that morning's front-page stories and the striking orange outfit the journalist had been dressed in, seemingly to resemble a prisoner in Guantanamo Bay. This was one of our colleagues kneeling in the desert sand, at the mercy of this black-clad, knife-wielding masked captor. It was shocking and heinous.

ISIS aimed to create a caliphate, ruled by an extreme version of Sharia law. Its militants took over Mosul on 10 June 2014. By the following year, ISIS controlled around one third of Iraq and Syria, with offshoots and linked groups in Africa and Asia too.[6] Mosul was the biggest city in this territory by far, but ISIS met no real resistance from the Iraqi army there. As its fighters advanced, Iraqi soldiers largely retreated, leaving military equipment behind them. It was an effective surrender that many citizens I spoke to still felt angry about.

The years leading up to the takeover had been punishing on the city's residents. People were tired of rampant corruption and the security forces' abuse. Yet now they found themselves characters inside a bewildering new plotline. Half a million people fled their homes, with many eking out a difficult existence in camps nearby, but more than one million stayed, for a range of reasons including not wanting to abandon everything they had worked their whole lives for. Soon, Mosul was being described as ISIS's 'crown jewel'.

In the city, the sound of music was replaced by the noise of violence and brutality. Black flags were raised. Restrictions seemed unpredictable and constraining, but the full extent of the stifling chokehold residents were caught in took time to be implemented and understood.

Dress codes became increasingly strict, with women ordered to wear loose black abayas, black gloves and shoes, burqas and chadors, and men instructed to grow beards and make sure their trousers stopped above their ankles. The Hisbah, or morality police, enforced the rules, preventing women from moving around without a male guardian. There were public executions for those found guilty of perceived crimes such as rejecting Islam, spying, adultery, treason, revenge, homosexuality, and refusing to fight. The punishments took the form of beheadings; firing squads; crucifixions; being burned to death; drowned in cages; or thrown from high buildings. People caught stealing could have their hand amputated. Locals described taking detours to avoid seeing bodies hanging from a bridge.

Previously, incidents of child marriage were far from unknown, though it was illegal under Iraqi law without judicial approval. But now a lengthy manual produced by ISIS members advised that girls be married between the ages of nine and sixteen or seventeen.[7] Thousands of Yazidi women and girls, whom ISIS fighters considered to be 'infidels', were forced into slavery. Of the 6,417 Yazidis thought to have been taken captive, 3,568 escaped or were rescued – often in complicated operations set up by good Samaritans, who paid smugglers to transport them out of ISIS territory. Many others could never be traced.

ISIS was also on a mission to erase Mosul's historical identity, so it became synonymous only with them. Its fighters blew up shrines, some of which were located inside mosques. One was believed to be the tomb of the prophet Jonah, also known as Yunus and 'the one of the fish', whose story is referenced in both the Bible and the Qur'an. Jonah was said to have been swallowed whole by a whale before he agreed to follow God's plan, and was vomited back out again. He was subsequently directed towards ancient Assyrian capital Nineveh – which Mosul was built around the ruins of – to promote repentance. Residents fasted, donned sackcloth, and thus avoided the destruction foretold.

The military offensive to retake Mosul began on 16 October 2016. It aligned Iraqi army troops, Shia militias and Kurdish peshmerga fighters, with support from a US-led coalition. The Americans saw it as part of their broader 'Operation Inherent Resolve' fight against ISIS; while the Iraqis called it 'Operation Nineveh, We Are Coming'. By that stage, more than three million Iraqis had been displaced from their homes in the northern provinces, the UN said.[8]

Other areas had already been liberated. One was Jalawla. The town in Diyala Governorate changed hands several times between ISIS and Kurdish forces and their allies in 2014. ISIS fighters were finally pushed out in November of that year.

It was in Jalawla two years later that I met Emam Mahdi Saleh, a thirty-six-year-old beautician in skinny jeans and slip-on shoes. She told me how her family were forced into a displacement camp and her salon was destroyed in her absence: electrical wires pulled from the walls, lights and fittings broken, cosmetic products stolen. When she reopened, it was with less stock and lower prices: a reflection of her customers' reduced financial means. But her business got an immediate boost from a rush of weddings: many engaged couples had resolved to marry only once they could return home. Emam gave facials to brides as the wedding approached and did their makeup when the day came. She considered expanding her business: she saw a market in giving botox injections to women, like her, who had been aged by the stress of war, she said. 'After two years as internally displaced people, the women have very tired faces,' she laughed.

This was late 2016, and fighting continued some hours' drive northwest of us. Troops and tanks were a common sight in the streets. Earlier in my trip, I had seen bombed-out buildings in nearby towns and cities. Sometimes they were booby-trapped, making it impossible for the former residents to return. So many aspirations – career paths, study plans, business schemes and romantic relationships – had been shattered or put on hold during the occupation and subsequent conflict. But by the time I reached Jalawla, a quest to rediscover joy felt tangible. Weddings represented one part of that.

When I first arrived in the region, the oil fields of Qayyarah,

A dress seen by the side of the road in northern Iraq, at the time of the offensive against ISIS.

around sixty kilometres south of Mosul, had been burning for four months. ISIS set fire to oil wells as they retreated: a scorched earth policy, one aim of which seemed to be attempting to impede coalition airstrikes. The resulting flames were almost impossible to put out. Smoke darkened and thickened the air. Black soot coated the ground for miles around. Pollution clogged lungs, proving particularly harmful for the elderly and children.

I still have videos from that time, driving through Qaraqosh, a once-Christian town on Mosul's outskirts, while carrying the knowledge that the buildings around us were likely laced with explosives. I remember the contrast between the human-made destruction and the dreamlike beauty of the purple skies as twilight descended; the contradictions of the people we encountered. I remember sitting on embroidered cushions on the floor with families who served sugary tea or coffee, exchanging pleasantries before describing the agonies they had been through. In one town, we stopped to find a bathroom. A genial woman led us to an outdoor toilet, then joked about cutting off my head, picking up and pulling a pair of scissors through the air in front of her neck while laughing.

Around thirty kilometres southeast of Mosul, I visited Nimrud, an ancient Assyrian city dating from around 1350 BCE. ISIS fighters had destroyed the site the previous year, posting videos online which appalled experts who considered Nimrud one of the world's greatest archeological treasures. Militants used sledgehammers to smash a winged bull and ancient tablets, eventually setting off explosives to obliterate what remained.

On the hill leading up to the site, stretched across the dirt road, were tubes which looked like three exposed improvised explosive devices – the full area had not yet been cleared, I learned later – though we somehow drove over them without realising it and survived. At the top, we met Iraqi archaeologists in their forties, who had dedicated much of their lives to teaching people about the site. They led us gingerly through chunks of ancient stone, each one treading on footmarks left by the person before, to avoid being blown up. 'It was so important, you can't imagine,' said archaeologist Kahtan Khalf about Nimrud. 'We were praying for it [to be saved],' added Abdullah Hamoud, who sighed whenever he picked up a fragment of a sculpture or tablet.

As we stood on the site, a rapid percussion of gunfire erupted nearby. Was it clashes? I asked, disturbed. More likely it was celebratory gunfire, one of the Iraqis replied. Probably part of a wedding.

So weddings could even happen at the height of a war, I thought then. That should have been obvious.

The battle to retake Mosul, between October 2016 and July 2017, was effectively the climax of the fight against ISIS in Iraq and Syria, with the commander of the US-led coalition calling it the most significant urban combat since World War II.[9] Civilians suffered through it all. They were used as human shields by ISIS fighters; bombed if they sheltered in place; and hit with mortars and artillery rounds while trying to get away. The American-led coalition carried out tens of thousands of airstrikes, which are thought to have killed thousands of civilians, though the coalition disputes those figures.[10] In March 2017 alone, more than 5,500 bombs, missiles and rockets were used by the coalition on Mosul. If locals broke free from the ISIS-held areas, they were suspected of being collaborators or sympathisers.[11]

Amara managed to escape. She had been with her husband for nearly a decade when ISIS took over: they had an arranged marriage, only meeting for the first time on their wedding day. 'For a year I didn't really want him, I was very young,' she confided to me. 'Even after I had my first daughter I still didn't feel comfortable when I slept with him, but he was always very kind, giving me comfort and words of endearment. We had a very simple house, just one room, and we were content and lived a happy life.' They would go on to have six daughters and one son.

As the coalition offensive neared its end, the family found themselves trapped in the middle of the clashes. 'About eight or nine rockets fell on our house during the liberation,' Amara said. 'We would jump over dead bodies just to escape. Many people got killed but thankfully we survived.' She watched her husband carry his father to safety; reporters near Mosul's frontlines saw civilians transporting the elderly, and people with disabilities, in wheelbarrows and makeshift wheelchairs. Amara's family sheltered in a refugee camp, but left again when the wives of ISIS fighters arrived there, and security forces became increasingly 'abusive'.

'Despite everything we are going through, our family are still together,' Amara said.

Before ISIS withdrew from many areas, they mined the buildings they had commandeered, placing explosives behind doors or even in ovens. One day, in December 2016, an Iraqi militia commander brought me around his own gutted home, which he had reclaimed just twenty-five days before. ISIS ripped the electronics out of the walls – even pilfering the wires from his air conditioner and lights. 'You want to see some bombs?' he asked, showing me twelve which his fighters had found since the previous day. He told me he personally knew people who were seduced by ISIS early on, to work as collaborators, and ended up holding powerful roles. In previous lives, they had been drug addicts or unemployed. ISIS allowed them to expropriate nice houses, and – perhaps more consequentially – to feel important. The commander's wife still refused to return home, she did not yet feel safe.

Mosul, and the famous al-Nuri mosque with its leaning minaret, known as 'Al-Hadba' or 'the hunchback', stood for more than eight hundred years until it was destroyed in the fighting. Its felling was perceived as symbolic of ISIS's failure, for it had been at the mosque that, on 4 July 2014, self-proclaimed caliph Abu Bakr al-Baghdadi announced the creation of the caliphate. The leaning minaret continued to be memorialised on Iraq's 10,000-dinar notes.

During their reign, ISIS promulgated prophecies. One was that there would be an apocalypse-style showdown between 'true' Muslims and 'infidels'. A belief that the 'end times' were coming did drive a lot of people to join the jihadist group. But Mosul was liberated from their control in July 2017, and the city continued to exist, as most of its residents always knew it would.

In early 2024, I returned to Iraq for the first time since ISIS were fully ousted. I flew to Baghdad, then on to the city of Erbil, arriving early on Valentine's Day. Erbil is the capital of autonomous Iraqi Kurdistan, at the foot of the Zagros Mountains, and an easy entry point. In a taxi from the airport, I passed a flower shop filled with giant bouquets of roses and bright red teddy bears. Later, in the train, I walked by a bakery displaying wedding cakes as tall as me, small figurines of brides and grooms perched on top of them. A heavy storm that night brought whistling wind as thunder and lightning cracked the sky.

The following day, I joined a shared taxi to Mosul, around eighty kilometres away. It was a joy to drive more effortlessly along roads that once felt so ominous. There were still checkpoints though, now guarded by Hashed al-Sha'abi, also known as the People's Mobilisation Force. Travellers of other nationalities – French, Americans, British – had recently been denied entry to the city, but I made it through.

Under ISIS, celebrating Valentine's Day could be punishable by death.[12] The year after Mosul's liberation, residents told reporters that they did not want to celebrate openly, out of respect for everyone who had lost loved ones. But, by 2024, the men of Mosul were under romantic pressure. More than one hundred of them streamed into Shahad Safadin's store in the days leading up to 14 February. Discarded rose stems piled up high on the floor behind the cash register. 'It was so tough,' Shahad told me. 'Each year the rush increases.'

The twenty-nine-year-old started selling her wares in 2019, after she graduated from university. Her latest premises, in eastern Mosul, had been open for a year. It was bright and beautiful, with carefully selected gifts and ornaments tastefully laid out – everything from teddy bears, tiaras, lamps and statues, to tea cups, body creams, candles and door mats. A fluffy black cat wearing a necklace of multicoloured bells prowled the floor, before leaping upwards to sprawl on a swivel chair. I was offered a red, heart-shaped sponge cake to eat.

Shahad wore a white hijab and shirt, a mustard-yellow sweater, jeans and brown fluffy boots. There were gold rings on her fingers – the hands she used to arrange flowers, and, when she had time, to craft her own handmade goods. She had perfected those skills during the ISIS occupation, when she was stuck at home due to the strict controls on women. Convinced eventual liberation was an inevitability, Shahad taught herself to decorate picture frames and baskets, incorporating beads. 'I had a lot of free time to work on myself,' she said. 'That period was my opening.'

It was in her store that Shahad met her husband, Muhammad Abdul al Karim. He first visited at the suggestion of a cousin, who mentioned its attractive and independent owner. Muhammad was there when I arrived, approaching sporadically to joke, or smiling at his wife from a distance. After their first meeting, he told me it had taken him five months to contemplate his feelings towards her and their potential together, before proposing. 'When I chose her, I took my mother to ask for her hand from her family.'

Shahad and her husband Muhammad sit in her store in Mosul, in February 2024.

The couple had one child, with another on the way. Shahad – whose business also decks out halls for wedding celebrations – said it had become 'more normal than before to marry for love', as they had, rather than through an arranged marriage. The strict controls implemented by ISIS had conversely made Mosul's residents, in the aftermath, feel more inclined towards 'doing whatever they want'.

Shahad's business made her a star in Mosul: her store had almost thirty thousand Instagram followers. She said local girls and women were envious but also came by to endorse her. 'They support me as a working girl from Mosul . . . Most of Mosul's girls, they want to open a store like mine.' As women, Shahad said, 'now we have huge opportunities to work on ourselves and do whatever we want, compared to the occupation of ISIS or before ISIS.'

*

Another city centre store belonged to forty-four-year-old Qutaiba Yassin Hamid. His photography business, specialising in weddings, began operating in 1999. But in the months after ISIS took over, everyone stopped working 'because we were afraid', Qutaiba said. Fighters pressured him to join their ranks, aware that Qutaiba competed internationally as a sports shooter in his younger days. In early 2015, he used a false ID to escape to Turkey. Two and a half years passed before his return. His business premises had been taken over by ISIS, then torched to the ground. Mosul's Old City, where it had been located, remained mostly in ruins even when I visited in 2024: graffiti on the walls of one destroyed building read: 'Here I used to have memories, home sweet home, what has time done to you?'

Ever resourceful, Qutaiba re-established his enterprise in a new area. He needed to borrow money – 'the financial side was zero' – but 'step by step' commercial rhythms resumed.

We chatted inside the store, camera accessories for sale around us. The walls were adorned with large photographs of a model couple posing. One showed them in a golden wheat field, the woman in a black sparkly dress, lace gloves and a headpiece, holding hands with a bearded man in a white suit jacket. In another, they sat in a sports car. A third saw the pair repositioned in front of a setting sun: she in a white dress with her hair in an updo; his hand on her chin, wrist angled to show off his silver watch. On a table in front of Qutaiba was a small red fish with a flared tail, swimming inside a bowl decorated with pearls. I recognised it as a male Siamese fighting fish, or betta – the type known for killing females after they mate. An amusing choice for a wedding-related shop, I thought to myself.

A wedding party in Mosul – for those that could afford it – cost $5,000 on average, Qutaiba said. Engagement celebrations could involve two hundred guests; the main day might have up to four hundred. The bride would spend the morning in the salon: Qutaiba's designated crews of female photographers and videographers were on hand to capture these preparations. The groom socialised with his 'company' before collecting her, maybe passing by some 'beautiful place' to take photographs. Renting a wedding hall could cost anywhere between $200 and $1,400.

Spring was the busiest time for weddings, Qutaiba said. Valentine's Day was proving progressively popular and 29 February was also a 'special day', highly in demand by couples who only wanted to celebrate their anniversary once every four years.

I asked Mahmoud Nashwan Ghanim, the manager of a Mosul wedding hall called Kingdom of Alez, what people did for fun under ISIS. We were sitting in a restaurant called Chef Omar, on the banks of the Tigris. A wedding party was in progress in his nearby hall – suited men and women in full-length dresses, heels and hijabs gathered under glaring lights. Freshly washed children scurried, ducking around adults, tables and chairs. The hall was booked every day that month, with families paying $800 for a package that included waiters, and sometimes a DJ and photographer.

Mahmoud shook his head, thinking back to the before times. 'People came beside the river and just sat,' he remembered. Shisha pipes, bubbling at tables around us, were banned then, as were playing cards or dominoes, and other recreational activities, like raising pigeons. The price of a contraband packet of cigarettes reached $20, Mahmoud recalled, the disgust notable on his face. Restaurants were open 'but not like this'. He gestured towards groups sitting and chatting, drinking juice. Dozens of women were among them, including one with her hair uncovered. Under ISIS, there had been separators between tables so no one could see each other. 'There were too many struggles, the families couldn't have mixed celebrations,' Mahmoud said. 'But now it's become more open-minded.' Mahmoud mixed genders at his own wedding, back in 2013. He advises other couples to do the same. 'It's happiness,' he said, smiling.

Even Moslawi women from less privileged backgrounds, financially locked out of the industry of expensive venues and photographers, said weddings changed after ISIS left. 'Social media has made a difference,' opined Tadhi Ghanim, a twice-married woman in her mid-forties. 'Before we didn't see anything, we didn't know how other people do things. Now we can see the whole world.'

Tadhi got married in a traditional black dress. Her personal highlight was the wedding procession, when she rode in a car covered with flowers. In contrast, her daughters both wore white when they married.

Saif and Marwa's wedding celebration under ISIS was notably restrained. 'I left my dream about the wedding day because of the occupation,' said Marwa. 'I wanted to make the celebration in a big huge wedding hall.' Her voice trailed off.

Dancing was banned, the couple recalled. Wedding halls had shut down. Music, if played at all, had to be turned down low because of the risk of severe punishment if the sound was detected. Their gathering took place in a relative's house, with less than forty guests, Saif said. There were two small speakers and Saif's cousin was the DJ. In one particular way, Saif felt lucky with the timing. It came shortly before ISIS issued a decree saying every man should have a beard, 'and this is very ugly to have for a wedding'.[13]

Saif's previous employment, as an election official, meant that even a secret celebration could be more perilous for him than for others. If ISIS religious police heard music, they could carry out a raid, ask for IDs and identify him. 'Maybe they would kill me then,' he said. 'Too many of my friends were killed during that period.' One, who ran a barber's shop, was IDed after he was deemed to be giving inappropriate hairstyles to clients: when he was found to be a former election official, he was murdered, Saif said. Another was apprehended at a checkpoint. A third was publicly stoned to death, said Saif, because of claims the man was having an illicit relationship with a woman who met the same fate. When I said I was sorry for his losses, he shrugged, as if to say nothing could be done about it.

'There were a lot of secret weddings,' continued Saif. 'Most of the guys, during the occupation of ISIS, they saw that it was actually easier to get married because it cost nothing. Before the occupation of ISIS, the concert halls, the food, it was very expensive. But during the occupation of ISIS it was very cheap.'

Obtaining legal recognition for the marriage posed a sizeable challenge though. Saif and Marwa had to go to the ISIS courts for a wedding certificate: they knew they would be punished harshly if they were found living together without it. Saif worried that his background would be discovered there too, but 'I went with my family, mother, father and the bride, her mother and father and it was routine.' The ISIS juror asked him how often he prayed and tested his knowledge of the Qur'an. Both Marwa and Saif had to take HIV tests. After Mosul was liberated from ISIS, they were required to procure a new marriage certificate. 'The Iraqi court warned me not to use the ISIS certificate any more because there is an ISIS logo on it,' Saif said.

I reflected on how marriage is regulated by religious institutions, states and societies, and what it means when those in

Saif, Marwa and their children at home in Mosul, in February 2024.

control shift and change in such drastic ways. Deciding to forge ahead with the traditional stages of life, regardless of the wider circumstances, felt brave in this situation. For Marwa and Saif, at least, it seemed to have worked out.

Saif now works as a computer science teacher, while Marwa – who was forced out of education under ISIS – teaches preschool. They have two lovely children. Eight-year-old Joury was born in the final days of the offensive. During her first days of life they were trapped in Marwa's family's house, without food and surrounded by fighting. 'I felt very sad because my child was just six days old and we were in danger,' Saif recalled. 'Twelve people in one home, shooting guns around us. I thought they would die and I didn't feel like I could protect them.' Soldiers eventually rescued the family.

The children entered the sitting room we sat in, holding hands. Joury was barefoot, in a purple fluffy jumper with a panda on the front, and purple-framed glasses. Two-year-old Jood was barefoot too; he ran his hands through his hair and stared at me in the serious, pondering way very small children sometimes do. The pair jumped up and wriggled onto the sofa, comfortable inside the love emanating from their parents.

'Mosul faced too many struggles,' Saif summarised, before I stood up to leave. After the ISIS occupation ended, the couple held a new wedding party, he told me – while they were financially constrained, they at least could celebrate without fear this time. Marwa wore the same dress and they invited their relatives, some of whom brought musical instruments to play there. A DJ played music, this time up loud.

Chapter 4

Uganda: Radical forgiveness

'The practice of love offers no place of safety. We risk loss, hurt, pain. We risk being acted upon by forces outside our control.'[1]

– bell hooks

'Amari.'

– Acholi for 'I love you'

Landlocked East African country Uganda is nicknamed the 'pearl of Africa' for its natural beauty, though internationally it might be associated as frequently with endemic poverty, the 1970s dictatorship of Idi Amin, or the more recent attacks on pop star turned opposition leader Bobi Wine and his red beret-clad followers. Even piled together, these disparate realities and historical moments are, of course, far from the whole story. Of all the countries I have visited, Uganda is one of my favourites. I adore the humour and am awed by the talent on display: how people find daily workarounds to life's grinding problems; the regular quips about the absurdity of the human condition. I am fascinated by the richness of its culture; the variety of geographical features; the street style.

Uganda was moreover the place where, in mid-2018, I came across an extraordinary manifestation of love for community, but also love for peace.

The hero of this story is David Ocitti. He was the mission orchestrator, driving us north on that momentous day. It was a routine the thirty-one-year-old had gone through countless times with different passengers, yet each of those journeys was special. Every one, in his thinking, was a stride towards peace and away from the harrowing past he and his countryfolk had lived through. He knew, on a deeply personal level, what it was like to be a victim of war and how excruciating forgiveness could be, yet how necessary.

I sat in the front seat beside him as we sped through a landscape steadily growing more verdant. Sharing the back were three men, the youngest in his mid-twenties and the eldest in his early thirties. Their faces were stern, almost frozen, shifting only when David told a joke, causing wide smiles to crack through the solemnity.

Charles, Ouma and Robert were all abducted from their homes when they were children. Up until recently, they had been members of the infamous Lord's Resistance Army (LRA), an armed group founded in northern Uganda in the late 1980s. Its leader was Joseph Kony, a despot who claimed to communicate with spirits, saying that was how he received the orders and guidance which he used to exert control over his forces.

Kony called himself a 'freedom fighter' and wanted to overthrow the Ugandan government. Essential to achieving this goal were the mass kidnappings that terrorised Uganda's north.[2] Between 1986 and 2004, more than fifty thousand Ugandans are believed to have been abducted by the LRA, around half of them children.[3] Kony's rebels called them *kuruts*, like recruits – that was how the LRA swelled its ranks.

As an initiation, kidnapped children were instructed to kill or be killed. Sometimes the targets were their own parents: a tactic used to make abductees feel guilty and shame them into never returning home. Others were commanded to rape or mutilate victims who might include relatives, neighbours or friends. As a strategy, this was both evil and effective. Its consequence was years of widening distance and aching silence between those abducted and the communities they left behind.

Now we were on a five-hour drive northwards from capital city Kampala. Our destination was Gulu, once the epicentre of Uganda's insurgency. That was where these men would be reunited with their families, after close to two decades apart.

The three had formed a friendship in what they called 'the bush'. Trust was hard to build there. Even a hint that someone was thinking of escaping from the LRA could see them executed by firing squad. Showing any sign of enjoyment, love or favouritism towards a particular person could constitute a death sentence. Kony was endlessly suspicious, his paranoia fuelled by informers keen for a promotion which they might earn by reporting any hint of wrongdoing. Alongside that, abductees truly believed Kony had supernatural powers, which made them terrified to defy him.

Charles, the youngest, was only nine years old when he was roused from sleep in the dead of night in 2001 and taken from his family. Ropes were tied around him – new *kuruts* were often strung together by their waists. 'We didn't get time to run,' Charles recalled. They were taken to a remote location where their 'training' would begin.

The eldest among the three was Robert, who had high cheekbones and was wearing a Ugandan football jersey and beige coat, a red, white and blue woven scarf wrapped around his head. Robert was abducted on 26 September 2002, along with three other boys he was sleeping in a hut with. He was appalled by the new life he was introduced to. 'The abductees were forced to kill people,' he told me. 'At home, where I grew up, I didn't see people forcefully killed, but in the bush such things are done.' Beyond that, perhaps the 'worst' other aspect for him 'was that there was no education . . . they want you to be a total fool.'

It was an environment where hours, focused purely on survival, stretched into years. Then, by chance, Robert started chatting to Ouma. This was later, after the LRA leadership signed a truce which compelled them to leave Uganda. The militants were largely nomadic, and roamed through lawless territory between the borders of South Sudan, the Central African Republic and the Democratic Republic of the Congo instead. These boys had grown into young men, their limits repeatedly tested. Like Robert, Ouma was distressed by the LRA's practice of killing without mercy. He had also secretly come to the conclusion that Kony was trying to 'destroy' their minds to control them, though he knew thoughts like this could never be articulated out loud. Instead, through conversation, the pair realised that they came from the same Ugandan sub-county and the same district. 'So we began sharing things, property, food items.' Robert also built up a rapport with Charles, who was six years younger. 'Charles also told his story to me . . . I realised we related well so I began loving him, I began loving Ouma. That's how we became close to each other.'

The three men were occasionally sent on ambush missions together. As time passed, the LRA's numbers dwindled and the violence and abductions the group were notorious for decreased, though the obstacle course of endurance wore on. LRA fighters would cut through thick forest with *pangas*, or machetes, searching for yams, honey, wild fruit, roots, and animals, including hippos, which they could shoot and eat. The weakest among them might die of thirst during these hunts, when water was hard to come by. Fighters ransacked civilian homes, or robbed passers-by, to procure cash or food, such as rice, maize, peanuts, peas and dry cassava. Kony's forces were also engaged in trading elephant tusks and minerals, like gold, diamonds and mercury, the escapees said – though they understood little about the mechanics of it. Life felt cheap and fraught with dangers.

It was Charles's idea to leave. He was the only one of the three men who had been 'allocated' a wife, a ghastly term for yet another crime which LRA victims came to accept as standard: that abducted girls and women would be divided between them. All three told me it was Kony deciding who was paired with each female captive; the men themselves had no say for or against it, or any input into who it was. Getting involved with a woman or girl who was not 'allocated' to you was punishable by death.

Charles's 'wife' was Congolese. After they had been together for more than a year, she became pregnant and gave birth to a girl. Charles remembered looking into the baby's eyes and realising his daughter would never be educated if they did not escape. He convinced the others to join him, saying their future would always be 'grey' in the bush. This was accompanied by a sharp warning: if they reported him, and he was killed prematurely, he insisted that they would regret losing this chance to get out.

During their long years in exile, Robert had come to have 'confidence' in his friends, calling them his 'partners'. 'When Charles came up with the idea of coming out of the bush I saw there was science in his message. He was a character who was not trying to betray us,' he recalled. The only other person who knew about the plan being hatched was Charles's wife. By the time they put it in motion, she had given birth to a second baby.

Their opportunity came when Kony called a meeting of his sector commanders, ordering them to come to Darfur, in Sudan, to convene with him in person. Charles, his wife and children, Ouma and Robert were all to join their commanders, trekking on foot to Kony. On the route back, after the gathering was over, they managed to steal away in the dead of night.

Ouma said the group was confident they would not be recaptured because they took guns with them. 'We had in mind that whoever comes to attack us, we would confront them straight away.' By that time, they estimated that there were only around sixty Ugandans left in the LRA, along with more from other nationalities: perhaps two hundred people in total, not enough to launch a major search operation. Still, it took them months to walk to Banda, a village in the Haut Uélé region of the DRC. They wanted to surrender to the authorities, but first they desired assurances that they could do it safely and would be treated well. They wrote a letter saying they were Ugandans who had been abducted by Joseph Kony. If the authorities were willing to welcome them, they specified, it should be announced on a certain radio station, until which time they would remain in hiding. The small group 'waylaid' a civilian – a 'woman with a human heart', as Charles described her – and asked her to bring their letter to a local government representative.

'The following day we heard them reading it on the news, saying they had received the letter,' Ouma remembered. 'When we heard the news about us we were very happy and we knew we would be pardoned.'

*

Northern Uganda has been the scene of extreme suffering. It is also a place where people dance in the streets of towns and cities, or in remote areas, between clusters of the huts with thatched roofs known as *ot-lum*, as portable speakers blare out the latest songs from a vast array of local musicians. Between early 2018 and 2021 – much of which I lived in Uganda – I made many trips to the country's north. I lived in Gulu itself for six months during the COVID-19 pandemic, beginning in March 2020. National borders had been shut, a 7 p.m. curfew was implemented, and even driving a car was prohibited without a special permit. Each week, I reported on the local coronavirus task force meetings, which took place outdoors, in the shade of a mango tree. The world going into lockdown offered me an unexpected opportunity to get better acquainted with this area and its people.

Gulu is more than 300 kilometres from Kampala. By the time I started going there, the journey north could last five hours in a private car with a fast driver. More regularly, I travelled in crammed buses. Official schedules were either non-existent or disregarded, with drivers only pulling away when the bus reached full capacity. This might take hours, as you sat, fending off women selling soft drinks from buckets on their heads, or gangly boys hawking plastic bags of peanuts, before the vehicles spluttered out of Kampala's bustling bus parks, stopping and stalling further along the route. While in the north, I would often bounce and career between interviews and meetings, along irregular dirt roads, on the back of a boda boda motorbike taxi.

Northern Uganda was peaceful by then, but that peace had been hard won. There is no accurate statistic for the number of people who died during the war – which lasted from the 1980s until LRA fighters were driven out of the country in 2006 – though Oxfam estimated that half a million people had been killed by 2005. Jan Egeland, the UN's former head of humanitarian affairs, described northern Uganda as the most neglected humanitarian crisis in the world.[4] By 2004, 90 per cent of the local population had been driven from their homes by LRA attacks or the government's military response, which saw more than one million Ugandans herded into ill-equipped camps. Around one thousand civilians died each week in the camps, prompting accusations of genocide and animosity towards a ruling regime that painted itself internationally as the good actors in the story.[5] Even today, Ugandans speak in hushed tones when they refer to those camps, which the Ugandan forces said were militarily necessary, but were widely perceived as a dictatorial tactic of repression and subjugation.

On the other side were the abductions. By 2004, the UN estimated that around 80 per cent of the LRA's fighters were children.[6] Northern Ugandans questioned why government soldiers had failed to protect these kidnapped young people. They even accused President Yoweri Museveni of prolonging the war as his allies siphoned off money received in aid, saying his supporters were happy to impoverish and brutally suppress the local Acholi people, who were known to oppose the government. In a bid to stay safe, children made evening journeys to more protected areas. Gulu market – where I later bought vegetables from gossiping women with rosy cheeks, whiffed the pungent smell emanating from lines of dried fish stalls, and was measured for clothes tailored from *kitenge* fabric – had once been a shelter for children who traipsed miles to sleep securely there at night. This phenomenon prompted a solidarity movement called the 'Global Night Commute', which saw groups in more than one hundred and thirty cities, across seven countries, participate in actions including organised walks and sleepovers in parks, in an effort to force their own governments to pay attention.

February 2015 was the first time I spoke to a former LRA fighter, after a researcher connected us. The work day was drawing to a close and my employer's East London office had quietened and emptied out. I remember pressing the corded phone to my ear to listen to the voice of this man who seemed far away in so many respects.

Milo Harrison was kidnapped as a teenager. He spent fifteen years in the bush. 'Too long,' he said. 'It is no good to stay there.' Like multitudes of others, he had gone through an initiation process. 'They train me to be something bad, even though from there I don't understand, I don't understand what I did.' The LRA's murdering sprees affected him for life. The weak connection – between a UK landline on my side and a Ugandan mobile phone on his – made his voice sound frail. He attempted to describe the whirl of emotions and memories stirring inside him as we spoke. On a normal day, his feelings veered between anger and 'annoyance', he said.

During his years in the LRA, Milo had envisaged the concept of home as a representation of 'good' – the only good he could fixate on. He tried to escape but was recaptured. 'When you're punished you have to do something, your friends order you to do something,' he said, though he did not want to clarify exactly what he was made to do.

When he finally arrived home, Milo was reunited with his brother and sister, though, tragically, his mother had died in the years he was away. Returning made him 'happy', Milo said. He felt 'free and relaxed'. The 'simple things' brought him joy, like growing crops. His sister was supporting him. 'People in my family, they love me, they stick together,' he said. 'They welcomed us and they kept us alive.'

He was speaking to me because he wanted to encourage others to defect. He had already cooperated with the security forces, recording his voice to be played on loudspeakers or put onto USB keys and smuggled to those who remained in the LRA. For a time, when there was still funding, defectors were even flown above the forests in helicopters, with loudspeakers projecting their voices through the blanket of vegetation below. This was a proof of life for the remaining fighters; a solid argument for leaving. Milo said he wanted others to understand that coming back home meant 'for you, the good life'. His words were pleading, addressed to his former fellow militants rather than me. 'There will be no badness for you,' he pronounced.

At the end of our call, Milo asked if we were friends now. It made me reflect on how people can have totally different backgrounds yet find common ground; how, all over the world, we have the same basic desire for connection.

It was their illicit friendship and growing love and trust in each other that enabled Charles, Ouma and Robert to escape. Firmly recovered from the wilderness, they had been told the Ugandan government was granting them amnesty, but would their relatives and broader communities be so kind?

Seventeen years had passed since Charles – now a stocky man, with a deep, sonorous voice – had seen his parents. On the day Charles was abducted as a nine-year-old, back in 2001, he had just returned from hospital, where he was treated for a head wound from being accidentally hit with a potato farming tool. The wound initially festered in the bush, though it eventually stopped bothering him. In preparation for the reunion with his family, Charles both cleaned his wellington boots and shaved his head to reveal his scar, so they could recognise him. 'The only ID I know is the scar on my son's head,' his father later confirmed to me. Charles's memory of this injury had enabled David to track his family down in the first place – David travelled around asking if any family had lost a boy who had been hurt in that way.

As we drove north, and the car wove in and out of phone range, David kept getting calls from eager yet still disbelieving family members. He put them on loudspeaker so the men in the back could hear. 'I really thank God for taking care of you and bringing you back home. I've been hearing of people coming out and I kept going to them thinking it was you, but it wasn't you,' came the quivering voice of Charles's sister, Alice. 'Now Mom gave me David's number, telling me you were back home.'

'I'm really back home and I'm so happy to hear your voice,' Charles responded, his voice heavy with emotion. 'People told me you were dead but I couldn't confirm until now . . . I know that you are actually alive.'

Alice had been abducted at the same time as Charles and later identified during an offensive by Ugandan forces. Charles long believed she had died then. Instead, Alice informed him that she was married and had her own children. She handed her young son the phone. 'Who are you?' asked the boy. 'Your uncle,' Charles replied, laughing and repeating his own name. 'Charles. Charles.'

Alice came back on the line, saying goodbye for the moment, at least. 'I'm so overwhelmed and excited to see you,' Charles told her.

David turned on an upbeat song and began to sing along. It was one the defectors had listened to in the bush – in fact, it was created specifically to convince LRA fighters to lay down their arms and come home. The song was played over a local radio station which covered areas the LRA moved in; its file was also loaded onto SD cards, some of which made their way to the remaining LRA fighters. The men's names were in the lyrics, which vowed they would be safe if they returned to Uganda. This was another factor which encouraged them to defect.

There is time for fighting. There is time for peace. But this time is the time to revive our homes. Let them come home, brothers and sisters, come back home. Why do you have to suffer in the bush? You have your family. Why do you starve in the bush? Why do you stay in the cold when you have homes?

We drove across a bridge above the River Nile, a marker that we were drawing close to Gulu. The men gawped at the rushing water. 'We crossed the Nile using a jerry can but now we're coming back using a car,' one quipped. When the LRA was forced out of Ugandan territory, its members, including masses of abductees, crossed the river on rafts made of jerry cans – the polyethylene carriers, which are usually yellow, commonly used in Uganda to transport water and fuel.

In Kamdini, a town an hour from Gulu, the schedule for the reunion hit a snag. Crowds had lined the roads, hoping for an early glimpse of the men in the car. We spotted women singing, dancing and ululating, dressed in colourful clothes picked out especially for the occasion. They were Charles's family. After David pulled over to the side of the road, an elderly man darted up to us.

David gestured back at Charles, who was sitting between the other two and wearing a black Tanzania football jersey. David warned Charles not to leave the vehicle – an effort to be

considerate towards the other families who were already waiting impatiently at the designated location in Gulu. But the
approaching man thrust his arm inside the car window, lifting
off the wine-coloured scarf wrapped around Charles's head
and tilting his chin downwards to see his scar. This was
Charles's father, who let out an audible noise of relief before
David directed him away again, reminding him that the real
reunion was almost upon them. 'It's a bit much,' reassured
David, seeing Charles's startled reaction. Charles's family
drove in front of us after that, acting as the homecoming
parade.

Our vehicle pulled into the car park of an old colonial house
in a part of Gulu known as senior quarters. When Uganda was
under British control, British officers hosted friends in this area
for gin and tonics, a local told me. Decades later, the Ugandan
military were known to torture detainees here, he said. By 2018,
the house had become a part-time rehabilitation centre.

Dozens of relatives from the three different families had
gathered. There was a strange quiet as our car drew up: the
waiting crowd seemed unexpectedly motionless, almost forming lines. Then the returnees stepped out of the car and a rush
of women advanced – ululating, shrieking – shooting forwards
as if they had been waiting for their cue. The men could not
walk far before they were surrounded, hugged tight, Charles's
feet even lifting off the ground as he was hoisted in the air and
onto a multitude of shoulders, to an ebullience of singing and
crying.

Formalities were initiated from there: prayers, speeches,
blessings and hand shaking. Family members took it in turns
to stand up and introduce themselves, while pointing out
which returnee was theirs, as if reclaiming them. 'You can tell
people are very excited but they don't know what to do,' said

Charles' mother hugs him after they were reunited following 17 years apart.

David. At one point it almost felt like time stood still, when Charles's mother pulled him onto her lap and sat with him there, her eyes closed, for around five minutes, Charles was smiling widely, his arms around his mother's neck. 'Propaganda was planted in us that once you escape and you come back home the people there would kill you,' Charles told me later. They even suspected that their own families might murder them, in retribution for the terrible things they had done. Yet the joyful welcome gave Charles a sense of certainty that he was being 'invited back'.

Ouma, who was kidnapped in 2001, appeared quietly euphoric. 'This really shows there's nothing that defeats God. One cannot compete with God. Everything has a beginning and an end. Nothing is impossible,' he pronounced at one point.

Robert was sixteen when he was abducted. After he escaped, David traced Robert's family through his uncle's unique name, Sabello Robertson. Robert hoped that the other boys who had been kidnapped with him had absconded earlier: it was only upon meeting his family – who had no further news – that he realised they must have died in the bush. This tinged the reunion with sorrow. 'They were all our sons,' explained Sabello. 'We have a tradition that my brother's son, we say he is also my son. That is Acholi,' he said, referring to their tribe. 'Now we know they are not there any more. We have to break the news to others at home.'

Sabello had long believed Robert was also dead, 'until David surprised us' three weeks before. Sabello was the eldest of three brothers. The youngest was Mugisha, Robert's father – a bicycle repairman who turned up in a pinstriped suit, including tie and waistcoat. Robert's mother wore a baby-pink dress with fluorescent pink rosary beads around her neck. 'Robert will have three dads,' Sabello beamed. 'There'll be blessings in the church when he gets back, then there's a welcome prayer at home, then we'll chat, dance and do whatever we can.'

Amid the chaos of their kinsfolk colliding, Robert and Ouma came to the realisation that, all this time, they had been distant relatives. While they knew that they both came from Uganda's Agago District, they discovered their households were related through Robert's mother. It added a supplemental lustre to the celebrations, their families stunned that, even so far from home, these men had connected and conspired together, helping each other make it back.

As the celebrations unfolded, David stood back and looked on, calm but encouraging. He knew intimately the challenges of reintegrating into a community you had been estranged from, and he was also familiar with the agony of losing a loved one. This man who assisted returnees had been abducted himself. His childhood – laced with memories of games of hide and seek and climbing mango trees – had abruptly terminated the night he was sixteen years old and rebels encircled his village. After they rounded the residents up, a militant asked David which parent he loved more. When he answered that it was his father, the militants took his father away and killed him.[7]

David remained in the LRA for six months before he escaped. Back in his home village, he was reunited with his mother and enrolled again in school, but faced stigma from his family and his community. 'I thought I was coming to my friends, to my people,' he said, but they regarded him as a 'killer, a murderer, a rapist'. The sting of this rejection, and the resulting sense of exclusion, was an ordeal he did not want anyone else to go through.

Regularly, David said he is asked what he would do if he came face to face with the person who killed his father.[8] His response was: 'I would forgive him.' If 'everyone takes the pain and everyone accepts to start a new page . . . then the cycle of violence has ended . . . Let him go tell the rest how it feels to be forgiven.'

David's non-profit organisation, Pathways to Peace, received funding from various foundations and private individuals. His Land Cruiser, which he nicknamed 'the tank', was purchased as a result of online crowdfunding – he drove tens of thousands of kilometres inside it, back and forth across northern Uganda's inconsistent roads and uneven terrain, searching for long-lost relatives and, when defections happened, supporting returnees. Sometimes, he even flew to central Africa to greet and accompany escapees making the journey home. David hoped donations would continue. 'For

David Ocitti during a reunion between LRA escapees and their family members.

me, this reintegration is not six months of work. This is a lifetime job that we have started here . . . Right now, we are only seeing reunion. But reintegration takes years and years and years. They have come home but they don't have a means to sustain their life and if we don't attend to them that means we have made a bigger problem. So we are going to continue supporting them. As long as we still have resources, we will not stop,' he said. 'Regardless of what happens these are my brothers, I'm not going to sit here and do nothing.'

The joyful atmosphere at the reunions he organised was something David wished he had personally experienced when he returned from the LRA. The initial reunion between Charles, Ouma, Robert and their families had gone well, he determined. 'We can see the excitement of the families and the excitement in their faces,' he told me. 'But at the same time, we also can tell how overwhelmed everybody is, because none of them believed either side was alive. The kids didn't believe their parents were alive, and apparently their parents also couldn't believe they were actually seeing their sons for the first time.'

The three men would stay together in Gulu a while longer, inching out into the world by degrees, beginning with a shopping trip the next day, alongside David. They would get medical checkups for 'splinters in their bodies that need to be inspected and unhealed bullet wounds, which might need surgery'. Other former LRA fighters would come to visit them, including the once fearsome commander turned fellow defector Caesar Achellam, who cycled to their interim accommodation on a bicycle and hung around long enough to teach me some new Acholi vocabulary.

The next big reunion would be in the men's home villages, attended by their extended families and the entire community. 'We have a ritual culture and we want to make sure everything is ready before we go home,' David explained. 'And then, after that, we are going to follow up with personalised livelihood support, which is on a case by case basis, based on what best fits their own society. As of now, you can see, everybody is really very excited. And it is very hard for them to know exactly what they want. We termed this period the "honeymoon period" . . . but once they get hit by real-life situations, we are going to provide them with real livelihood support. We have a lot in store for them, but we don't want to rush them in the whole process.'

In 2000, an Amnesty Act was passed by the Ugandan government, offering pardons to everyone who had engaged in rebellion with the LRA or other groups since 1986, the year President Museveni came to power. It was introduced following an effort spearheaded by Ugandan religious and cultural leaders, which focused on reconciliation and charting a peaceful way forward. This, they believed, could not be achieved through military means. More than twelve thousand former LRA combatants received amnesty over the next twelve years.[9]

Getting amnesty was contingent upon defectors reporting themselves to a recognised official, renouncing conflict and surrendering their weapons, at which point they would receive a certificate. Separately, some also underwent a cleansing ritual which involved stepping on an egg, a symbol of innocence, to signify rebirth. They might also take part in a traditional ceremony known as *Mato Oput*, which involved confessing wrongdoing, apologising to those who were hurt, paying compensation, and drinking a liquid brewed from a bitter root together, to symbolise the bitterness caused by the crimes that had taken place. That bitter taste truly marked the beginning of peace, David was fond of saying. At that point, the families of the perpetrator and the victims were considered to be reconciled.

Information about amnesty was spread through the radio, including during a Mega FM programme called *Dwog Paco*, meaning 'come back home'. A report compiled five years later by Ugandan human rights organisation the Refugee Law Project concluded that there was overwhelming support for the amnesty process across Uganda, though it said the involvement of the International Criminal Court was undermining efforts to reach a peaceful resolution to the conflict.[10] The ICC's first ever arrest warrants were issued, in 2005, for five LRA commanders, including Kony, Dominic Ongwen, and three others who later died. Critics said the warrants had stymied peace talks, preventing the LRA from agreeing to lay down their arms in the following years and supplying Kony with a strong argument that the fighters should not give up, because they would be punished if they left.[11] Ongwen was apprehended a decade later. In 2021, he was convicted of sixty-one counts of war crimes and crimes against humanity. I was with his family in their village, Coorom, that day, as they strained to hear a translation of the ruling from a tinny radio placed on top of a wooden bench. They felt the result was unfair, given that Ongwen had been kidnapped as a child, making him a victim himself.

The Refugee Law Project report certainly suggested that there was widespread support for a broad amnesty and widespread forgiveness. It said numerous Ugandan interviewees had emphasised how giving amnesty resonated with their cultural understandings of justice, where the possibility of legal and social pardons, rather than punishment within formal legal structures, was more likely to lead to long-term reconciliation. 'Although the amnesty does not fit with "conventional" or western understandings of justice, it would be a mistake to simply write it off as somehow weak or as rewarding impunity . . . The fact that the Amnesty Law was in keeping with wishes of the victims of conflict, rather than by perpetrators trying to negotiate their own safety, is a crucial aspect,' it noted.

This is not to suggest that Ugandans were not appalled by the atrocities that had been carried out. Yet many had an empathy, or else a pragmatism, and a love for their wider communities that stretched into an overwhelming desire for peace. Northern Ugandans would say they recognised LRA fighters as their own people, even when they had committed abhorrent crimes. I saw it as a policy of radical forgiveness. Curiously, the report even found that, though there were mixed opinions about how exactly Kony should be treated and where he should go if he was caught, a significant number of civilians supported giving him amnesty too, because of a belief that this might be necessary to end the violence forever. I regularly thought back to the response of a Ugandan friend when I told him I was accompanying Charles, Ouma and Robert back home. Without pause for thought, without questioning what they had individually done, he immediately said that I should tell them 'they are welcome'.

Though there could be stigma towards returnees in the form of name-calling, that report noted no incidents of physical violence towards them: 'Given the extraordinary level of brutality employed by the LRA . . . the capacity of the communities to resist taking revenge is remarkable,' it said. Friends and other sources later told me that tension and occasional attacks upon former LRA members did happen: they were most likely to occur in the context of disputes over land or resources, or when other people were stressed or drunk: common flashpoints in many a situation when one person might seize on anything from another's background to hurt them.

Though LRA defectors continued to return in trickles, by the time I lived in northern Uganda in 2020, memories of the war had more broadly been reformulated into digestible tales, the fighting somewhat refashioned into a backdrop for amusing stories. In a post-conflict society, I have learnt that this is part of the process of resistance and recovery; it is a necessity for endurance.

Running errands one day, a Ugandan friend and former child soldier laughed while noting that he still walks like he is marching. He showed me how LRA fighters taught him to hold his gun; how he always slings bags across himself like that. On innumerable evenings, I sat in dark, concrete-walled rooms, drinking beer or Bond 7 whisky as other friends cheerily recalled outwitting rebels, sprinting for their lives, or being detained and questioned by the LRA or government soldiers, who were always suspicious of the local population. They told stories of both stupidity and cunning, but I was endlessly in awe of how they managed to withstand this hostile environment, when so many did not.

A post-war society holds secrets, of course. One was confided to me by a woman I will call Daisy, with whom I sat outdoors amid long grasses and sunflowers as she told me her dilemma. She was trying to decide when exactly she should divulge the truth of his past to the boy she was raising as her own son. After Daisy was abducted by the LRA, this baby was born to a fellow captive and Daisy was forced to kill the baby's mother. With no way to trace the rest of his family, she vowed to save and care for the child to atone for her sin. She loved him deeply, but she felt she had to tell the boy eventually, maybe once he turned eighteen.

The Amnesty Act was what Charles, Ouma and Robert would avail themselves of nearly two decades after it was signed into law, as they emerged into their new lives. The following months would be hard, beginning a slow reintroduction to villages they had varying and distant memories of. Economic challenges were one key hurdle. Of the three defectors whose reunion I attended, Robert was the only one who could read, write a bit and speak some English, despite it being an official language of Uganda. Charles and Ouma could neither read nor write, though Charles told me he could copy words if someone else wrote them on a page, he just had no idea what they meant.

Robert remembered being talented at arts and crafts before he was kidnapped. In captivity, he learnt to fix the radios which the LRA commanders used to communicate. He hoped to re-enter education to improve his skills with electronics. Being the eldest child in his family meant he had been kidnapped before some of his siblings were born. His return prompted him to meet his youngest brother, aged just nine, for the first time: at one point, I saw Robert slip the boy 1,000 shillings, or around 20 cents – a discreet gift to form a bond between them. 'What surprised me is that my parents are still healthy and both are alive. Imagine the long time the war took. Thank God for that,' Robert said. 'I was really very excited to see my parents coming here. I even saw my uncles, my sisters, another sister is coming tomorrow.'

Despite his joy, he was uncertain how reintegration would go. 'The living conditions in the bush are really quite different from an open place here, like the village,' Robert noted, 'but I hope [it] is going to be OK. All in all, what is important now is working together without discrimination . . . I hope it can be done best with the help of my parents.'

'My dream is that I want to study and join hands in the development of the country,' said Ouma, who planned on becoming a 'businessman'. He, too, was stunned by the warm welcome they received. 'What really surprised me was the propaganda that whoever escaped from the LRA and came back would be killed. I found this was really a total lie. In the bush they were saying that if you went back to Uganda you'd be taken to farm as prisoners, as labourers.'

Charles's thoughts remained focused on his two children and the woman he still called his wife, who remained in the Democratic Republic of the Congo. Relationships formed forcibly between two abducted people are tough to understand and to navigate. Charles wanted to formally marry the woman. They had been together for six years; she was abducted aged about sixteen. She had to stay in the DRC for the moment because she is not Ugandan, but Charles had spoken to her on the phone. He planned to talk to her parents, to explain to them 'how I came to be in a relationship with her'. Charles wanted his children to come and live with him in Uganda, but the challenge, as he perceived it, was financial – how to pay for their travel, as 'all this movement requires money'.

'I had a very good relationship with my wife,' Charles said about the woman who was 'allocated' to him. 'We related together very well. I really love my wife and two children . . . I will do everything possible to marry her and get my children back. I don't want my children to remain in a different country, it's very painful for me.'

Amid this uncertainty, Charles's other lost relationships were being restored to him. He had been close to his parents once and felt certain he could be again. 'Whenever I came back from school, my dad or mom would help me, guide me with my homework and school exercises,' he said, as we sat in the grounds of the old colonial house in Gulu, the day after their reunion. The air was warm, though sudden rain forced us to leave the spacious garden and take shelter. A rooster crowed intermittently.

'There are times my parents would correct me when I made mistakes,' Charles said. 'That really helped me to know more about my parents and become closer to them. Whenever my mom was busy working or cooking I'd be with my father, him carrying me, chatting with him, playing with him. When I was abducted I kept building pictures of them in my mind.'

His parents were asleep in another building when Charles was abducted: he suspected they had been murdered or captured too, or even that they might have died from heartbreak. Not knowing for sure was a torment. But it was the images of them which he held in his mind that helped him 'immediately' recognise his parents when he saw them again. The only difference was that his father had 'gotten fatter', Charles laughed. Notwithstanding all of this time away, he felt deference; a boy's desire to absorb parental guidance, a pull to abide by their decisions. 'I am still waiting to hear from my parents as to what I should do with my future. We will sit together and discuss when I go back home,' he said.

This second chance at a relationship with them had started off well, at least, he smiled. 'I was extremely, extremely happy yesterday when I saw my family members, especially my mother who served me with a loving breast when I was still young. I thought I would not see my mom, but when I came back yesterday, I saw her inviting me back.'

Chapter 5

Ghana: Love under siege

> *Odo nnyew fie kwan* (Fante)
> *Odo nyera fie kwan* (Asante)
>
> – 'love does not lose its way home', a proverb represented by an
> Adinkra symbol, which are used in fabrics, textiles and jewellery
> in Ghana, West Africa

On 23 May 2015, I stood on a stage in Dublin Castle looking out
over a sea of cheering, jubilant faces. Ireland had just become the
first country in the world to legalise same-sex marriage by popular vote. Onlookers joked that it felt preordained when, hours
before, a rainbow appeared in the sky. There was a festival atmosphere, with multicoloured flags and outfits; the crowds singing
and whooping. My friend Conor pointed upwards, joking:
'Even the sun has come out.'

The Catholic Church traditionally held huge sway in Ireland.
Homosexuality was illegal until 1993, while divorce, for hetero-
sexual married couples, was barred until 1996. Generations
grapple with the fallout from abuse by priests and the cruel
treatment of women and girls who became pregnant outside of
marriage. The majority of Irish children – including me –
attended state-funded Catholic schools. In my primary school,

confession was mandatory and the teachings of the Church went unquestioned. Our lives were steeped in religion.

Ireland had no postal vote, so flights back home, in the days before the referendum, were crammed with diasporans keen to have a say. They saw this as a defining moment for a country once considered staunchly conservative to an extent that many felt pushed into exile.

I flew home as well: the same-sex marriage referendum was one of the first and only stories I reported on in my birth country. 'I think the hardest thing about getting married should be trying to find a husband,' said Ciaran Hewitt, a twenty-two-year-old wearing a 'yes' badge whom I met in the queue at airport immigration in Dublin. He, too, was coming from London, though others travelled from as far afield as Australia, the Democratic Republic of the Congo, Thailand, Mozambique and the US.

In Dublin Castle, as the result came through, citizens mixed with celebrities: various public figures had come out as gay in the preceding months and they were welcomed with raucous cheers. I ducked out of camera shots as health minister Leo Varadkar emerged on stage behind me: he would go on to become Ireland's first openly gay Taoiseach two years later. Even a priest was praised for revealing his sexuality ahead of the referendum: Father Martin Dolan, at Dublin's Church of Saint Nicholas of Myra, was reportedly greeted with a standing ovation when he announced during mass that he was gay.

When I report on homophobia and state-sanctioned oppression of LGBTQI+ people, I often think back to that joyous day, its euphoria and triumph, and how legal protection for human rights – in a way that was once unthinkable – so rapidly became the status quo. Of course, it is not the same everywhere.

*

Nine years later, and thousands of kilometres away, I was at one of Ed Hanson's regular haunts. We sat at a plastic table beside a roadside bar in Ghana, sipping beer from big bottles. It was mid-afternoon and we were the only customers. Afrobeats played somewhere in the distance.

I had come to West Africa to hear about queer love in a time of unprecedented repression. My communication with Ed started shortly after Ghana's parliament voted in favour of the Human Sexual Rights and Family Values Bill, on 28 February 2024. If signed into law by the president, it would become one of the most repressive anti-LGBTQI+ laws in the world, giving security forces sweeping powers to arrest anyone who even identified as queer.

When I told Ed that I was looking for a couple to spend time with, to illustrate love amid crisis, he informed me he was single but willing to be profiled as a person who was searching. I travelled to Ghana in June 2024. It was Pride month: the first since persecution on a new scale had begun. 'We'll show you the queer side of Accra,' Ed promised. The thirty-three-year-old was a key figure in what Ghanaian activists call 'the community'. These are LGBTQI+ people – more or less open, more or less obvious – who have found each other amid an assault on their very existence. Meeting me and agreeing to be interviewed was a courageous move on his part.

It was dusk when I landed in Accra, during that shimmering transition period when a smattering of electric lights are switched on and then multiply, resembling a globular cluster of earthly stars from above. How preposterous to move so quickly from a place where love could be explored and developed out in the open, to one where even efforts to seek it must remain hidden, I thought.

Ghana – a coastal country almost exactly the same size as

the UK – is considered to be a beacon of democracy in Africa. It was the first sub-Saharan African state to break free of colonial rule, with its declaration of independence in 1957 providing motivation for many others to follow suit. Fundamental rights for all citizens are enshrined in Ghana's constitution. Since 1992, it has been a multi-party democracy.

But democracy does not always mean the best for everyone. Since the British colonial era in Ghana, 'unlawful carnal knowledge' had been punishable by up to three years in prison.[1] This was widely interpreted as prohibiting sex between men, though no prosecutions were documented by human rights organisations.[2] The new anti-LGBTQI+ bill was an appalling regression, activists, advocates and queer people said. It was homegrown, but also fuelled by the US far right and by evangelical groups that are active across much of Africa.[3] The proposed legislation targeted people who 'hold out as lesbian, gay, bisexual, transgender' and even their 'allies', with possible prison sentences of up to three years. It hinted at other potential forms of abuse too, suggesting that sentencing could be 'flexible' only if the person 'openly recants and requests access to an approved medical help or approved medical treatment'. In 2022, British news website openDemocracy revealed that a two-day workshop organised by the National Coalition for Proper Human Sexual Rights and Family Values – a campaign group backing the bill – appeared to promote conversion therapy to Ghanaian medical professionals.[4]

Groups that supported or advocated for LGBTQI+ people would also have to disband or face charges. Sharing information 'aimed at changing public opinion' was deemed a crime deserving of between five and ten years in prison. Funding activities supporting LGBTQI+ people could mean a five-year sentence. Perhaps most terrifyingly, when it came to maintaining relationships between families and friends, the bill said citizens had a duty to actively report any LGBTQI+ person to the police or other authorities, and to assist with any subsequent investigation and prosecution.[5]

Amid this jeopardy, Ed was keen to emphasise what should have been obvious: that Ghanaian voices needed to be centred in any relevant discussion. He specifically meant those who lived there. Outsiders, and even the Ghanaian diaspora, had been known to make loud public statements on LGBTQI+ rights from the relative comfort of Europe and North America, or during brief trips to the country, leaving behind a firestorm which locals had to suffer the implications of. With this in mind, I began taking submissions, through WhatsApp voice notes, from queer Ghanaians who were willing to share their thoughts on resistance and love: both platonic and the romantic love that still, somehow, managed to endure.[6]

Charlie (31, pronouns: they/them)

On a romantic memory: *Two or three years ago, I was emotionally and romantically involved with this individual. It was a good experience, honestly. And this particular memory happened at night spontaneously. He texted me, 'would you like to go to a bar?' So I dressed up, and I met him at his place. Then we took an Uber to one of the most vibrant, colourful parts of the city. When we got there, I took a shot, I had a glass of wine, we ate fried yams. We had fried rice as well, and then I danced, and I found it very romantic because it wasn't planned at all. It was just spontaneous. But our energy was a good mix. And if you were inclined during that particular time, if you were an observer, you would realise that something was going on between us.*

*I remember any time I stood up to dance he would just lock his
ankles around my leg so I would dance in between his legs . . .
People weren't really judgy. People were not staring much, I
believe. Remember I was tipsy, but I don't think we encountered
any extreme homophobia. It was fun. And the bar we went to was
a space for a lot of diverse people to mingle and a lot of diasporans
to come and hang out at, so they are inclined to other forms of
expression. I believe that also added to why we were not really
harassed. It was fabulous. I danced for quite some time. I took
more shots. And, you know, he was very protective, and we
ordered an Uber back home.*

*I remember a day before, I told him that I wanted to see the
documentary* Amy. *So when we got home, although he was very,
very drunk, he told me 'I have downloaded* Amy *so we can watch
it together'. And it was fun. He didn't finish watching with me
because he passed out, but I finished it, and it's a memory. I hold
it here, although we are no longer together, bless him.*

On the community: *There is platonic love between people in
the community. I have an amazing group of friends. We respect
each other, we do our best to love and support each other. We trust
each other, and this is something I hold very dear. We try as much
as possible to hold each other accountable, to always remind each
other that this is where we live, this is who we are, these are the
precautions we need to take.*

*I have also been able to observe another form of queer platonic
relationship, where a group of boys live together under one roof,
cook for each other. Most of the time one person owns the place, but
they make it a safe space for all their friends. And they get to hang
out. They get to express. They could share experiences, advise one
another on men, society, job opportunities, everything in between.*

Advice for others: *This is what I would like to share to other
queer people living in repressive countries, especially to queer men*

who are feminine in their expression, and also to non-binary people: it is important you validate your own self, and it is important you inspire your own self, and it is important you tell yourself that you are loved, because no one is going to do it for you. If you are waiting for the country to validate you, if you wait for the government to validate you, if you're waiting for your family to validate you, even if you're waiting for your partner to validate you, it might not come. You need to be your own muse, unfortunately. And you also have to remind yourself, as much as possible, that you are of value. You form a vital part of the socio-economic development of your country. Whenever you encounter challenges – whether it be unemployment, whether it be a lack of validation from men because of how you express – just know that you are of value. You are beyond your sexuality. You have your mind, you have your heart, you have your abilities, you have your character, you have your personality. These are things that form your being. So just be proud of who you are.

If you cannot be your own muse, try as much as possible to find a chosen family, people you can trust, to share a part of yourself with.

There's a possibility it might never get better. But if you believe within yourself that you are of value, and if you believe within yourself that you are free to be and to love as much as you can, then it does get better for you. So just soldier on, cry when you need to, affirm yourself. Resist oppressors' rule. Love loudly. Be loved loudly by the community, or love yourself as loudly as you can.

Ed Hanson was born in 1991, in Cameroon, a Central-West African country with a population of nearly twelve million people at the time – a figure that had doubled fifteen years later. Though Cameroon is largely French-speaking, Ed comes from the restive Anglophone area along the Nigerian border, where separatist rebels have been fighting to gain independence and form a state called Ambazonia. Yet Ed's childhood was full of positive memories.

As to becoming aware of his sexuality, 'most queer stories are the same,' Ed said, almost dismissively. When he was a schoolchild, he remembered students 'playing house', pretending to take on the roles of father, mother and children, which gave him a chance to explore different identities. 'You hide behind the fact that sometimes there are no girls around,' he recalled. 'So you start kissing boys here and there. I kissed my first boy when I was in Primary Four.'

While he realised he was queer and 'accepted it', his family was 'not really aware per se'. He said he was lucky to be able to 'easily pass as a straight man' but remained sensitive to comments from relatives who seemed to have some inkling of what he was hiding. One of his aunts, on a futile mission to encourage him to become a doctor, told him to 'go to the medical school and stop acting all gay'. Another said she 'hopes you don't become like one of those men who sleep with other men'. He responded with silence or by telling them to focus on their own marriages. Ed's mother, who has passed away, had an inkling, he believes. 'I think she knew that I was queer, she couldn't ask me directly. [But] I think mothers always know.' She 'had a very open heart and I take after her a lot'.

Ed was sitting on a bench beside me, wearing a red beanie hat, white shorts, a gold necklace and a blue-and-green-patterned T-shirt. 'I'm a Gemini in case you're wondering,' he said. 'Geminis are fluent, they are articulate, charming, they are natural communicators, natural charmers. We are spontaneous, we are mysterious in our own way. People would naturally gravitate towards Geminis because they're also good-looking.' He paused, then chuckled.

I had reported on abuses of LGBTQI+ rights across Africa before I met Ed. More than half of African countries criminalised same-sex relations. Throughout much of the vast and diverse continent, conservative religious and political voices painted homosexuality and queerness as 'un-African', even though many states, like Ghana, adopted their initial laws criminalising same-sex relations from colonial ones.

The risk of unanticipated intensification was always simmering. Bashing homosexuality seemed to be embraced almost as a diversion technique by certain politicians – a way to deflect attention from the myriad of ways they were failing their people. At the same time, many queer people hated hearing it described as a distraction tactic. The threat to them was far too real.

When I lived in Uganda, between 2019 and 2021, I witnessed the impact firsthand. An Anti-Homosexuality Act, which became known as the 'Kill the Gays' bill in the western media, was signed into law by President Museveni in February 2014. Though it was struck down by the courts less than six months later, its passing, and the debate surrounding it, unleashed a nationwide wave of homophobia. As a result of my housemates' efforts, our home in Kampala sometimes served as a safe space and venue for queer-friendly parties. It was a relatively secluded hideaway, reached by turning off a potholed road onto a suburban hill dense with greenery, then climbing another road, this one steep and winding. Those present flirted, danced, and could dress and feel like themselves. There were checks on the door and a carefully selected guest list. The risk of a raid hung over any gathering.

Safe spaces and allies did little to halt the advance of repressive movements. A new anti-LGBTQI+ Act, which included the death sentence in certain circumstances, became law in Uganda in 2023. Many of the young, gifted, stylish people whom I'd once partied with found ways to reach Europe. They, of course, were the lucky ones. In an isolated refugee camp in northern Kenya, I visited LGBTQI+ Ugandans who put their faith in trying to get resettled to the US. They ended up spending years in a semi-desert climate, reliant on aid rations and handouts of ever-decreasing sizes, while persistently stigmatised by the other refugees whose own experience of persecution did not necessarily make them more sympathetic to alternative forms of it.

Queer people who claim asylum in countries apart from their own are sometimes called 'rainbow refugees'. In 2024, the North America-based organisation Rainbow Railroad received more than thirteen thousand requests for help; the year before, it was more than fifteen thousand. Afghanistan, Pakistan, Uganda and Turkey were listed among the countries where LGBTQI+ people were most likely to seek assistance, but the US itself shot to the top spot after the 2024 re-election of US president Donald Trump, with the charity saying this 'dramatically accelerated global regression on [both] LGBTQI+ and asylum rights'.

More than seven hundred Ghanaians were supported by Rainbow Railroad in 2024, but none of this assistance helped them leave the country. The charity said that was because shifting international restrictions, visa regulations and other controls on movement meant 'their passports cannot take them anywhere to claim asylum.'

Ed was just eighteen when he moved to Ghana, more than 1,000 kilometres away from Cameroon, in 2009. He told me he did this out of a desire to be 'independent', to become 'anonymous . . . live the life that I want to live'. Then he paused. 'Now this is where my story gets a bit interesting.' Ed first came to Ghana while training to become a religious brother in a Catholic order. The initial phase, known as postulancy, was in Cameroon. Then he moved to Ghana for the novitiate. I have seen a photograph of him from that time, smiling in a long tunic with other brothers-in-training, the knots in the cord tied around his waist representing chastity, poverty and obedience.

After Ghana, Ed spent four years in Kenya, East Africa, for his scholasticate, where he also trained to become a biology and chemistry teacher. There, he began a secret relationship with a man he met on Facebook. When Ed received his qualification, he was asked where he wanted to be based. 'I chose Ghana again, because Ghana was the country that I had felt comfortable in.'

Ed quit the religious order in 2017, right before he was due to take his final vows: 'I decided that it was not my thing.' The decision was 'only difficult because I had to start life afresh'. Self-sufficiency was 'a whole process' and Ed was anxious, if excited. 'But, I don't know, Mother Nature or heavens, whatever power you believe in, I think it was very favourable to me, because as soon as I did that, three schools offered me employment. I chose the school I'm working with now.'

Over the coming years, Ghana would become the latest flashpoint for LGBTQI+ rights, and Ed played a key role in lighting the spark. In 2018, he was one of the founders of an organisation called LGBT+ Rights Ghana, where he eventually became the communications director. Initially, 'our goal was basically cyber-activism, to call out discrimination against queer people, to call out human rights abuses,' he said.

He traces his decision to become more outspoken back to Oprah Winfrey's talk show. Winfrey was interviewing a man who said 'a country that believes there are no queer people in it is a delusional country,' Ed recalled. In Ghana at the time 'it was just assumed that there were no queer people.' Ed felt that the wider Ghanaian population needed to realise that people like him existed.

In January 2021, LGBT+ Rights Ghana opened a centre in Accra. Multicoloured umbrellas were strung upside down in a line. There was a huge Pride flag hanging beside the black-starred green, yellow and red Ghanaian one. The launch event was attended by EU delegates, the Danish ambassador and the Australian high commissioner. 'When we launched this safe space, it became a whole national issue,' Ed said, though 'we didn't think about it that way.'

Within a month, the centre was shut down by the police. Salacious media reports claimed men were having sex in the building, and teenage students were being 'recruited' using laptops loaded with pornography. One journalist threatened to reveal where LGBTQI+ individuals lived, saying 'if Ghanaians want to beat them up, so be it.' The overall commotion led to the genesis of the anti-LGBTQI+ bill that March.

Sam Nartey George, one of eight MPS who sponsored the bill, told Al Jazeera it was drafted as a response to 'provocation' by the LGBTQI+ community.[7] But the bill's introduction also followed various visits to Ghana by notable US evangelical Christian groups. Between 2007 and 2020, an openDemocracy investigation found that at least $54 million had been spent across Africa by US Christian groups known for fighting against LGBTQI+ rights and comprehensive sexuality educa-tion.[8] Many were closely linked to US president Trump's administration, the investigation noted. It said they were running initiatives which also included bringing African politicians to the US and training them in tactics to oppose LGBTQI+ rights.[9] US-based right-wing Christian coalition the World Congress of Families even organised a regional conference in Accra in 2019.[10]

Before the bill, there might be multiple community events every week – not just during Pride month. There were beach hangouts, film screenings, potlucks; the Accra Lesbian Visibility Festival; and a New Year's Eve party with bottomless cocktails. These were 'packed', but now 'very few people will come. They are afraid for themselves,' Ed said. As in Uganda, events went semi-underground. It was easy enough to get information about them if you knew the correct people and terminology, but the location was often released at the last minute, an RSVP was mandatory and there was always uncertainty about whether they would actually go ahead.

The passing of the bill in Ghana prompted many queer people to isolate. This might be because they were worried about their personal safety, or because they wanted to insulate themselves from the misery of others. The queer community in Ghana, like everywhere else, is affected by 'elitism, classism', Ed said. Some stood to lose a lot because of their positions and their perceived hypocrisy: they were pastors, priests, politicians, or the children of those people. The LGBT+ Rights Ghana welfare team began encouraging everyone to 'stick to the people they have', which meant they would 'cut down on the number of partners, cut down on the blackmail, be free from diseases and all the nonsense and the complications that come with it'.

In Ghana there has long been a 'hook-up culture', Ed said. In the past, people had met through HIV and AIDS campaigns. Then came Facebook, and afterwards the apps:

Grindr, Blued, Jodel, Tondo, Tinder. The internet revolution-ised relationships globally. It made marginalised people feel much less alone but it also made them vulnerable, enabling blackmail and extortion. Online, anyone could pose as a potential date, then demand money, or assault and rob their victim in person, after luring them to certain places. Ed heard accounts of people being photographed or videoed naked, with abusers threatening to post videos and photo-graphs online if the victim did not hand over large sums of money. The extortionists were confident that their victim would never go to the police. Sometimes the extortionists themselves were LGBTQI+. In response, LGBT+ Rights Ghana began producing a 'blackmail broadcast list', where queer people could check the names of whom to avoid and locations that were dangerous to go to.

When I first visited Ghana, in early 2022, it was mostly to produce reports for a series focused on interesting things young Africans were doing across the continent. I had lived most of the previous year in Sierra Leone – a country rich in minerals but very poor economically – and the transition three coun-tries east felt like moving forward in time. In Ghana, a cost of living crisis was about to escalate, but there was also nonstop electricity, Uber, Domino's Pizza and an authorised Apple Store. I repeatedly encountered the same pop-up karaoke com-pany. Accra seemed like a sleepy city, but fun.

I wrote an article about how Ghana had officially rebranded Valentine's Day as 'Chocolate Day'. This was partially a bid to grow the country's domestic cocoa market, though a govern-ment minister also said it 'would minimise social vices'. 'Other people think Valentine's Day is about sex, sex, sex, but it is a day for love and chocolate,' declared Mabel Sallah, a sales manager for a cocoa spice business, standing behind her stall at an outdoor Chocolate Day fair.

It seemed like an amusing topic to report on, but the reference to social vices linked in with a tendency from political figures to see themselves as moral and religious enforcers, in a way that was also used to target sexual minorities. I understood the implications of that more after I travelled to Kumasi, the capital city of the Ashanti Region, which lay 250 kilometres northwest of Accra. There, I spent much of a day at the artists' residency set up in 2018 by transwoman Va-Bene Elikem Fiatsi. 'We are all the same,' was written at the entrance to the compound, alongside a painting of a person whose finger was shaped like a gun and pointed at a huddled mass of multicoloured others. Va-Bene regularly travelled abroad to perform and exhibit, and used her earnings, along with donations, to fund the residency, which she saw as a 'community space'. Inside, she both hosted an evolving roster of artists and gave shelter to queer people who needed it.

Va-Bene had recently visited Ghana's parliament to listen to a debate over the new anti-LGBTQI+ bill. 'They started comparing us to armed robbers, terrorists, paedophiles,' she said. 'It was so exhausting to listen to all that . . . without having a chance to respond.' So she created a video, which later played on a big screen, of her hair being unbraided by many hands and her extensions being removed. It was a ritual to convey shedding the negativity she had weathered.

As we walked around the residency's premises, ahead of a series of performances by those living there, she told me that she strongly felt she had a duty to remain in her birth country, because other transgender people had been cowed into silence and she was willing to speak out. 'Relocating from

Va-Bene Elikem Fiatsi removes her hair extensions in an artistic video response to the negativity around Ghana's anti-LGBTQI+ bill.

Ghana is the last thing I'll ever dream about. Even if I'm chased with machetes and bullets, I may prefer to die in Ghana than to relocate to Europe,' she said. 'If I wanted asylum, I would have got it long ago. I owe it to Ghanaians. Ghanaian vulnerable, marginalised communities. Not only LGBTQ Ghanaians. [All] Ghanaians, even the homophobes, I owe them the responsibility to change them from thinking what they're thinking. What I'm doing . . . it's a way to help people reflect.'

Va-Bene saw her art as 'a radical act of empathy'. Inserting her work and body into public spaces was 'intervention and confrontation'. In 2015, Va-Bene played dead, lying naked and covered in black paint, in the arms of a white woman wearing only underwear, in front of the headquarters of the Bible Society for Ghana. On Good Friday 2021,

Va-Bene acted out a crucifixion: a remembrance of 'those Ghanaians, blacks and queers, who suffered similar violence and death'.

Like Ed, she came from a religious background: she was once a Christian preacher and teacher of 'religion and moral studies'. She would continue preaching what she saw as a message of love over the coming years.

In September 2025, on her birthday, Va-Bene posted on Facebook:

I dedicate this milestone to the work I've accomplished and the work yet to come, to the seeds I've sown, and the creative spaces I've brought to life.

I offer my life-changing gratitude to my mother and grandmother, who shaped me into a vessel of love, and to my father, who fostered my growth into a selfless mother. Sadly, none of them is alive today to witness this moment and appreciate the joy they brought to so many faces and future generations.

To all those I've met throughout my forty-four years, friends, lovers, and even enemies, I say thank you. Every encounter, whether filled with love, hate, abuse, care, or violence, has contributed to making me stronger, compassionate and wiser. My sole desire is to die without any hate in my heart.

Gem (25, pronouns: she/her)

On how the community help each other: *We have a little society which is very hush hush. You have to know someone in the community to know the community. A lot of times people who are outed by their friends or come out to their families need places to stay. And a lot of times the community has found ways to raise money to support people.*

*We create a safe space where queer people can just come
and be themselves. It's a very inclusive, very excluded community.
There is a lot of platonic love. I'm a very loving person, so I don't
necessarily have to be in a romantic relationship to show someone
I love them . . . Anytime I go on a trip, I try to get a gift for my
friends.*

On love within the community itself: *I have a group of
friends, a lot of gay men and lesbian women, and a lot of time
when we are out in public people think we are couples. And it's
funny, because people are so homophobic that they would rather
see queer people and think there's no way this will exist, right?
They would rather think we are just weird.*

*You tend to find a lot of people who have dated still
being friends, because we can't find the community we
need outside of the community we've created. So it creates a
very familiar or family-like institution. In those cases they
talk things out. They see that, oh, you know, it happens. You
don't have to marry each other because, I mean, we cannot
marry each other . . . Sometimes it doesn't work out for both
parties.*

On having a long-term relationship: *'The thing with
long-term relationships here is, because of how uncertain our
stance is, nobody wants to do like a fulsome thing, where now you
are deep in this and then you have to have a lavender
marriage . . . So, yeah, a lot of our relationships aren't long term.
You go on a break, we are friends, we date other people, and then
we come back. It's a little mismatched. To have a long-term
relationship would include us going on dates, going in public
together, and this is a society where we are not accepted. So we
even have to hide who we are or change how we dress . . . It is
possible, especially if a couple have plans to leave the country
together. But it's safer to avoid being that target.*

Advice for others: The goal is to survive, right? It's to stay alive and to just continue this, to continue whatever community or whatever love or whatever space we find ourselves in. We're not trying to make any noise or cause any problems for anybody. And the best thing you can do is to be hush hush about your relationship . . . It's hard to have your family not see you for who you are, but I think your safety is more important than your coming out story.

Across Africa, queer activists are keen to point out how obvious the presence of LGBTQI+ people is throughout history. Queerness was taken as normal in certain traditional cultures, Ed expounded, 'and not just in a sexual sense'. Ghana's Fantes, for example, are said to have perceived gender roles through the belief that those with 'heavy souls' desired women, while those with 'light souls' desired men.[11] Even in more recent discourse Ghanaians had terms like *Kojo besia* for an effeminate man, and 'doing *supi*', describing close relationships between girls that may be sexual.

Researching this, I thought about how much queer history must have gone unrecorded, from Ghana and across the rest of the world. After photographing queer friends and acquaintances for a 2016 project named *Just Like Us*, Ghanaian photographer Eric Gyamfi expressed a similar notion. He felt 'these stories are important, because if they are not told, then a part of our history as a people has vanished . . . If queer life is not archived, in years to come, bad people who want to erase queerness can boldly say that this has never existed.' He hoped for a world where 'people can understand and appreciate other people's differences'.[12]

A community-generated mapping platform, called Queering the Map, began as a class assignment by a student in Canada in

2017. It is another effort to ensure queer visibility. It lets LGBTQI+ people tag locations globally which mean something to them with messages or memories. While more than half a million submissions had been pinned across the world by 2025, including more than 180,000 in the US,[13] there were less than twenty in Ghana. 'I love that I'm queer. I love that I have queer friends. I love that we're thriving despite the erasure we face. I want every queer Ghanaian to find this map. I'm overwhelmed by the number of queer people who have left messages,' read one.

I again considered how it must feel to be constantly on guard as Ed and I drove between drinking locations in Accra. A smiling monkey-nut seller in a tangerine T-shirt, standing in the busy traffic, started in recognition upon spotting him. 'This your wife?' the seller asked, gesturing at me in the taxi's back seat. Ed said the seller double-jobbed as a cleaner in the school where he was a teacher.

In his professional life, Ed said he works hard and is recognised for his diligence. As far as he knows, no one there knows that he is queer. He believes in 'compartmentalising . . . when people do that, life becomes a bit easier for you . . . If you are at work you are basically just working, your sexuality doesn't need to come in to it.'

For the first time, though, the walls between his different lives were being chipped away by the new bill. In school he felt 'distracted'. The bill was passed on a Wednesday. 'I had to put out statements, issue press releases, do interviews, attend meetings online to strategise. I have to talk to people who are a bit wary, people who are confused.' He told everyone he was convinced that the bill was unconstitutional and his organisation was ready to challenge and stall it. Nevertheless, many of 'the community' were frantic.

Even if it never became legislation, a new wave of homophobia was proliferating. Citizens interpret a bill passed by
parliament as one given broad approval. There were 'damage
controls' to do, Ed explained.

Ed was griping. He was tired of going to weddings – he had
watched too many closeted gay men marrying women,
forced into a performance of straightness not reflective of
their authentic self. They made vows surrounded by men
they had slept with, their new bride none the wiser. I wondered about their wives, and how much unhappiness this
could mean for the women. Societal pressure was twisting
lives into wrongful directions.

Ed's longest relationship had lasted a year, and he was
not in a rush to enter a new one. Ideals of romantic love are
difficult to maintain in a society with widespread poverty
and no social security net, not to mention state-sanctioned
persecution. Committing yourself to one person means
taking on extra risk. Ed seemed conscious of this when he
said that because of the 'plan that I have in mind, I don't
think I want to commit myself to an exclusive relationship
right now'. But he had 'people that I can still roll with . . .
I'm focusing on my life. I'm trying to build something.
Being the high achiever that I am, until I get there I will not
be satisfied.'

Later, a few drinks down, Ed chastised me for not asking
him how he imagined his wedding. I checked my assumptions
then – I hadn't considered it as an option. Twenty-two people
were arrested in Ghana in 2021 for attending what authorities
called a 'lesbian wedding', though those present said it was a
birthday party.[14] The idea seemed dangerous, as well as legally
impossible. But Ed had pictured it.

'As I age, and when I know that I'm settled, I want to be in a committed relationship . . . I want to do it with someone that I care about, who cares about me as well.' Each person would give up 'things on the side' because they were focused on building their own lives, 'both individually and as a couple'. By that point, Ed would own a home, a car, and have money in his bank account. His wedding would not be 'too elaborate . . . just a few friends and their family, my family'. He would wear a plain suit 'tailored in a very particular way', or a casual outfit in soft colours: grey or ash, or maybe off-white rather than cream white. He liked the idea that, in the years that followed, whatever occurred during the day, he could go back home and relax with someone, let go, deconstruct anything that had happened and be 'fresh' to face the world again the following morning.

In the meantime, one love he expressed certainty over was his love for the queer community as a whole. That was why he wanted to advocate for everyone, he said. 'We speak for the voiceless. I have defended people even that I didn't like . . . I think I love human beings.'

We went to another roadside bar that Friday night. The DJ seemed entranced in his own world, head bumping to the beat of the music, surrounded by fairy lights. Ed smiled benevolently and sipped his beer. We were sitting at a table separate from everyone else, though it was clear he knew many of the other customers. Sometimes, he had emphasised earlier, it is better to keep yourself apart and alone.

Berry (34, pronouns: she/they)

On the support the community give each other: *I like tea a lot. I like to share tea with my friends and my people. So I organise slow days for people like that. And there are a few people*

*that do that as well, and there are also community organisations
that do that.*

*Among my friends, we check in on each other. Calls, when we
have that time. Visits. Nature visits. Once in a while, I call some
of my friends to just catch up with them, to find out what's going
on with them, if they need me to be of help in any way that I'm
capable.*

*Whether there's platonic love is a very interesting question,
because on the broader level, if you are standing outside of a
community or a sub-community and looking in, you would notice
that people are very hyper-sexual, like people move to people for
sexual reasons. There is that, however I feel like if you delve
deeper, into the individual communities or circles, you realise that
there is also a deeper level of platonic love and affection . . . It's
something I'm very grateful for.*

*For most of us, the kind of support we need is not the kind of
support a general Ghanaian populace think they should offer to
their friends or their loved ones. So in as much as you might have
support systems outside of the community, there is a deeper kind of
support that you can only find from your friends within the
community.*

On long-term relationships: *I like to think of myself
as a romantic. I've had – does a year and a half fall within
what a long-term relationship is? I think the major challenge
was differences in values. We both claimed to be polyamorous.
But then at the end of the day, one of us was more autonomy
driven, and the other was more, let me say, information
driven . . . I think that problem was something that could
have been avoided by having conversations about these things
before even the relationship started. I think it was at this stage
of both our lives where we were just doing relationships on
vibes.*

Advice for others: *Life is full of negotiations. As people, I feel
like our natural instinct is to want to do the things that we want
to do whenever we want to do, to live your life the way that pleases
you. However, with the kind of cards we are dealt, with the kind
of place you find yourself in, with the kind of people you find
yourself among, sometimes you have to be strategic with your
negotiations in life. Put your safety first, then your mental health,
also your development.*

*I grew up in a very religious and strict home. I had to learn
from a very tender age that I'm very different from my people.
However, I also knew that resources at home were very limited,
and I didn't even know anywhere else that I would find any form
of resource if I decided to leave home. So from a very tender age I
started negotiating my life, the things that I could do that would
not kill me, the things that I could do that would not make me
feel like I was selling off my soul for food. Especially when I was
still a child, and in my parents' care, I was basically using my
family to get what I wanted, which was my education and the
care and everything. But then, if you get to a point where you feel
like you can somehow manage your own affairs, you can take care
of yourself and yours, then maybe you can start having these
conversations around how you want to relate with them, who you
are and everything. Because, much as we would love for everybody
to accept us . . . I feel like that is still a long way from here and
yes, we need to work towards that, but also we need to take our
own safety and security into account when we are doing these
things.*

On love and resistance: *Resistance is a very important thing.
Sometimes, when we say 'resistance', people are inclined to look
outward, right? To look to the external things. You say resistance
and automatically, everybody's thinking of resisting government
policies, resisting the oppressors in your family. That's true, that's*

right and all. But then there is also resistance that has to do with internal stuff, mental stuff, right? Because we are conditioned from young ages to believe in certain things, to think certain ways. And as you grow and do the work on yourself to try and get to where you want to be, one form of resistance that you don't have to let go is the one that has to do with certain ideologies that you've been imbibed with, something like internalised misogyny, internalised homophobia, internalised racism and all of that. You have to do constant work.

Also, love is not ownership. Love is not lordship. I say love is freedom. So if you see that thing that you love, that person that you're thinking of, you should always think of how to make them freer and not monopolise them, or not monopolise that thing that you see in them that you think you love.

At half past nine in the morning, on the last Saturday of Pride month – June 2024 – Ed and I boarded a rented bus across from the upmarket Accra Mall. In our bags were large packets of crisps, snacks, and two litres of whisky, our contribution to the secret event taking place that day.

'Where should we sit?' Ed asked me.

'Back seat queens,' came a welcoming voice from the bus's rear.

Ed greeted a few friends and acquaintances and they chatted. An hour passed but the bus was less than half full. Ed put on his headphones and began to sing the lyrics to 'Cheerleader' by Jamaican singer Omi, one foot tapping along; then changed over to the Soweto Gospel Choir. He'd stayed out late dancing the night before, long after I withdrew to my hostel, and he looked tired but still luminous: 'part freak', as he explained it.

Organisers peered out hopefully when anyone new approached, but the arrivals never picked up past a trickle. 'We would have loved the bus to get full but it has been here since nine thirty a.m. and now it's almost eleven,' one said eventually. It seemed like another reminder of how anxious potential attendees must be. I wondered how many had regretfully opted to stay away. We were ready to depart.

Street sellers with cork boards of sunglasses, or buckets of soft drinks in ice, rushed by as the bus moved out of the city centre. Nigerian musician Omah Lay's mellow tunes played on a speaker. We passed schools and chapels bleached by sun; water trucks and a bike pulling a cart of water sachets for drinking. We came to a stop an hour later, in a grassy area surrounded by trees, including plantain and oil palms, as well as bougainvillea. In this secluded location, the group would not be disturbed.

Some had already taken magic mushrooms, they announced. Ed pulled out one of our whisky bottles – it was time for shots. There were colourful mats to laze on and chatter about hairstyles.

We sat at a table topped with yellow cards – a game of truth or dare – along with two other men and one woman, a student from Nigeria. 'Let's dirty this shit up,' said Ed gleefully, though in reality it remained quite tame. On another day, I could imagine Ed, the secondary school teacher, in this clearing with his students, explaining the natural ecosystem to them, as he paused to do to me.

The game switched to Uno. Rain began pattering against the trees' wide leaves, and birds, undeterred, sang around us. More people arrived, the music was turned up and wine was uncorked. I spoke to a Liberian woman about the difficulties and advantages of leaving her birth country for Ghana. The conversation, where she spoke about her longing for acceptance, reminded me how a lawyer working on LGBTQI+

rights issues once told me that it was the countries where most
of us never hear about crackdowns that might actually be the
hardest for queer people to live in, because a visible community never formed in the first place.

As the crowd grew, a new plan was announced: different
teams, relay races, volleyball. There was flip cup, a sack race
and 'lime', a game like the egg and spoon race, with a lot of
arguing over the results. Someone offered around a bottle of a
weed-infused hibiscus drink. People wore heels, sandals, run-
ners, jeans or sequins. Some had braids, dreadlocks, or their
hair half dyed. Ampe, a clapping and stamping game Ghanaian children play in school, caused more shouting about the
rules, winners and losers. Ghanaians are very competitive, several people told me, laughing.

Then, we sat around plastic tables again. There were more
jokes and gossip about romantic entanglements. A man in a
bright pink tank top said he had been feeling despondent at
the beginning of the day, but now he felt happy; he had realised there could be comfort and joy in Pride.

We stayed later than planned, eating communally, then gathering up the mats, bottles, plates, rubbish; and making sure
the site was left exactly as we had found it. Everyone piled into
vehicles, some in Ubers or taxis from the Yango app, and some
in their own cars. Three women sat in the cargo bed of a pickup
truck, their heads bobbing in and out of sight amid the head-
lights and beeping and pollution of rush hour in a city without
properly planned road systems. Accra could feel like Europe –
a man in my car posited – if you only drove in the middle of
the night, when the streets were mostly empty. That's when
'you see the place that you actually want to be', Ed said,
wistfully.

Before we left the park, the larger group discussed where to go next – it was only twilight, after all. Ed suggested the bar that he and I had been in the previous night.

'Is it queer friendly? Is there a place inside that we can be?' asked a doe-eyed woman in a bright orange dress. 'Don't worry, the owner is my friend,' Ed responded.

Right as we arrived at the venue, the vehicle driven by another attendee broke down. Community members gathered around, trying to come up with ways to fix it. Several pushed the car into various positions. A mechanic was found and a new battery fetched. No one went inside the bar – they were all together, supporting each other, in the semi-darkness, the only illumination emanating from two weak lamp posts and a few roadside stalls selling packets of spices and sachets of coffee, soft drinks, eggs and other basic goods.

This scene seemed meaningful. Everyone there would ultim-ately retreat, have another drink, maybe even a dance, all the time hoping that they were only noticed by each other; that no one more sinister was paying attention. It felt like they were pro-tecting and bolstering each other. In Ghana, they were forced to live in the semi-shade, however much they longed to shine. I thought about love as I watched this group of people, most of whom I had met just that day, stand together in the middle of that road.

Ed believed queer people found solace through forming a community. 'Even if the government is trying to ostracise us and separate us and make us feel like you are less than a human, we still have found ways of making people feel like they matter and they belong and they feel loved and cherished,' he told me in one of our conversations.

He felt some gratification with how Pride month had gone, despite all the hurdles. 'The most important [thing] to highlight is the fact that we are a resilient set of people,' he said. 'We are working tirelessly to make sure our voices are heard, to make sure that we counter the prejudices and the abuses that we face every day here in Ghana . . . The queer community in Ghana is a very united community. We will not allow anyone to come between us.'

Chapter 6

Nigeria: Motherly love and acts of bravery

'In times of crisis, we must all decide again and again whom we love.'

– Frank O'Hara

When she heard reports that Islamist insurgent group Boko Haram was approaching her hometown, Madagali, Zainabeu Hamayaji had to think quickly. The group – whose name roughly translates as 'Western Education is Forbidden' – had been terrorising northeast Nigeria since 2009, with the goal of establishing an Islamic caliphate. Its fighters were known for slaughtering men en masse, and kidnapping women and children to become wives, recruits or slaves carrying out domestic work.

Months before, in April 2014, Boko Haram had abducted nearly three hundred schoolgirls from a school in Chibok, a town roughly 150 kilometres away by road. News of that incident was slow to filter out, but it eventually came to global attention through the social media hashtag #BringBackOur-Girls, which was shared millions of times, including by Nobel laureate Malala Yousafzai and Michelle Obama, the wife of then-US president Barack Obama.

With more than 200 million inhabitants, Nigeria is the

most populous country in Africa. That means a lot goes under the radar, hidden by the chaos of multitudes on a planet where global attention is not fairly distributed. A spotlight was completely unexpected, especially one pointed towards the north of the country – where locals felt ignored and abandoned even by their own government, far away in capital city Abuja. As often happens with the news cycle, the narrative that did emerge was a simplistic one which glossed over the history and scale of this long-running crisis, where kidnappings and killings had been taking place for years. Neither did the concentration of international consciousness translate to protection for those in danger; it made scant difference to Zainabeu Hamayaji, for example, and the jeopardy she was now facing.

Zainabeu's biggest concern was her eldest daughter, Hassana Isa. At twelve years old, Hassana was still a child: suitably young to enjoy spirited games with her siblings, yet old enough to be chosen as a wife for one of the violent Boko Haram militants. So Zainabeu made a decision. Speaking about it years later, a range of expressions flickered across her face: exhaustion, sorrow, pride.

We were sitting in an old classroom, on a school campus which had been turned into a camp for the displaced in the rural northeast Nigerian town of Gwoza. It was 2017. I had arrived in Gwoza that morning in a helicopter, alongside staff from Unicef, the UN children's agency. We soared above the dry landscape, headphones on and conversation impossible with the noisy rotor chopping above. The helicopter landed at an army base in an old government lodge, where poorly paid soldiers from the Nigerian Army's 192 Battalion leaned against walls or sat moodily beside sandbags. Gwoza had become a garrison town, a secured oasis of relative safety from those who still roamed its perimeters relatively freely.

For almost a year, from August 2014, the town had served as the headquarters of Boko Haram's 'caliphate'. By then, Boko Haram controlled an area of Nigerian territory roughly the same size as Belgium, including around nineteen of the sixty-five local government areas in the country's northeast. Gwoza was the command centre, from where insurgents pushed out orders across the region. As ISIS had in northern Iraq and Syria, Boko Haram exerted total control.

Former captives described militants marching through Gwoza waving black flags, performing brutal executions and celebrating in the streets after suicide bombings, which often targeted markets and other busy places in areas under government control. One woman, who told me she was sold as a 'slave' inside the group, said Gwoza's militants would even exchange videos with IS fighters inside Iraq and Syria by phone, boasting about their conquests and barbarity. The Nigerian militant group's leader, Abubakar Shekau, declared allegiance to IS in March 2015, branding his organisation the Islamic State's West African province. The following year, he fell out of favour with them, splintering Boko Haram into two factions.

On one side of Gwoza are the Mandara Mountains. Thousands of the town's residents fled there to hide in caves when Boko Haram first seized control. It took a Nigerian military offensive, launched in early 2015, for them to come back. Displaced people from other parts of the region made their way there too. They were in limbo, waiting for safety and the chance to return home.

Reporting on the insurgency in northeast Nigeria made me consider the lengths a parent might go to protect a child, or to find one. In 2015, the Global Terrorism Index ranked Boko Haram as the deadliest terrorist group in the world.[1] Its militants attacked Christians and Muslims alike, men and women. Yet Boko Haram's war was largely a war on children and their futures, as clearly evidenced by their frequent attacks on schools. As a result, the insurgency also morphed into a test of parents, and an examination of the extent to which they would, or would not, push themselves to save their children. In particular, it was a place where I recognised motherly love as a powerful force. I noticed that on my very first visit to the area, in April 2016, and on further trips in the six years after that.

Through a large bullet hole in the blackboard of the schoolroom I sat in with Zainabeu, I could see small boys playing in the blazing sun. I was only allowed to stay in Gwoza for a few hours, with the army and aid organisations limiting access for security reasons. They worried about Boko Haram learning that foreigners were present, potentially increasing the possibility of suicide bombings and kidnapping attempts. That risk was there anyway. Soldiers manned barriers on the town's outskirts, firing early warning shots into the air if they spotted anyone emerging from the lush vegetation that surrounded them. Nearby was the Sambisa Forest, a vast, colonial-era game reserve believed to be hiding a combination of Islamist militants, the region's disappearing wildlife, and – locals repeatedly told me – a hub of charms and magic. Sheltered by baobab, rubber, tamarind and acacia trees, that was where Boko Haram maintained its bases, following their withdrawal from Gwoza.

The soldiers conducted a rapid assessment each time a figure appeared in the distance. These could be farmers who had ventured out earlier in the day, desperate to harvest crops on farmland outside the town's perimeter and stave off starvation; women collecting firewood to sell at low prices; or individuals, including mothers cradling infants, who managed to escape the militants and were attempting to come home. Soldiers ordered anyone approaching to hold up their hands and empty bags or even raise their dresses to prove they were not wearing a suicide vest. Some complied without hesitation, keen to do whatever was necessary to ensure a peaceful welcome. Those who did not risked being shot. The soldiers were aware that their barked commands could prompt hasty reactions. A few months earlier, they had watched a panicking teenager blow herself up in front of them, too far away to hurt anyone but herself.

Inside Gwoza, a modicum of civilian life had come back. Young girls walked arm-in-arm down the streets. A speaker blasted a cover version of Michael Jackson's 'We Are the World'. Yet burned-out cars lay beside burned-out buildings: husks and skeletons of what once was. Saeed Salisu Sambo, the town's

Drawings by Boko Haram militants on a wall in Gwoza, northeast Nigeria.

chairman, said around 30 per cent of its residents had returned to the town. Many rushed to repaint their homes, eager to conceal the numerous markings that militants left behind them. 'Even the house I live in [had] "Allah" painted all over it,' Sambo told me.

Boko Haram fighters destroyed key sites before retreating. A former medical centre was set on fire, its records incinerated. On the cement outside, where patients had surely once waited wearily on plastic chairs, a laptop had been smashed and then burned, its memory rendered unreadable.

Unicef set up tents on the same grounds to act as a new healthcare facility. In a corner behind them was a mass grave. 'That's where Boko Haram buried their own,' a medical worker told me. Staff had to be careful of where they stood – besides the hidden bodies, there was a risk of undetonated explosives.

On the remaining walls in one of the destroyed buildings, drawings seemingly left by the militants were visible. They were childish pictures of weapons, cars or tanks. I looked at them, trying to grasp what was inside the minds of people who could cause such devastation. It was surreal for me to be there, after years of covering the militant group from afar. It was even more incredible to encounter people, like Zainabeu, who had found a way to resist them.

'I dug a ditch within my compound,' Zainabeu told me about the decision she made as Boko Haram were approaching her town. Inside what sounded more like a dugout, she said she had stored jerry cans of water, sacks of non-perishable food and some leather bags to use in lieu of a toilet. Then she instructed her daughter to get inside. Zainabeu says she covered the top of the 'ditch' with corrugated iron, and erected a tent above that. She kept her daughter hidden there for months.

Within days, Boko Haram had murdered Zainabeu's husband and other local men. I heard about this mass slaughter from displaced people who had been scattered from Madagali all over the region. Another witness told Amnesty International that hundreds of men who refused to join Boko Haram had their throats slit in the town on a single date in December 2014, while at least six hundred were killed twenty-six kilometres north in Gwoza on another dark day, four months before.[2] Zainabeu said she saw many of her neighbours being killed as they tried to abscond. 'So I couldn't leave,' she said.

Next, as she had anticipated, the militants went door to door looking for young women. Tipped off about Zainabeu's eldest, they turned up at her house. 'I swore and swore I didn't have a[n older] daughter but they didn't believe me and kept beating me,' she said. 'They came every day to beat me and they were constantly terrorising me. So I decided to strip myself of all of my clothing and just walk around naked in the village. I unplaited my hair to look like a mad woman. I urinated and put faeces on my hair and my body. I'd go to the town centre and roll around in trash so they would think I was mentally unstable.' As Zainabeu detailed this, she gesticulated wildly, almost re-enacting the persona she says she adopted to get her through those gruelling months.

Zainabeu's younger three children – aged seven, ten and eleven – backed up the charade, telling the sceptical militants that their mother had attended a psychiatric hospital before the town was captured. She demonstrated how, while pretending to be mentally unwell, she would pull her other daughters close to her. Flies swarmed around her, attracted to the excrement. This was another ploy to save her younger children.

'Boko Haram decided they did not want a child from a madwoman. Previously they had killed a madwoman and the curse from the madwoman prevented them from any military successes. They didn't want to kill another, so I was spared because of their belief. They wrote something on the wall saying nobody should attack this madwoman, it will be a curse. So I was protected.' The irony, a local later commented to me, was that the level of trauma and stress people from these areas had experienced had probably driven them all quite 'mad' anyway.

The next sizeable challenge was convincing the Nigerian soldiers, once they recaptured the town, that she had not been a collaborator or been married to a Boko Haram fighter herself. Zainabeu said this was easy enough: she just took them to the dugout where her daughter was hiding. 'We went there

Zainabeu Hamayaji sits in a classroom in a school turned displacement camp in Gwoza, in 2017.

together. When we opened up the hole, there she was . . . Hassana came out.'

Their life in the Gwoza camp was difficult, with her daughter out of school and Zainabeu reduced to begging for scraps to feed her family. She had a dislocated shoulder from beatings by Boko Haram militants, along with a scar on her forehead and a missing tooth. Her headaches were constant. 'I will see what the future holds. I don't know what will happen,' she told me, the commotion of hundreds of other displaced people audible around us. 'I just know we're safe now.'

I wish I could have had more time with Zainabeu. I wanted to meet her daughter, hear more of her memories and find others who corroborated her story of survival. But I could not stay longer and there would be no way to contact her again. Gwoza was completely cut off from mobile phone communications at the time: the insurgents routinely felled telecommunications lines, to prevent locals from leaking information about their activities or calling for help. None of the displaced people I met had phones anyway; many had nothing but the clothes they were wearing.

As I got up to leave, to walk back to the helicopter that would spirit me away, I realised Zainabeu was one of the relatively lucky ones, still in the presence of her children. Other women, sitting hunched in groups on the ground, appealed for me – a rare outsider – to find their families for them. Even if they could get to a place penetrated by phone networks, they had no numbers, no Facebook accounts or other ways to track down their offspring, spouses, siblings and parents.

Among them was Rahila Madaki, a twenty-five-year-old whose husband was killed during the assault on Gwoza. She told me she had spent fourteen months travelling across the northeast – visiting the cities and towns of Yola, Mubi,

Maiduguri and Kano – looking for her two missing children: a ten-year-old son and eight-year-old daughter. Also vanished were her mother, her teenage brother and her sister, who had been coerced into marrying a Boko Haram fighter. Three years had passed since she last saw them. I took a photograph of her and posted her appeal online, but heard nothing further.

I met many mothers who had made similarly lengthy and often meandering journeys, hitching lifts or paying for a seat in a private car, bus or van, travelling through dangerous territory where roads could be dotted with military checkpoints but vehicles were also regularly ambushed by militants, and travellers shot, kidnapped or killed. On specific days, travellers could join a convoy escorted by armed military personnel and members of the local vigilante group, wielding sticks and cutlasses.

When the mothers arrived in new schools, churches and mosques transformed into displacement camps, they would ask anyone they met for information, naming and physically describing each child's appearance when they did not possess a photograph. These trips were expensive, costing as much as 40,000 naira in one direction: more than many earned in a month. In some cases, families sold their belongings to pay. Taking a longer but safer route could push the price up tenfold. While many aid agency staff used helicopters to move between projects – reaching the Nigerian military-protected enclaves by air, as I had – that option was not available to the vast majority of local Nigerians.

Informal networks transmitted rumours and reported sightings: sometimes a woman would, by chance, run into an old neighbour, friend or acquaintance who told her to go here or there, claiming to have some precious piece of knowledge. It felt like playing a schoolyard whisper game, but maybe this was better than the alternative: completely giving up.

Rahila's search proved futile. She was slumped in despondency, like she was resigned to this hot, dusty camp for displaced persons being her final resting place. 'I get nostalgic when I see people with their parents or husbands,' Rahila told me. 'I think too much and cannot sleep at night.'

To get to northeast Nigeria, on my initial trip in 2016, I had flown from London to Abuja, then boarded a small United Nations-operated plane to Yola, in Adamawa State. I reported there for a while, before flying on again to Maiduguri, the Borno State capital. I was twenty-six and more commonly worked as a desk reporter, so I was grateful to be away from my UK office, if anxious about what I might find. In my rucksack was a satellite phone, which my editor told me I should use to send out a distress signal if I ended up in danger.

When I conjure memories of that trip, every scene is overlaid by glaring sunlight, which reflected off the ground as well as beaming from the sky. It glinted from the metal water pumps which children hung from in the camps, the yellow *keke napep* tuk-tuks ubiquitous on the streets, and the white aid agency land cruisers, sightings of which prompted local people to assemble in case any charity would soon be distributed. I registered the tragic irony of the slogan on many local licence plates, which proclaimed Borno State the 'home of peace'.

Suicide bombings were common. I travelled that first time with the International Rescue Committee, an aid organisation whose staff advised me not to stay in any location, besides their safe houses, for more than twenty minutes. This was how long it could take for word to spread that I was there and for me to become a target, they said.

The threat was different to any I had encountered before. Boko Haram was using young female captives as suicide bombers. Of the forty-four minors who carried out attacks in 2015, more than 75 per cent of them were girls.[3] They could be convinced or forced: often given a choice between doing this and getting married. Some reports suggested the girls might be fed what many believed were enchanted dates, or *dabino*, and given what they were told was holy water to drink, then instructed to walk towards crowded locations loaded with explosives that could be detonated remotely, meaning the carrier herself might have no idea when her end was coming. Often, they were directed towards markets, displacement camps or places of worship: the locations where quotidian life usually continues, even in times of crisis. It was unnerving to scan my surroundings for girls or young women who might be approaching too fast, looking apprehensive or out of place; to train my brain to perceive females as the most plausible danger. A year later, from inside a UN compound in Maiduguri, I listened in the dark as seven bombs went off in a row. Five of the bombers turned out to be women or girls.

At night, when the Nigerian army patrolled the streets, anyone moving could be considered an enemy. For that reason, the aid agency I was travelling with placed me under a 6 p.m. curfew – meaning I spent far longer than I was comfortable with cooped up in compounds, pondering all that I did not understand and everything taking place beyond the walls around me. I was missing out. Locals told me about the nightclub they went to in the evening before the military curfew kicked in, staying until 6 a.m. the following morning when it was lifted. Everywhere, under every circumstance, people will find a way to live.

On that 2016 trip, more than a hundred kilometres from the isolated location where I would meet Zainabeu the following

year, I heard testimony from another woman who had protected her children using surprisingly similar strategies. These
mothers had never met each other, yet they both demonstrated
the same audacious capacity for quick thinking, making use of
whatever was around them at the time. Their efforts could
have easily gone wrong.

'My husband was killed in front of me, he was slaughtered
by ten men,' Esther Bello recalled. 'My house was burned
down. Lots of people were killed.' She was sitting under a fan
in a white plastic chair with the words 'Grace of God' emblazoned on the back. Outside this small reception room, the
temperature was a sweltering forty-three degrees Celsius. For
Esther, the shelter offered a reprieve from the dusty, hot camp
that had become her home, shared with nearly six thousand
others. This was the National Youth Service Corps government camp in Maiduguri: just one of the many formal, and
vastly more informal, settlements the region's more than two
million displaced people lived in at the time.

Esther was another example of a woman who displayed
extreme love and care for her children; a quiet hero among the
victims of this crisis. Her hometown Bama, the second largest
town in Borno State, was attacked repeatedly. Boko Haram
first concentrated on the military barracks stationed there,
then used the base as a launch pad to capture the rest of the
town in September 2014. Esther and her children – aged
eleven, nine, seven, five and three – were among those taken
hostage.

'Lots of women were abducted with me: the majority of
females in my locality,' she said. Some did manage to run
away, 'but I had my children with me. I couldn't run away and
leave my kids behind.'

She was held captive for three months, watching on as 'lots

of women were forced into marriage and those that resisted were shot.' The militants were solidifying their hold on Bama: Boko Haram controlled it until March 2015, when they were ousted by the Nigerian military. 'They put us in a large compound and locked the gates. When they came around with foodstuffs . . . mostly women cooked for them.'

Esther could see only one way out. 'I had to pretend that I was insane, that I was mad,' she explained. 'I put dirt, mud, everything on my body. It was difficult to convince them, I had to use whatever was at my disposal. Even if it was vegetable oil, I would pour that on my body. It wasn't easy. When I began pretending that I was insane they left me with my children. It wasn't even worth holding me. Once I started portraying madness I was no longer of use to them . . . They were able to let me go.'

Esther and her five children walked barefoot for three days to find safety. They had nothing to eat and she worried they would die on the way. 'At one point, I thought I was going to lose my kids.' She pointed to her bare toes, showing me where sharp, dry plants in the bush had punctured them as they walked, and blisters quickly erupted.

'When we came here, my children were admitted to the medical centre in the camp, where they were treated,' she said. The camp's conditions were far from ideal: residents were crammed together with little privacy. They were only guaranteed two meals a day of rice, beans, cornmeal or soup.

During sleep, nightmares transported Esther back to the bush and to captivity, until she would gasp awake, her heart hammering. She received no counselling. 'Compared to being in the hands of Boko Haram, it is OK here,' Esther conceded, though she was keen to return home. 'If things get better I would want to go back,' she confirmed, but she was not sure how her family would survive in practice. 'When I was staying before in my town I was supported by my husband – whatever he got he would bring back home. So I'm not really sure what I'm going to do.'

From 2009, when Boko Haram began its armed rebellion, Nigerians ran for their lives. More than two and a half million people were estimated to have been forced from their homes by 2016.[4] I always think the word 'displaced' sounds strangely antiseptic, considering that it equates to an obliteration of the life that existed before. People scattered in all directions, losing track of even their nearest and dearest; not knowing whether their neighbours or relatives survived or who had been brutally murdered, unless eyewitness accounts trickled out in the months and years that followed.

One consequence was that minors disappeared en masse. In April 2016 I visited a dozen formal and informal camps and settlements for internally displaced people across Borno State and Adamawa State. At each one I met multiple parents who were missing their children. Their stories were shocking in their repetition: 'I don't know where they are' seemed to be the most common refrain. This made the accounts of those who managed to protect their children especially striking.

The main organisation working to reunite separated family members in Nigeria was the International Committee of the Red Cross (ICRC). By 2023, it had registered more than twenty-five thousand missing people in the country, more than half of them children.[5] 'It likely only represents a fraction of the total number,' said Tatjana Halpaap, the ICRC's team lead for what they call the 'protection of family links'. She spoke to me on the phone from Maiduguri.

That year the ICRC had a staff of thirty-five working on

registering missing people and family tracing, she said. Assisting them were more than four hundred volunteers operating in tandem with community leaders. They mostly focused on Nigeria's northeast, but also examined cases elsewhere. In northern Nigeria, 'there are many [areas] that are not covered by phone networks. Internet, forget about it. So of course it makes it very difficult if they cannot use technology.' She described the search for a missing person there as 'like looking for a needle in a haystack. Sometimes you get frustrated.' Between 2018 and 2023, the ICRC were involved in just ninety-one physical reunifications between adults and children.

Anyone could open a 'tracing request'. They just needed to provide the missing person's name, their mother's name, a physical description and the location where they were last seen. The ICRC used this information to create booklets of photographs, also calling out the names of the missing in camps for displaced people. For a year, the organisation supported a radio programme on the Hausa-language service of Radio France Internationale called *We'll See Each Other Again One Day*. Tatjana said they planned to dedicate certain broadcasts to particular areas. They would advertise their area of focus in advance so that anyone from that locale could tune in.

In the Dawari settlement in Adamawa State, more than three hundred households set up camps on borrowed land which had been previously used for farming. There was some class differentiation: those who escaped with money could afford mud bricks to build huts, while others crafted shelters out of reeds and wood. Everyone there originally came from the local government areas of Gwoza, Bama and Madagali.

Amid stifling heat, a group of men sat on mats in the shade

while sand blew past. Women's eyes peered out from between the slats of a nearby hut – tradition kept the genders segregated.

These ten men, all Christians from Gwoza, had lost eighteen children between them while fleeing a Boko Haram attack. One man's wife and two children had disappeared. 'There is no access to Gwoza, so there is no way to go back,' he told me. A second was missing his wife and six children. A third had lost two wives and three children, while a fourth had lost seven children. 'I don't know anything about [them],' this man said despondently. 'Only God knows.' A fifth man witnessed his elder brother and his two wives being killed, while a sixth man saw his fifteen-year-old son murdered in front of him.

Even as I heard heroic stories from mothers who had risked their lives to save their children, a lot of estranged fathers seemed notably hesitant to say they would welcome them unconditionally if they were found.

'Yes, we'd take them back, we'd rejoice,' one of the ten men in Yola said, explaining that this was primarily because their offspring were very young when they were kidnapped. However, that group all agreed that if their children had 'matured' and gone through forced conversions to Islam, or become involved with Boko Haram in other ways, they would not be so accepting.

Some children were put in harm's way because of their parents' beliefs, or even traded to Boko Haram militants for money.

In the dark office of a transit centre for people recently released from Nigerian military custody, I met seven-year-old Mustafa. He wore ripped jeans and a stained red T-shirt. His legs dangled from his chair, too short to touch the ground.

Mustafa's father was the one who had delivered him to Boko Haram with his mother and his three siblings, after packing them into a car together, saying they were going to spend the day with relatives a short drive away. Mustafa's father was later murdered by a man Mustafa called his father's 'friend', after he had a public disagreement with Boko Haram leader Shekau. 'Dad's friends then took us to another town. My mother and siblings were crying,' Mustafa recalled. 'When father died, mother remarried a man with multiple wives. She told us to run if we heard gunshots.'

Mustafa was collecting firewood when he heard a staccato burst of gunfire in the distance. Despite his mother's clear instructions, he hurried back to their shelter to find her, but she was gone. Mustafa was on his own when he was discovered by the Nigerian military.

As an unaccompanied child, Mustafa's future was uncertain. Authorities said he could only stay in this transit centre for a maximum of six months; they were considering sending him to live with a local politician. The boy shook his head and

Mustafa sits in a transit centre in Maiduguri in 2017.

stared at the ground when asked for his thoughts on what would happen next. Instead, he started speaking about the lessons he was attending in the transit centre. 'I can't write but I can read the ABCs,' Mustafa said. The boy also spoke shyly about his life before this turmoil, though his memories were fading quickly. 'My town before was very peaceful,' he said. 'My father was so nice to me.'

Many abductions were carried out by close relatives, said Labaram Babangida, a Unicef child protection officer working with Mustafa. Labaram said he had recently heard a story of a father in neighbouring Yobe State who sold his fourteen-year-old daughter to Boko Haram as a suicide bomber for 400,000 naira, close to $1,000 at the time. This was discovered when his daughter turned herself over to the authorities, strapped with the explosives she refused to detonate. Back in Madagali, Zainabeu said her neighbours gave away their daughters for 'selfish' reasons – they might be given money or stolen land as a 'dowry', or food to feed the rest of their family. The money they received was usually between 100,000 and 200,000 naira, worth roughly $250 to $500.

Children in northeast Nigeria, as everywhere, were highly vulnerable to abuse on all sides. They were used as labourers or bombers by Boko Haram, or recruited as spies or guards by vigilante groups fighting them. Minors who escaped could be turned into 'trackers', ordered to lead and direct soldiers to the sites where they had been held, where Boko Haram camped, a vigilante told me.

The Boko Haram insurgency created forty thousand orphans by 2017, Borno State authorities said, and governor Kashim Shettima suggested the figure could be above 100,000. 'Without educating these youth, they will be monsters that consume us all,' he told journalists.

Children who spent time with Boko Haram immediately fell under a cloud of suspicion. Despite his age, Mustafa was detained for more than a month in a cell in Maiduguri's dreaded Giwa Barracks, where anyone suspected of association with Boko Haram could be held without charge.[6] Mustafa spoke of being packed into a room with countless others, in temperatures as hot as forty-five degrees Celsius. Amnesty International, which labelled Giwa Barracks a 'place of death' because of its poor conditions and high prisoner fatalities, found that nearly one hundred and fifty detainees died there between January and May 2016 alone, including eleven children under the age of six, and a boy of around fifteen.[7]

Through all of my reporting, the Nigerian military proved an unreliable source of information – often stonewalling or failing to respond to queries. At the same time, evidence implicated it in atrocities, including extrajudicial killings, summary executions, and the dumping of bodies in secret burial sites.[8] The Nigerian military rejected the allegations, but local people repeatedly described treatment by soldiers which they saw as harmful and dehumanising.

'They were very skinny, collarbones sticking out,' a witness told me about the day one batch of detainees were released from Giwa Barracks. A seventy-year-old man died then, shortly after scrawling his wife's phone number into the sand on the ground of the transit centre. He did not live long enough to see her again.

When I visited, several children were milling about the enclosed centre, which comprised a few dormitories and three dusty courtyards. Women lay on beds, or stood outdoors in quiet reflection. A tall Cameroonian man, awaiting repatriation, sat on a concrete slab, his head in his hands.

I asked gentle questions to fidgeting children. Should I have been talking to them at all, I wondered later. One boy crawled under a big wooden table, another rested his feet on top of it. Labaram, the child protection officer present, said it was hard to know with certainty what they had been through. Boko Haram fighters had schooled them on what to say, he posited, telling children that they would be killed if they admitted to doing anything wrong. What did come through plainly was the attachment these children had to their parents, how they were unwilling to judge their actions, how they longed to be with them again.

One hot day, I stood at the point in Maiduguri's Railway district where Boko Haram had established its base, years before it launched its insurgency. Mohammed Yusuf, a charismatic speaker, was Boko Haram's founder. He was said to have begun as an *almajiri*.[9] In northern Nigeria, this is a child, usually from an impoverished background, who is sent away by his family to get a Qur'anic education, combined with begging on the streets to support his living costs. Yusuf began travelling and preaching publicly, then established his own mosque right where I was standing. In 2009, Yusuf was captured and killed by Nigerian security forces, prompting the violent backlash that grew to become a full-blown insurgency, and would forever change millions of lives.

Yusuf's death meant that Shekau, previously his second in command, took over the top job (he also reportedly married one of Yusuf's wives).[10] Shekau seemed to have fewer qualms about killing civilians. I learnt more about Shekau from Maiduguri's vigilantes. Often untrained and unpaid, these men welcomed me to their headquarters, regaling me with accounts of having fought insurgents with whatever weapons they could find: hunters' guns, bows with rusty arrows, cutlasses. They

Members of a vigilante group, formed to stop Boko Haram, pictured at their base in Maiduguri.

told me how their all-consuming quest to defeat Boko Haram had led to them becoming alienated from their own families – another reminder of the contorting effects war can have on personal relationships. One claimed to have played football with Shekau in his younger days. 'He was always strange. He had psychological problems,' the man recalled.

Shekau was said to be another former *almajiri*.[11] Maybe it is notable, given my focus on motherly love, that both of the two men most responsible for the insurgency appeared to have been parted from their mothers at a young age.

Over his years at the helm of Boko Haram, Shekau would be reported dead multiple times, springing back to life in gleeful and rambling videos where he made threats and mocked his attackers. His repeated resurrections sparked persistent rumours that he used doubles, or clones, to avoid detection, and even a belief that he kept being replaced by newer versions. Shekau eventually killed himself by detonating explosives in 2021, while battling the increasingly powerful Islamic State-aligned faction who had detached themselves from his group, and were pressuring him to surrender to them.[12]

During her many years reporting on the crisis in her country's northeast, Nigerian conflict reporter Hauwa Shaffii Nuhu told me that the powerful force of motherly love was clear to her too. Within that term, she included love that 'transcends biological connections. It manifests even in the ways that women are able to just adopt a kid whose parents are missing, or a baby who's been abandoned by a dump site. Women, even when they do not have much, will simply never leave an unaccompanied child alone ... I don't know if adopt is the word, because it's not really done through any official process.'

She said she saw Nigerian women going to great lengths to give their children a sense of safety, even when it was a false one. That included depriving themselves of food so their children had enough, or boiling water and pretending to cook to make the children think a meal was coming when stocks had run out. In the rainy season, mothers living in tents would position themselves in a leaking part so their children could be dry.

Hauwa said she interviewed a woman who had been locked up unfairly for more than a decade, due to suspicions that her dead husband had an affiliation with Boko Haram. The woman was clearly traumatised, staying indoors, mostly in darkness, and showing little animation. But her face lit up as soon as she saw her son, even though they had spent most of his childhood apart. 'She smiled, she hugged him, she even pecked him on the cheek,' Hauwa recalled. While incarcerated, the woman told Hauwa that she dreamed of her son, though 'he appeared as that three-year-old that she had been separated from, not as this fourteen-year-old who was now staring at her. And still she found a way to connect with him. He was quite literally the centre of her universe throughout that time that I spent with her.'

When Boko Haram attacked, Hauwa said some women actually surrendered their children into the arms of the insurgents, believing this was the only way to save their lives. 'The militants often respond very violently if they see people running, they feel compelled to gun down people, whether they be children or adults.' In that situation, Hauwa said, the mothers envisaged that boys, in particular, will 'be armed, they will be radicalised, but they will not be killed'. Many held out hope that they would find their children again later.

Like me, Hauwa noticed a more accepting reaction from mothers than fathers when their daughters had spent time with Boko Haram. This included when they were forcibly married or raped, which might result in a baby. 'I think perhaps patriarchy might have something to do with it,' she said. Fathers in the northeast 'usually feel a responsibility to appear tough, to appear as though they do not tolerate any sign of weakness. And so sometimes they think that showing love is a sign of weakness. So they feel the need to exert themselves, to act in ways that maintain that idea of the father as the head of the house.'

When she asked mothers about their hopes for their children, 'almost without fail, every interview I have done and asked that question, the answer has always been education. They want their children to have an education, to go to school.' She said this was true even among women who had willingly been in Boko Haram, who had at some point subscribed to their teachings.

*

I heard that sentiment shift expressed by a father too, when I went back to northeast Nigeria in late 2021. I seized the opportunity that came with having another assignment in Nigeria's economic capital, Lagos, where I interviewed tech entrepreneurs and Afrobeats musicians, and walked the red carpet at the All Africa Music Awards. The glitterati had assembled that night: a reminder of the opulence and prosperity that exists in Nigeria too.

Maiduguri lies more than 1,000 kilometres from Lagos, and it can feel even farther away. Despite the short-lived burst of global attention, the northern conflict remained out of sight and mind for many Nigerians. I caught an early flight: Maiduguri's airport, previously closed to commercial airlines, was functioning again.

I found the city in certain ways transformed, partially as the result of a new trench, which had been dug around its perimeter to keep away Boko Haram and the increasingly powerful splinter group, the Islamic State of West Africa. Some of the tense urban hum seemed to have dissipated, though the territory outside the trench remained effectively no man's land. Electricity had also been cut off, due to insurgents blowing up the power lines, so some of my interviews on that trip were carried out in near darkness.

I found the authorities dealing with a new phenomenon: mass Boko Haram defections. What should be done with those who swore commitment to a new, law-abiding way of life in such an impoverished place? A group like Boko Haram seems most likely to thrive alongside a lack of opportunity. I interviewed former militants who claimed they had only joined for economic reasons, because they needed a way to support their families. After surrendering, they lived in camps which were supposed to be guarded, though some traipsed freely in and out. Mohammed, one former commander, said Boko Haram first hired him to procure supplies for them, paying 'good money'. Opting to become a fighter meant his family were better provided for, he contended earnestly.

Worn out by violence, Mohammed defected with his family after his child found a leaflet on the ground promising that the Nigerian authorities would not kill them, and would instead give the family a place to live and training for Mohammed to start a small business. Ten others who left with him later rejoined the militants, complaining that government promises of economic assistance had not materialised.

Mohammed wanted to remain on the side of the state. His children were finally getting an education – something impossible while he was part of an insurgent group known for destroying schools, abducting students and murdering teachers. Like many of the mothers I had spoken to, Mohammed's love for his children made them his priority, and that included giving serious consideration to their future prospects. 'It's one of the factors that will stop me from going back, because my children are going to school and they like it.'

Chapter 7

Lebanon: Crimes in the name of love

> 'All of us were toys in the hands of fate.'
>
> – Kahlil Gibran, *The Broken Wings*

> 'You'll always be my person.'
>
> – Graffiti on a road out of Beirut

Bassam al-Sheikh Hussein had reached the end of his tether. The forty-two-year-old had been making regular visits to his bank in Hamra, west Beirut, trying to take out money. There was roughly $210,000 in his account – savings he had been adding to since 2009, including the proceeds from selling his car and property he was gifted by his parents. Despite that, Bassam was limited to withdrawing a little over $400 every month.

Even procuring that much could be a challenge. Regularly, bank staff told him to come back another day, because there was not enough cash available.

Then, in 2022, a calamity occurred. Bassam's beloved father Aqil had a fall. Aqil was in his seventies, with Alzheimer's, and needed to be hospitalised for broken bones. Unable to access his savings, Bassam pawned gold jewellery belonging to his wife and sister to pay his father's medical bills. Friends remembered him 'begging' for assistance. 'I wanted to help my dad,' he recalled. 'I was really in a tight moment with money.'

So Bassam began to plan a bank raid. He spent around three months frequenting the bank to puzzle out the logistics: figuring out which employee had access to the keys for the safe; who held the front door keys; and whether there was a back door, which someone might access to subdue him from behind. In what would follow, love was a motivator: both Bassam's love for his father and the wider pressure to support and care for his family amid a monumental economic collapse.

Lebanon, a small Middle Eastern country of roughly five million people, has faced persistent struggles, and Bassam's life has been shaped by many of them. He was once employed as a lifeguard supervisor in hotels, but lost his job due to a reduction in tourism following the 2006 war, during which around 1,200 Lebanese people and 165 Israelis were killed.[1] Bassam began working in his family's small grocery store instead. That business became untenable amid the economic meltdown which started in 2019. Bassam's hope that he could fund his family's move to a better apartment was put on hold.

The day before he raided the bank, in August 2022, Bassam carried out a final reconnaissance mission. His father had been back home for around two weeks and had all the medication he needed, but Bassam was in debt, and keenly aware that if his father had another accident, or any other family members needed help in the future, he could not provide it. He told the bank manager he wanted to speak to someone more senior, but the man refused. 'I don't care what you will do. Do whatever you want,' Bassam remembers the manager saying. He identifies that as the breaking point – though it seemed more likely that there were many. I imagined the slow humiliation and sense of injustice that comes from dealing with unfair and corrupt bureaucracy and authority figures; fissures cracking and lengthening under pressure.

The following day was a Thursday. Bassam woke up early and ate breakfast with his father and brother. Then he drove back to Hamra with a gun and a gallon of petroleum. 'I parked the car to block the entrance of the bank, and went inside to make sure the manager was there,' he said. They made eye contact, and the manager told him to leave. 'I had threatened the manager before but now I was ready for action,' Bassam determined.

He returned to his car, picked up the gun and petroleum bottle, and stormed back again. He remembers ramming the bank's iron door open so forcefully that it sounded like an explosion: 'I wasn't seeing anything, if anyone had tried to have a discussion with me I would have shot them immediately, I was in that mindset. I wasn't understanding myself what was happening. It was like I was possessed by God's power. But I remember every single detail.' As Bassam said that, he lit a cigarette.

We sat, months later, in his third-floor apartment which overlooked an airport runway. Bassam had long black hair and his beard was a mixture of black and grey, like he had rubbed it in icing sugar. He wore khaki-coloured tracksuit bottoms and a black, long-sleeved T-shirt emblazoned with hands seemingly in prayer, the words 'focus and win' in white lettering. He smoked Grey Cedars cigarettes. A guitar hung on the sitting room wall, alongside framed photographs of Bassam and his wife at their wedding, and a statue of the Eiffel Tower. In another photograph, their young son, Reda, was dressed in a polka-dot bowtie, balloons visible behind him. Somewhere below us, the notes of an ice cream truck chimed out. This neighbourhood, Ouzai, had been home to luxurious beach resorts before the Lebanese civil war, but now residents described it as 'poor' and outsiders called it a slum. The wider area, Dahiyeh, was recognised as a stronghold of militant group and political party Hezbollah. It sustained the heaviest bombing by Israel during the 2006 bombardment, and would be heavily hit again in 2024 and 2026.

Conflict was far from the only threat. Months before I first met Bassam, concrete and steel in his building had been cracked by the shock 7.8 magnitude earthquake that devastated parts of Turkey and Syria and he did not have the finances to fix it. Electricity inside the apartment came from solar power: Bassam used his phone's light to lead our way upstairs. On warm summer nights, he slept on the rooftop in an effort to get some relief from the encasing heat.

Bassam's wife, Maryam, offered me almonds, cake and orange juice. The couple originally connected around eight years earlier, when Maryam was employed by Bassam's dentist. Their child, Reda, was born in 2018, a year before the economic situation deteriorated so badly and four years before the bank raid. By the time we met, Bassam had told his story many times, but the recounting still animated him. It had been one of the most notable days of his life.

'People were shocked,' he recalled, about his dramatic entry to the bank. 'I wasn't understanding what's happening. Even the employees were very scared. It was a hard moment for all of them. One woman, a customer coming to take her money, fell over on the ground from fear.' Bassam ordered a staff member to give him the bank's keys, and he guided the woman outside the building so she could receive medical help if she needed it. Then he locked the bank's door.

'The plan was to take what was in the safe and go away. There were only the employees, the manager and two customers left.' First he doused the floor in petrol, splashing computers and even the employees. 'I told them that if anyone moves I will burn the bank with you all inside.' He pointed the gun at the bank manager, instructing him to open the safe and hand over his $210,000 of savings. 'He only gave me four hundred dollars.' After further threats, the manager offered Bassam a few thousand dollars. The safe contained barely anything, Bassam realised. The money he wanted did not exist. 'So I changed the plan. I said no one will go out from here unless I get my money.'

When a country falls apart, do its people become more, or less, divided? Some flee into exile. Others stay and suffer, alone or together. Under pressure, the usual rules fall apart. In desperation, a number are even willing to commit crimes for the people they love – though maybe a crime is no longer truly a crime anyway, when those determining the law are corrupted.

Bassam was far from the only person in Lebanon who dreamed of raiding a bank that year. The week before he did it, the World Bank published a report accusing the Lebanese authorities of carrying out a giant Ponzi scheme over the previous three decades.[2] It said the country's financial and economic crisis was 'one of the most severe globally since the mid-1800s', and that this was the result of 'deliberate' actions. Basic services had been removed or hollowed out, while the savings earned by hardworking people, who trusted the banks to take care of them, had been squandered. 'These are earnings by expats who toil in foreign lands; they are retirement funds for citizens and perhaps the sole resource for a dignified living; they are necessary financing for essential medical and education services that consecutive governments have failed to provide; they are funds to pay for electricity,' the report said.

In Hamra, the same neighbourhood where Bassam held up the bank, I met Mohamad Faour. The thirty-three-year-old was an assistant professor of finance at the American University of Beirut, as well as a research fellow at my alma mater, University College Dublin. We sat in the garden of Café Younes, a Beirut staple since 1935. It was mid-afternoon. Faour – who had thick, curly hair, and wore round black glasses and a navy puffer jacket – was fasting for Ramadan. Pop music played in the background.

To understand how things got to this point it was important to understand the historical context, he said. The end of Lebanon's civil war in 1990 culminated in a power-sharing agreement, which led to 'paralysis in every facet of decision-making in the country' and a broken political system. Militia leaders and armed groups were given immunity from prosecution, despite having committed terrible atrocities during the war. Various commentators have described Lebanon's leadership since then as a 'sectarian mafia'.

To maintain stability, a decision was made to transform the Lebanese economy into an 'incredibly consumerist' one, Faour said. At the heart of that was the currency peg which guaranteed 1,500 Lebanese lira to $1, and was maintained artificially, through debt. Lebanese expatriates were encouraged to put their money in Lebanese banks in return for extremely high interest rates.

'There was a point beyond which the music would stop. And the music did stop,' said Faour. From 2019, everything 'started deteriorating'. The debt became unsustainable and Lebanon's banking system collapsed. Investors scarpered. Inflation became the highest in the world. People began to call the Lebanese pound 'Monopoly money'.

'Do you think that there need to be people held responsible for this?' I asked Faour. 'And what would it look like?'

'Absolutely,' he responded, saying he would like to see politicians held accountable, but also bankers paying a financial price for what had been done. 'Bankers need to be held accountable for their decisions. Bankers need to take the hit . . . Their capital needs to get wiped out but also their personal money, their personal assets.'

After I left Faour, I walked around Hamra for a while. Before the civil war, this area was a key cultural hub, where Arab intellectuals would debate the issues of the day. Beloved Lebanese singer Fairuz performed sold-out shows at Hamra's Piccadilly Theatre in the 1970s. Hamra was a place I'd stayed in before the economic crisis. I had fond memories of bustling streets and shops lit up with Christmas lights, a wide array of goods on sale. It seemed darker now, more faded, more empty. I passed the Barzakh bookshop, library and events space, on the site of what used to be the Horseshoe café, a gathering point for artists and writers. Across the street was graffiti that included a love heart. 'Love is giving something you don't have to someone who doesn't want it,' it read. Beside that were the words: 'We miss you.'

In Lebanon, residents often said, problems piled upon problems, leaving no recovery time. It is impossible to understand the full depth of despair affecting any potential bank raider's state of mind without knowing that, at 6.08 p.m. on 4 August 2020, Beirut also became the site of one of the biggest non-nuclear explosions in history. It took place after a fire broke out at the city's port, where around 2,750 tonnes of ammonium nitrate was being stored inside a warehouse. Where it came from and why is not fully certain. How it could have been kept in an urban location, where it posed such a colossal hazard, has never been properly ascertained.

Nearly two million people lived within three miles of the explosion. Its force hit mothers giving birth; couples posing for wedding photographs; young people commuting from work. It ended the lives of firefighters responding to an emergency call. Around half of the city was damaged and more than two hundred people were killed.[3] When I asked anyone about the blast, the first thing they usually mentioned was trauma. While the government resigned, no one was officially held accountable. As with the financial crisis, it was the poor and powerless who suffered the most.

'It's OK to feel like you're on the verge of exploding . . . It's OK to cry every day . . . It's OK to feel numb, indifferent, yet suffocate at the sight of every funeral,' emphasised a Lebanese mental health organisation's campaign in the aftermath, encouraging affected people to talk to counsellors. Its website said one person was attempting suicide every six hours.

The legacy of the port explosion came up unexpectedly at the end of a visit I made to Beirut in August 2023. Another anniversary had just passed. I was en route to the airport with a friendly taxi driver who asked me my profession. I said I was a *sahafiyyeh* – a journalist – and he told me his wife and two daughters had been killed that day. 'Boom. Boom,' he said, his eyes crinkling, his hand lifting from the wheel to grip at nothing. He pulled up his T-shirt to show me the scars on his stomach. On his phone was a photo of his wife and girls. 'Gone,' he said.

*

I visited Lebanon for the first time in 2016, returning multiple times the following year. I downed shots in nightclubs and cappuccinos in coffee shops. I attended house parties on the roofs of old buildings, with music blaring from speakers and a fashionable milieu joking, flirting and debating everything and nothing meaningful. Many European journalists I knew had moved to Beirut to begin their careers on English-language newspaper the *Daily Star* – this was seen as a common route into becoming an international correspondent.

At that time, Lebanon was described as a 'playground for the rich', a place where wealthy Arabs from conservative societies like Saudi Arabia came to cut loose. I remember buzzing, thronged streets, and employees in dessert shops handing me free tasters. Beirut was also a city of contrasts, a place where a Palestinian teenager whom I chatted with, who was living in a crowded urban refugee camp, could present on Instagram as an affluent influencer, posing on beaches or beside the expensive cars ubiquitous in the city.

Those extremes became sharper and more sinister once the economic crisis began. I did wonder, wandering around in later years, how restaurants selling duck and escargots stayed in business, or stores selling outfits for small dogs. Electricity was one key marker of wealth. State power was already subject to blackouts when I visited in 2016 and 2017. By 2023, it was on for barely four hours a day, with those who could afford it paying private 'generator mafias' for power the rest of the time, while everyone else went without.

I stayed away from Lebanon for almost six years. Lebanese politicians have been condemned as self-serving and fickle, with little regard for the impact their actions had on the broader populace, and possibly nothing illustrated this as strikingly as when Lebanon split into two time zones the week of my next trip back, amid a last-minute governmental change and disputes over which leadership should be listened to.[4] Passengers on the plane I was on broke out in laughter as the air hostess first announced that the local time was 2.58 p.m., then made a 'correction' as she had 'just been informed that the clocks hadn't gone forward'. Even more confusingly, my phone, my computer, and Google – normally all in sync – began showing three different times. 'Waking up not knowing what time it is is yet another level of lowest you can reach in screwing up the very little left of a nation's mental health [with a population] barely making it from one day to the next,' tweeted clinical psychologist Mia Atoui.

Dusk had turned everything hazy that first evening, in March 2023, by the time I ventured out of my friend's apartment to find food. I ordered a salad in a restaurant chain I had eaten at before, but when I tried to hand over banknotes to pay for it the waitress laughed at my drastic underestimation of how many were needed. The price was now 980,000 Lebanese lira; up from the 12,500 lira listed on their Google page. A dollar, worth 1,500 lira before the crisis, had hit 140,000 a few weeks earlier. Unable to deal with the constant fluctuations, many businesses were 'dollarising' – giving up on the lira altogether when it came to listing prices, or creating QR codes which customers could scan to see figures that changed by the day or even the hour.

Driving around the city as a foreigner in Beirut, it is always hard to discern what is damaged as a result of the civil war, what was caused by the port explosion and what is just general decay. The shattered windows, crumbling buildings and shards of glass on the ground contrast with towers, hotels and apartment blocks that exude a sheen of luxury. Beirut feels like a city of unfinished dreams and unfulfilled promises. There are buildings high, fantastical in their design and ambition, that look abandoned, tattered, frayed, symbols of the endless optimistic or capitalist efforts to rebuild and retry.

Painted words under a bridge at an intersection read: 'Before I die I want Lebanon to'. In a scrawl beside it someone had added: 'hold me right when I come back'. On the side of another highway, 'eat the rich' was emblazoned on concrete in black. I saw a sculpture made of disused radiators – a commentary on the country's electricity troubles. More graffiti by the roadside questioned: 'If this is a free country then why are we trapped by the cost of living?' In the bar district of Gemmayze was a painted picture of Lebanon's symbolic cedar tree, alongside words penned in the early twentieth century by Lebanese-American poet Khalil Gibran: 'You have your Lebanon and its dilemma. I have my Lebanon and its beauty.' Nearby was a plaque commemorating those killed in the 2020 explosion.

As in every crisis, there were dark jokes. On Instagram, I read a post that said: 'so now in Lebanon, we can ski, swim and go to hell the same day.'

When Bassam's raid on his bank began, employees used their phones to appeal for help. Quickly, the neighbourhood filled up with police; Bassam discerned their voices outside. Officers were talking to him, saying 'Please calm down, the money will come, please calm down, we don't need blood.'

'No one from my family knew what was happening,' Bassam remembered. That morning, he only told his wife that he was going to the bank 'like normal'. She texted later, asking if he had been delayed there. 'I texted back saying what I did and "don't call me again". I didn't need anyone to convince me not to do it,' he said. After that, he turned off his phone.

Maryam, back at home, said she had a feeling 'something was wrong.' The evening before, Bassam had been ruminating about injustice, as usual. He said he wanted to 'drive the bank manager mad'. Maryam warned him that he could end up in jail – but this was still a joke for her then. They were watching a movie and drinking coffee. Bassam was calm, Maryam felt. 'Nothing was suspicious.' She was not taking his words seriously.

That sense of ease dissipated the next day. 'When he went to the bank, I was texting him so much – "where are you, it's not normal for you to be late at this time".'

Maryam started getting messages. There were rumours circulating on WhatsApp about her husband, 'saying he was shooting, burning the bank'. She headed to Hamra 'to see with my own eyes'. Once there, she pushed through the police lines.

Bassam was worried that the police would start shooting at him. His gun was pointed at the bank manager; he wanted the police to understand that he was willing to use it, and that producing members of his family to plead with him was pointless. 'My brother turned up and said "please calm down", and I threatened to kill him too,' Bassam recalled. 'My state of mind was that I could not be talked down. No negotiations, nothing, I just wanted them to bring the money.'

The standoff would last more than six hours, making international news. 'Armed man takes hostages at Beirut bank demanding return of frozen funds' ran a CNN headline. 'Robin Hood in Hamra?' asked Lebanese news platform L'Orient Today.[5]

Inside the building, the smell of sprinkled petrol was making the hostages feel sick. Bassam allowed a customer in his eighties to leave. He instructed a pregnant bank employee to move to another room to avoid inhaling the fumes.

A crowd of cheerleaders had gathered outside: they came with the explicit purpose of showing solidarity with Bassam.

'Every one of us has been robbed from different directions, from banks and from the government,' Sandy Chamoun, a thirty-five-year-old artist, told a *Washington Post* journalist. 'I thought we should be outside, supporting him, so he doesn't give up, so he doesn't feel alone or besieged.' Both Chamoun's parents had been bank employees: even their savings were locked away from them, Chamoun said.[6]

Through a window, security forces offered Bassam cigarettes and coffee, trying to pacify him. Reporters arrived. Photographs show Bassam communicating through a barred door. The journalists asked him to give advice to other depositors, whose money was being held too. 'I said everyone should take their own rights into their own hands.' He grinned and stretched his arm out along a sofa decorated with blue, beige and rose-coloured flowers, as he narrated this part of the story.

The police began offering him more money: $5,000; then $10,000. They said they were sending representatives to different banks, gathering reserves of cash. That made Bassam angrier: he told them to go to the Central Bank and only come back when they had the full amount.

The single customer still inside the bank asked if he could leave. The man's daughter had cancer and was very worried; she had heard rumours that there had been gunshots, he said. At that point, Bassam remembers, the phone rang. 'It was a restaurant in Hamra, offering me food, saying "we support you".' T-Marbouta delivered them shawarma, salad, spicy potato and drinkable yoghurt. Bassam consumed nothing apart from one drink, suspicious that the food had been 'spiked'. But the others ate – apart from the bank manager, whom Bassam would not allow to. As the food arrived, that last remaining customer left.

The negotiation continued, reaching $35,000. Authorities said they would give Bassam a further $400 every day for a year and he would not be arrested; in fact, he could meet the interior minister. 'I said "I don't have faith in you",' Bassam recalled. One of the security generals warned that he had to accept the offer or they would summon special forces and compel him to leave. Bassam saw security men preparing to advance, so he raised his gun again and came to an agreement: they should bring him $35,000 and his brother would count the money at the door, take it home and call Bassam from there. Only at that point would Bassam end his raid.

The deal was done. When he finally walked outside, Bassam remembers civilians saluting him. Another brother was waiting for him in a car (Bassam's family is big, five brothers and a sister). Unexpectedly, they did not drive towards home; instead, they were guided to the police headquarters. There, someone he described as a 'general' showed Bassam the keys to the bank.

'All the time we had the keys, but we took the decision not to raid it because we knew there would be blood,' the man said, according to Bassam's account. At the police station, Bassam said he also met Lebanon's head of internal security. Bassam says the official called him 'brave' but said engaging with the judicial system was now unavoidable, so Bassam would need to sleep in the station that night. 'For me that was tough, because I thought we already had an agreement.'

The following day, Bassam was informed that the bank wanted to sue him. In response, his extended family began making calls, threatening to burn down every branch. They protested, shutting down roads. 'My cousins, even my neighbours, the whole neighbourhood . . . They were pushing hard on the bank so they wouldn't sue me.' Other depositors in the same situation joined in too.

Bassam's young son, Reda, had been asking for his father

while the raid was happening. He recognised Bassam on TV. During the days that Bassam was held by the police the boy refused to eat, remembered Maryam. 'He's really attached to his father.' Later, when their son saw protests by Lebanese depositors on the TV news, he would pronounce the words 'Bassam bank'.

Bassam was released five days after the raid. The police lent him a private driver, because there were riots near the police station. The media was waiting at his home. He was welcomed as a champion: 'Hey, let's take a picture, tell us the story, what happened.' He remembers people beckoning him over for a long time afterwards. They would ask where he got the idea; how he mustered up so much courage. In shops, he was given discounts and free goods. A large portrait of him appeared on a main road.

'Man who took hostages demanding his own money becomes public hero in Lebanon', ran a *Guardian* newspaper headline. The article said that Bassam's action had 'resonated with hundreds of thousands of people held hostage by a staggering economic collapse',[7] noting that the soldiers and police who tried to encourage Bassam to leave had had their own salaries reduced more than twentyfold over the previous two years, with many earning the equivalent of $70 a month by then. 'No one will say he did the wrong thing,' said one bystander, Ahmad Yatoum. 'Desperate people do desperate things. We are all like him, even the soldiers and the riot police liked him.'

'I was the most famous person,' Bassam said, the surprise evident in his tone. He began being approached by people who wanted advice on carrying out bank raids themselves: they asked about his planning process, whether he had consulted a lawyer beforehand. A fictionalised version of Bassam's raid was now immortalised in an Arabic-language television series; he showed me a TikTok clip on his phone. 'Netflix came, VICE, BBC,' he said, leaning back on the couch.

An aircraft flew close to the house – landing or taking off, I wasn't sure. Maryam was six months pregnant with their second baby. Their eldest, dressed in a blue Nike tracksuit, played on the floor with a red keyboard.

I asked Maryam whether she supported her husband's actions. 'It's his right to do what he did, it's his money,' she said. 'He saved for a long time. We exhausted ourselves earning all this money and saving it in the banks.' She said she felt proud, even if she was startled when it happened.

'I only regret that I went out without the money, I think I could have got it all,' Bassam said. He was waiting on a legal decision. 'I promise if the court doesn't give me my right I will do something bigger than I did before.'

Due to his Alzheimer's, Bassam's father Aqil had no idea

Bassam and Maryam pictured at home together.

what had happened. Bassam's mother, just one year younger, was 'really angry' with her son though, Maryam said. 'His mom was tired and sick, we were about to lose her from shock.'

Our conversation over for the day, I looked up the cost of a ride home through a taxi app. When Bassam heard it came to roughly seven dollars, he jumped up. For that price, he said, he would drive me himself: he was still stuck for money, after all. He pulled on a cap and black puffer jacket, threw away his cigarette and we got into his car, speeding through the roads he knew so well, in the only country he had.

Bassam was one of the highest-profile bank raiders in Lebanon, but his attempted heist was not the first or the last. For a time, these raids became commonplace. When asked why they found it necessary to take such drastic action, a notable number of the people carrying them out said they were trying to get money for loved ones who needed expensive medical care. The decimation of their country's health system, as a result of the economic crisis, meant that very sick people often had to travel abroad to get adequate treatment. By 2021, according to the World Health Organization, nearly 40 per cent of Lebanese doctors and 30 per cent of nurses had left the country.[8]

The very first known bank raid happened in January 2022, when a thirty-seven-year-old coffee shop owner in eastern Lebanon held bank staff hostage, managing to leave with $50,000 of his own money.[9] In September 2022, a month after Bassam's raid, twenty-eight-year-old Sali Hafez carried a toy gun into another Beirut bank branch, pouring petrol on the ground and threatening to light it. She said she needed cash to fund her sister's cancer treatment. Videos captured her standing with the fake weapon on a table, inside the bank's premises. Sali made it out with at least $13,000. She told Reuters news agency that she should not be considered a criminal: 'We are in the country of mafias. If you are not a wolf, the wolves will eat you.' To Al Jazeera, she declared she would do it all over again. 'I had four options: commit suicide; work in a [morally] wrong way to get money; see my sister dying; or go inside the bank. I decided to use the last solution. I wish everyone would do the same. Many people are committing suicide because they are not able to help their relatives.'[10] (When I contacted Sali, asking for an interview, she said I would have to pay her for it. I declined, explaining that paying for interviews is against journalistic rules, though I had to admire her gumption.)

Georges Siam, the honorary Irish consul in Lebanon, tweeted calling Sali a 'hero . . . we need more of that'.[11] Two days after her raid, on 16 September 2022, there were further hold-ups in at least five different banks across Lebanon.[12] In early October 2022, Siam took part in a sit-in at his own bank, which was reported on by CNN and other media.[13] (When I contacted him, he said rules set by the Irish Department of Foreign Affairs meant he could not give interviews about this, though he was available for any consular advice I needed.)

A range of associations and organisations became involved in campaigning on behalf of Lebanese people missing their money. One was called Depositors' Outcry. 'Just a minute, one of our friends is having a problem in the bank too,' said its founder, Alaa Khorchid, in place of a greeting, when I met him in his friend's apartment. The man he was on the phone to was missing $2 million, Khorchid explained after he hung up. 'Everybody thinks I have a magic stick,' he complained. He was sitting in an armchair, his legs crossed, one arm over the back.

Khorchid, by then fifty-four, had spent two decades in West Africa, working long hours managing factories. He kept a low profile there, he said: he barely had friends because 'more friends mean more problems'. Not having a family was a sacrifice he made to succeed at business, he said; he figured he would marry and procreate once he had 'fixed money, fixed a life, so my son will not suffer like me'. He envisaged being a provider. 'I stayed away by myself, I studied by myself, I worked hard by myself, I did it for myself,' he said. 'And in the end, you see what's happened . . . I cannot accept that all what's happened in my life just goes like that.' He made a gesture, with his fingers, suggesting evaporation.

Khorchid's plan had always been to return to Lebanon when he got older, 'take a rest a little bit' and do some 'small business'. All that time he was away, he stored his earnings in Lebanon's banks. It never crossed his mind that the money would not be safe – he had never heard of a bank seizing everyone's deposits.

Many affected people had worked for decades, he emphasised. Some could no longer find employment because of their age. He knew people who had died from what he saw as stress-related heart attacks, and others who lost close family members who only required basic medical treatment. 'It's affecting people. It's killing people,' he said. I thought about the torment of not being able to support and help your family, despite working for a lifetime, or the feeling of not being able to start a family in the first place. I thought about the older generations, including a long-time Lebanese pharmacist I met, who told me courageous stories from the height of the civil war. To get to his pharmacy each day he had crossed the Green Line: effectively a no man's land between warring parties. When the economic crisis started, the pharmacist confessed, he began drinking gin in the mornings to get through the day.

After bank raids were planned, Khorchid's organisation called the media to inform them – that was one way to ensure the security forces would not become too aggressive, he posited, because popular support had remained on the side of the bank raiders. The raiders themselves 'are not violent people', he said. 'It's enough that we are suffering, we don't want somebody else to suffer . . . But what's going on, it's outrageous.' About the people responsible – the bankers and the political leaders – they believe 'they are not guilty, and that's the worst thing. They cannot accept that they destroyed this country.' In the longer term, he wanted to see major political change. 'It's a moral problem. Lebanon should be rebuilt again.'

Not too far away, in the Debs & Associates law firm, in the upscale Achrafieh district of Beirut, I drank tea with Fouad Debs, Bassam's lawyer. The thirty-five-year-old was one of the founding members of the Depositors Union, another depositors' rights group.

The economic crisis made Lebanese people pick sides, he said. In the past, Debs had represented banks, as his father did for decades before him. But 'relationships soured and they're very unethical, so that is no longer the case'. He recalled a mass outbreak of protests in 2019: meeting activists on the streets on the first day. One of his friends was shot and beaten but survived, Debs said. Later, they found another way to protest: taking on lawsuits. His organisation filed hundreds on behalf of depositors in Lebanon and abroad, most of whom were trying to seek access to money to pay for healthcare or education. Only around five people had managed to get their money back this way, by the time we met. At least the banks felt pressured, Debs sighed. Around five or six thousand people had become extremely rich, he said, and they were treating the rest of Lebanon's citizens as 'slaves'.

Later, on the phone, I spoke to a member of Lebanon's banks association, who did not want to be named. 'Yes, yes, yes,' he responded when I asked him if Sali Hafez's description of Lebanon as a 'country of mafias' was accurate, before saying that perhaps it was not exactly right, and that the reality was complicated. He said he would rank responsibility in this order: first, governments and politicians over the previous three decades; second, the Central Bank; third, commercial banks; and last, depositors who put more than half a million dollars in the banks, who would have known there was a risk. It was only 'small' depositors, with amounts less than this, who bore no responsibility, he said. And bankers abided by the expression 'you cannot fight the Fed', he added. While corruption existed, he put it as the second or third cause of the crisis. While he did not agree that bank raiders were doing 'the right thing, I understand it', he said.

A year later, I had moved to Beirut more permanently. It was summertime, June 2024, when the claggy heat was so smothering it woke me in the early morning. If lucky, I would fall back asleep again, half conscious in a sweaty stupor.

News headlines were focused on Israel's brutal assault on Gaza. Tens of thousands of Palestinians had been killed – many of them children – in what seemed like genocidal revenge for the Hamas attacks of 7 October 2023. The besieged enclave was less than 300 kilometres down the coast. I watched footage of bombings, displacement and starvation on the big television in our sitting room, or on my phone screen, first thing after I woke up and right before I went to sleep. A key topic of conversation in Beirut was what many obliquely called 'the situation'. Open conflict between Israel and Hezbollah had been going on since 8 October 2023, when Hezbollah fired rockets into Israeli-occupied Shebaa Farms 'in solidarity' with Hamas. Since then, the majority of violent attacks had come from the Israeli side, where prominent figures and politicians were advocating for a ground invasion, saying they wanted to protect their northern border and enable displaced Israelis to return home. Israeli Defense Minister Yoav Gallant had just seemingly escalated the threats by publicly saying that Israel had the capacity to send Lebanon back to the 'Stone Age' in a 'potentially apocalyptic' escalation.[14]

When there was thunder or fireworks people would ask each other whether the bombing had begun. Sometimes there were sonic booms, caused by Israeli jets flying faster than the speed of sound above us. As I had found in Ukraine with Russia, many people in Lebanon hesitated to even say the word Israel out loud, with foreigners and some Lebanese referring to it as 'Disneyland' or 'Dixie', while older Lebanese people were known to speak about 'wled el 3am', or 'the cousins'.

Amid this, Bassam was grieving. His father had passed away just over a month earlier. Before his death, Aqil, who was already very fragile, lost the ability to swallow food. The various illnesses plaguing the elderly man for the previous six years seemed to have merged into one mass affliction, dragging him under.

Bassam's eyes welled up at the thought of his father. He was sitting in his family's newly opened furniture shop – his area was known for selling affordable furnishings, with merchants making use of the fact that it lay on the road connecting Beirut to southern Lebanon. On one bicep, the claws of a tiger tattoo curled out from under his black T-shirt. It bulged as he pulled out his phone, using it to scroll through old photographs of Aqil: smiling and relaxing; looking very frail.

Bassam still lived in the same apartment, in the same damaged building, where I had visited him before. As a result of signal jamming by Israel, Google Maps, and other apps, showed people's GPS location as being close to Beirut's airport and Bassam's home, no matter where they were in the city.[15] Another unexpected side effect of the jamming was that Lebanese singles kept matching with Israelis on dating apps, because their GPS location positioned them together even if an app user in Beirut set their maximum acceptable distance to five kilometres away. Many singles rushed to reject these profiles, aware that even communicating with an Israeli was illegal in Lebanon, and meeting in person would be impossible; there was even speculation that this was some kind of covert intelligence-gathering tactic.

Halfway through my catch-up with Bassam, Maryam walked in with baby Yusuf, who was now seven months old. She was with the children all the time, Bassam said fondly. 'Nom nom nom,' he feigned munching as he pretended to bite the baby's head. Yusuf's hair was clumped together in the humidity. The infant was beautiful, and, in his tininess, a reminder that every new generation deserves a fresh start and chance at life. I asked Bassam how he felt about his children's futures, and he sighed. Bassam's brother was sick now. He had what Bassam described as a problem with his brain: a 'vein exploding', and 'pimples' being found inside it. His surgery would cost around $40,000, Bassam said.

He was frustrated with the legal system too, he could not understand why everything was so slow: 'I speak daily with my lawyer to make things move faster.' He was still owed $175,000 of his own savings from the bank. He longed to pay off his debts and make improvements to his business so he could live off it. He had briefly tried storming the bank again: this time, the manager was not even present. 'I will always repeat this, until I get my rights back,' he said, his voice devoid of any sense of contrition.

Reda, Bassam's older son, came in to the furniture shop now. He was skinny, in the awkward way of children who have recently had a growth spurt. Reda flicked through a brochure pulled from his father's table. The cost of living was going up, Bassam explained. Reda's school cost a payment each of $600 and 8 million lira for the previous year; the next year would be $1,200 and 18 million lira. 'I can't drop him out of school,' Bassam fretted, adding that the family would have left the country long ago if they were able to.

Bassam's father Aqil had worked in Lebanon's state electricity company for around forty years, only retiring when his Alzheimer's became undeniable. Aqil was an introvert who enjoyed playing Tawle, a game similar to backgammon. As a child, Bassam said, 'I was always with my dad.' The pair would go to the beach, or more frequently to Aitaroun, the village where Bassam's father was born. His father loved to be immersed in nature and planted lemon trees there. 'For us, the southern people, no matter what, even if you lived all of your life in Beirut, you will bury your loved ones in their villages,' Bassam said. The village is 'one of the most beautiful villages. It's my happy place.'

Aitaroun is 125 kilometres south of Beirut, around two kilometres from the border with Israel. When Aqil died, the conflict meant his family had to coordinate permission with Lebanon's security forces to bury him there and hold his funeral. Lebanese military intelligence allowed them just one hour in the village, Bassam said, because of the Israeli attacks. They could only bring close family, though other villagers – former neighbours of Aqil's – turned up too: around forty people in total. Bassam's brother returned from Australia.

Bassam holds up a photograph of himself with his father Aqil, taken before his father's death in 2024.

Maryam stayed in Beirut with the children. Bassam said they could hear the humming of surveillance drones above. The next village was attacked shortly after the mourners left.

I finally visited Aitaroun, almost a year later, for another funeral: the mass burial of ninety-five people killed during the war. By that stage, it was largely destroyed. Hebrew-language graffiti – including the phrase 'death to Arabs' – marked the walls of some of the remaining buildings, acting as a reminder of the Israeli occupation and subsequent withdrawal.

Bassam said that his love for his family – including his father, and more recently his sick brother – had been key motivations for his decision to carry out the bank raid and his willingness to do it again. Family gave him purpose, influencing how he chose to live his life. Other families were different, chimed in Maryam, who said she knew of couples who had divorced and relatives who turned against each other when faced with debt and similar challenges. 'It depends on the mindset,' she said.

The national economic meltdown only made his own family's ties stronger, said Bassam, some pride in his voice. 'For us, it's like one for all, all for one. If one is hurting, it's like all of us are hurt.' However, despite his devotion to his father, Bassam said his quest for survival came with a conscious decision not to emulate the man. 'My dad was calm, I'm an angry person, I always want to do things quickly . . . I don't want to make the same mistakes my father did.'

'Your father didn't make any mistakes because he made you, he raised you, he helped you, supported you to become yourself,' interjected Maryam.

'My father was kindhearted. For me, this doesn't work nowadays,' argued Bassam. It seemed like a sorry determination when he concluded that, from his perspective, gentle humans 'always get the bad things, they always get hurt. The people will take advantage of that.'

Chapter 8

Syria: A quest for justice

> *'Talking to him was very difficult. For instance, he doesn't
> know what a road is, or what a tree is.'*
>
> – A Médecins Sans Frontières staff member, on treating a boy
> who survived Syrian detention[1]

I first spoke to Fadwa Mahmoud on a Zoom call in 2022,
when she was about to mark the tenth anniversary of her husband's and son's disappearance. With a cigarette in one hand,
she described the mission that had taken over her life.

Her conviction and energy seemed so powerful that they
stuck with me until the day, nearly a year later, when I found
myself sitting beside her, in her apartment in central Berlin.
Beside us, her cat Zeitouna snoozed in a fluffy multi-level cat
box illuminated by the glow of a red lava lamp. On the walls
were photographs of her missing men.

Political activist Abdulaziz Al Khair, and his stepson
Maher Tahan, disappeared on 20 September 2012. Abdulaziz
had been involved in meetings in China regarding the eighteen-
month-old conflict in Syria, and Maher had gone to the airport
in Damascus to collect him. They were apprehended by security forces and vanished, presumably into Syria's complex
prison and detention system. It was not clear what the men

were accused of, if anything. Their disappearances were two of many that set off a years-long, continents-wide quest for justice, bonding together thousands of Syrian women who would spend their lives searching for answers.

The shirt Fadwa was wearing had a pattern of hearts and stars. Her sandals were beaded, and on her left hand she wore a red-jewelled ring. Her bed, in the same room, was topped by a colourful throw. There was a table with four chairs and a separate dresser. She offered me a Marlboro and her Egyptian housemate brought in a pot of Arabic coffee and small white cups. Fadwa, now in her late sixties – with short grey hair and a perceptive demeanour – began to tell me her story again, this time from the beginning.

Fadwa had heard of Abdulaziz long before she met him, though she only knew his alias, Abu Ahmed. Three years older than her, he was already a 'great opposition leader' in the regime-banned Communist Labour Party. In the 1980s, in her late twenties, Fadwa became a member too. 'It was a secret activism, we were not allowed to actually meet and know each other's real names,' she recalled.

Both Fadwa and Abdulaziz came from close to Latakia, a seaside city in western Syria. Abdulaziz was more specifically from Qardaha, the same town as Hafez al-Assad, the authoritarian dictator who had ruled Syria from 1971. Like Bashar al-Assad – Hafez's second son, who would go on to succeed him as president – Abdulaziz qualified as a doctor.

Fadwa was born into a wealthy family. 'My father was one of the people who had money, vast lands. I saw the people who worked for him on the land as peasants, how they worked hard and at the end [how little] they got. My father and all people like him, I used to see them suck the life out of those people who actually work on the land. It was injustice,' she said.

Unknown to Fadwa, she had friends who were quietly on the lookout for potential recruits for the Communist Labour Party. They registered Fadwa's discomfort and idealism, and slipped her banned reading materials. 'It resonated with me a lot. I finally saw something that represented me, that said something I wanted to say. They wanted Syria to be democratic and free. Social justice, equality, those were the goals of the party and that was what mattered to me. That's why I was not only a member, I was a very active member. I knew that one day I would pay the price.'

Though she concealed it from her family, Fadwa joined the campaign. She distributed flyers 'to educate people about their rights, [saying that] they shouldn't be silent when they face the atrocities of the regime'. She wanted to highlight the inequality in Syria's economic system, where 'the majority of people couldn't find bread to eat while the regime had everything.' She acted as the liaison between her party and other political groups.

One day, she was asked to facilitate a meeting at which Abdulaziz was speaking. It was their first time coming face to face. 'I saw how he communicated his ideas, how he spoke. My heart was pounding and that was it.' She laughed, cigarette in hand. 'This was how we met the first time. So I got to know him.'

Fadwa was already married to someone else. There were other complications too. Her brother was a senior intelligence officer, working for the Syrian regime. The siblings had been close as children, but his decision to join the intelligence forces created a rift. 'I told him that one day you might be the person who arrests me,' she recalled. 'The position was probably very tempting, the power and the money. He wanted to be with the system and I took another way.'

In the early 1990s, Abdulaziz needed a place to hide and Fadwa offered up her own home. She was living alone with her children, after separating from her husband. No one would think to search there, she figured, given her brother's position. Abdulaziz and a female friend, who was also involved in their political struggle, lived with her for more than a year. Decades later, Fadwa's eyes glowed remembering her own daringness. 'I'm very strong and I'm very different from your normal Arab girl,' she grinned.

Alas, the subterfuge ended badly. Abdulaziz was apprehended on 2 February 1992, after the details of a meeting he was attending were extracted from a contact through torture. Afraid he might be executed, their party issued a statement. This was before they had internet access, so Fadwa drove a few hours to Beirut, the capital of neighbouring Lebanon, hoping the statement could be distributed from there. While she was en route, another party colleague was arrested and tortured. 'They threatened that they will rape his sixteen-year-old daughter in front of him,' she said. The man broke down and named Fadwa as a collaborator. This meant she was caught upon her return. Her brother headed the unit that found her. He 'didn't really have a choice. That's what power does in Syria, it corrupts people.'

The two years Fadwa spent in prison were 'really hard'. At first, security forces 'asked me to give in all of my comrades', she said. 'Of course I refused, no way I would tell them anything. I spent one year and two months in a basement. All the time I was still in the pyjamas that they arrested me in. The only thing that was on my mind was that my kids are young, I have small kids and they were alone then. That was my biggest suffering.' The prison guards 'asked me for many things. But I just couldn't accept. I never did. Sometimes you lose track of time and I waited for the night to come to be able to sleep because during the day there were the sound of torture and screams all around. It was just inhumane, especially when you hear younger people screaming of pain and torture.'

Fadwa was transferred into a prison in the city of Douma. Despite the conditions being 'cruel and hard . . . when they put me with my comrade in one cell in the prison they used to hit us because we were singing.' Improbably, she laughed. 'It was horrible . . . they wanted to break our spirits, they couldn't.'

Abdulaziz was locked up for nearly fourteen years. Fadwa says he never left her mind. 'We just loved each other from far away,' she said, growing quiet and smiling. After she got out of prison, Fadwa managed to see him just once, when he was on trial. 'The meeting was a bit hard because it was in a situation where we were not allowed to talk freely . . . We just hugged each other, we reassured each other that everything is going

Fadwa Mahmoud in her Berlin apartment in June 2023.

well . . . He told me that he would keep going and I know that he's a tough guy, he's not afraid of jail and detention . . . It was a sweet meeting, a beautiful meeting, but also, at the same time, a very tough meeting, because it was in these circumstances.'

During the following years Fadwa discovered ways to send Abdulaziz essential provisions he needed through a mediator. She would get a box of cigarettes, take one out, remove the tobacco and roll up a letter inside the cigarette, packing in some tobacco again on top, so the intelligence agents would not find it. These were not 'love letters', but 'missing messages', she said. 'When someone is in prison you need to always encourage the person who is inside, send reassurances, keep them updated, keep up their hope.' It was her way to care for him, though she also sent news: updates about their political party and the latest manoeuvring of the regime.

In late 2005, Abdulaziz was finally released. Three years later, the couple wed in a religious ceremony. 'There was no proposal, we just went and got it done,' she said. Her family were not supportive. 'They were very sceptical and afraid of him.' This may have been expected, not only on account of their political differences but because of the insecurity Fadwa was taking on; the feeling of borrowed time.

For former political prisoners, freedom was never absolute. Both Fadwa and Abdulaziz were prohibited from exercising certain civil rights, including the right to register their marriage with the state. Abdulaziz was barred from working as a doctor, though he practised under another doctor's name. 'In addition to the pressure we were facing, Abdulaziz was always chased, he was always listed by the intelligence who wanted to arrest him.' Despite the persecution and harassment, Fadwa remembers these years fondly. 'Of course, these were the most beautiful days of my life. We lived an amazing period of time.' The memories they made then have become an anchor which 'keeps me strong', Fadwa said, even though the duration was 'short'.

Then, in 2011, Syria's revolution began. There was no question but that the couple would support it. 'It was dangerous for both of us. But we didn't really have a choice, the only choice was to be involved in it. That's our dream, to have change in Syria.'

Fadwa and Abdulaziz hosted meetings for young revolutionaries, sharing tactics and giving advice on how to organise protests; ways to interact with or evade intelligence agents; tricks not to get detained. Abdulaziz was a co-founder and the external relations manager of an umbrella group for different political parties. It kept him in contact with delegations from other countries, whom he would speak to about Syria's future. It was after one of those trips that he and Maher disappeared.

By the time I first spoke to Fadwa, more than 100,000 Syrians were thought to have gone missing in similar ways.[2] While thousands of women and children were among this figure, the majority of the disappeared were men. This meant it was the women who loved them who ended up fronting the brave campaign that pushed for answers.

In Arabic, there are many ways to speak about love.

Habibi (male) or *habibti* (female), meaning 'my dear', can be used casually, but also as a term of deep endearment. *Ya rouhi* can also be used to say 'my dear', but it literally translates as 'my soul'. *Hayati* means 'my life', while *eayni* means 'my eyes'. Calling someone *ya amar*, or 'oh moon', means that they are incredibly beautiful – a use of language that confused me the first time a Sudanese man said it to me, in a park turned refugee camp in the coastal Tunisian city of Sfax. I thought he was saying I had a large, round, pale face.

The term *Qalb 3ala Qalb* translates loosely as 'hearts on hearts', but means 'hearts in sync', denoting a telepathy between people who have a love for each other. It describes a deep connection caused by any type of love, not just romantic.

Tu'burni for a man, or *Toborini* towards a woman, means 'may you bury me' in Levantine Arabic – effectively, it is a way of saying you want to die before the person you love because you would not be able to live without them, though this is a phrase often used humorously. In classical Arabic, there is also, specifically, a word for a parent who has lost a child: *thakla*.[3] Usually, a *thakla* is a grieving mother. Syria is filled with them. Many still hold hope that they are not truly bereaved, that their loved ones may come back to them some day. Others pray that their missing are already dead: the alternative – that they have existed and suffered all of this time – is immensely more frightening.

Years of reporting on Syria taught me how love can be weaponised and harnessed as a means of domination.

For decades, even before the 2011 revolution and civil war began, Syrians were controlled by fear. It was the Assad family's strongest weapon: a current so potent that it shaped what it means to be Syrian at all. Everything from academic papers and photographic projects to novels have been produced analysing the impact of fear on the psyche of Syrians. How it was omnipresent, like a boot slowly crushing a skull, making it hard to look the world in the eye; how it necessitated each person to shrink in size and to develop, as one resident of Aleppo described it, 'a small policeman' inside their hearts.[4]

It was fear for themselves, but also for their family members. Fear made silence the safest option: there was a lot that Syrians could not discuss openly, though they spoke in codes when necessary. 'Prison', for example, could be referred to as *bayt khaltu* or 'your aunt's house'. Because trading in foreign currency was illegal, dollars could be referred to as 'green', 'mint' or *molokhiyeh*, a dish made from jute leaves.

There was an air of suspicion, a hum of distrust because no one knew who was in the *mukhabarat*, the intelligence service. Anyone, from a corn seller on the street to a teacher in your child's school, could be an informant: the shady figures who were known to some as 'the birds'. Being in the wrong place at the wrong time could get you subjected to interrogation tactics including electrocution, being hung from the ceiling in a practice known as *shabeh*, or *dulab*, where detainees were forced to bend their body into a car tyre before being beaten. The relatives of an individual under suspicion could be seized and humiliated: ordered to kiss the feet of an officer, or refused access to medication or a bathroom. Even while walking near their own homes, Syrians averted their eyes from regime-associated buildings: onerous when they were so numerous, but necessary for the preservation of life.

'There is no way to govern our society except with the shoe over people's head,' Bashar al-Assad has been quoted as saying.[5] An ophthalmologist by training, Assad practised in London and married a British wife, Asma. He was thirty-four when he ascended to Syria's presidency, upon the death of his father in 2000. Though Bashar was initially heralded as a reformer, that perception quickly evaporated.

The Syrian war, which began in March 2011, started with a period of hope. Popular protests spread across the country, as Syrians dared to dream of a new nation. In response, the regime chose violence. Cities were barrel bombed, civilians massacred, and tens of thousands more people disappeared into the network of regime prisons and detention sites, never to be seen again. Numerous other actors became involved, carrying out their own atrocities, as the frontlines morphed and expanded. The UN stopped counting the number of dead as early as 2014, though estimates reach 600,000. The regime itself, and its allies, were responsible for the vast majority of civilian deaths.[6] For the bloodiness of his clampdown, Assad would come to earn the nickname the 'butcher of Damascus'.

I set out to meet more of the women whose lives had been changed forever.

As I was messaging Wafa Mustafa to set up an interview, I scrutinised her WhatsApp photo. It was a picture of her father, sitting, looking past the camera at something, or someone, that made his eyes light up. He had dark hair and wore a shirt with the top button undone. He was sitting in a white chair on what seemed to be on a balcony with a balustrade behind him. Beyond that was a tangle of green plants, maybe ferns. '3,620 days . . .' read Wafa's text next to it.

We met at lunchtime on a Friday, at a trendy coffee shop in Kreuzberg, Berlin. Wafa wore orange trousers, a cropped white T-shirt and gold hoop earrings, with her dark hair half tied up. She leant forward as she told me about her childhood.

The oldest of three girls, she was born on 4 August 1990. Her family came from Masyaf, near Hama, in western-central Syria. She lived her first seven years in Damascus, then they moved back to Masyaf.

Even when she was very young, Wafa idolised her father, Ali Mustafa. 'My dad was very passionate about politics, about music, about love stories, but at the same time he was just like all other fathers. He was quite strict, not very expressive, he worked so hard.'

Ali cared deeply about his children's education. He liked to remind them that 'we started from scratch and we should not take things for granted.' Sometimes the pressure felt too heavy, Wafa said. He desperately wanted them to learn musical instruments, for example, though they had no talent for it. 'My dad grew up in a very poor family in very difficult circum- stances,' she explained, suggesting that he was trying to give them everything he had gone without as a child.

Her father bought a cottage in the mountains and reno- vated it himself. There, he hosted gatherings for friends, preparing food as they played music and sang. 'For Arab men it wasn't easy to express emotions, so I think my dad had this way to express love and passion,' Wafa said. Setting off from the cottage, he would take his young children on road trips, driving at night around the mountains in the truck he used for business. Wafa remembers him playing the *Titanic* movie soundtrack. 'We would spend hours in the mountains and say no words and listen to music. That was scary but very calming.'

Ali was born fourteen years after the 1948 mass displace- ment that Palestinians call the Nakba, or 'catastrophe', and he believed deeply in the importance of self-determination for the Palestinian people. Aged around twenty, he travelled to Leba- non to fight against the Israeli occupation in that country's south. WAFA was the moniker of the Palestinian news service he listened to there and he decided to name his future daugh- ter after it. 'The first thing you learn about yourself is your name . . . I think it's the thing on which I built my character and my personality,' Wafa said. She grew up proclaiming that she wanted to be a war correspondent. Listening to her father's stories, she regarded him as a heroic figure who 'loved to live life, but is willing to die, if this is what it takes, to seek his beliefs and values. This is the kind of character that you see in films, you see in series, you read about.'

As a young man back in Syria, Ali had studied psychology, but he quickly realised it came with few professional opportunities. Instead, he started his own company selling frozen food and vegetables. He fell in love with Wafa's mother 'immediately', Wafa said. 'For years, my dad wrote my mom love letters. We did not read them because my mom said they are private but she said they were full of poetry and songs.'

Their family home was filled with books, music and art. It was more political than other households, with her father airing opinions openly, something Wafa says made other children afraid to talk to her. 'The first thing you learn when you're a kid in Syria is that walls have ears . . . People did not really want to be friends with me because they thought it would put them at risk.'

Wafa and her father were living together in Damascus the year he disappeared. By then a journalism and media student, she had started participating in protests. Here was a chance, finally, to step into history; to bring about change. 'I genuinely believed, and still believe, that we deserve freedom and we deserve a country where we don't get killed just for walking in the streets and chanting freedom,' she explained. Ali was delighted. 'I fought for this my whole life and I did not even expect to witness its beginning,' she remembered him telling her.

Tragedy struck when Wafa's friend was killed during shelling by regime forces. Her grief was so extreme that she says she could barely walk. It changed the dynamic of their relationship. 'My dad was there for me, not only as a father but as a friend,' she recalled. Ali cooked for her and showed his care purely by being present. After three months, he encouraged her to return to Masyaf to see a doctor. Days later, a group of armed men came to their door and took Ali away.

Ali had instructed his family to leave the country if he was taken, knowing that the relatives of detainees could be rounded up too, with their arrests used to increase pressure on the initial prisoner. Wafa, her mother and younger siblings, escaped Syria on 9 July 2013, one week after his disappearance. In Turkey, 'we knew no one there, we had nothing,' she said. Wafa was twenty-two.

That is when the extortion began. A 2021 report by a Syrian prison victims and survivors group determined that extortion was one way the Syrian regime sustained itself financially, with officials at one prison alone estimated to have extorted about $2.7 million from families.[7] All of the women I spoke to experienced extortion attempts. Even a few weeks before we first met, in June 2023, Wafa's family had handed over €500 to someone offering information, she said. In return, they received a death certificate that turned out to be a forgery. 'You cannot say no,' Wafa emphasised, explaining why extortion attempts are so successful. 'Even if I know they're lying to us, if there is one per cent chance . . . I cannot live with this guilt . . .'

In Turkey, Wafa posted appeals related to her father on Facebook, but much of her energy went towards supporting her mother and siblings. She was also severely depressed.

Eventually, she began to work with the citizen journalist group Raqqa Is Being Slaughtered Silently, documenting human rights abuses under ISIS from afar. That work was dangerous: in 2015, at least three journalists associated with the group were targeted and murdered.[8] As a result, Wafa and other colleagues were offered the chance to travel to Germany to ensure their safety. There, she received a scholarship to Bard College Berlin, where she studied humanities. 'I was all the time feeling very guilty because going to school and studying felt like a luxury. My father was somewhere between life and death and everyone I know was in refugee camps or still in Syria, it was surreal.' Her mother and sister stayed in Turkey, later travelling to Canada. When Wafa graduated, she devoted herself to activism full time.

Wafa is a compelling public speaker. She would go on to address the UN General Assembly and the UN Security Council,[9] but 'to be very honest this is the part I'm least proud of . . . this is not an accomplishment. I'm sad for myself that I had to talk to a group of old men and convince them that my father deserves freedom and my country deserves freedom. That was three years ago and look at us, nothing has changed.'

In 2021, Wafa staged a solo vigil outside a courtroom in Koblenz, Germany, where two former senior Syrian intelligence officers – Anwar Raslan and Eyad al-Gharib – were on trial. Raslan was said to have overseen the torture of more than four thousand people: he was only caught because he was spotted by victims in Germany, where he had claimed asylum. He would be found guilty of crimes against humanity, with Gharib found complicit in the same. In a closing witness statement, plaintiff and former prisoner Hussein Gherir said enforced disappearance should be considered not just a crime against humanity, but also a terrorist act, because it aimed to terrorise society. Even the lowest ranks of Syria's security forces knew its impact, he added, and 'that is precisely why it is practised'.

Those locked up were 'banished from life', Gherir said. In prison, time stops mattering. 'After a few days you won't know if it's day or night, as if they don't exist for you at all. The light and the dark will no longer make any sense; you will forget the shape of the leaf and the scent of the rose. And what is life other than those little details?'

Gherir was released in 2015 and escaped to Europe. 'Do you know why I fled from Syria?' he asked the German court. 'Not out of fear of dying by a bullet or under bombardment, but precisely out of fear of disappearing again . . . I ran away because I didn't want my family to live the nightmare a third time, the nightmare of the questions that keep messing with their lives: "Did they kill him? Is he still alive? Is he hanging at the moment? Did they break his back? Are they torturing him now while we eat?" '[10]

Communication with the families of detainees from other countries made Wafa feel most 'grounded', she said – they could show each other solidarity. Still, she was frustrated that individuals like her could be characterised as either victims or heroes, when they were simply normal people caught up in something horrendous; when she felt like there was no other choice. Her life was agonising, she said. She could not even be in a relationship, experiencing that type of stability, without guilt overwhelming her.

'This is definitely not the reality I wanted for myself . . . and not what my father would have wanted for me . . . I literally don't have a life, everything in my life is about my father,' she said. 'My last ten years, nothing in that life was about me, it feels like I'm living the life of someone else. This is painful beyond words. But to be honest, forgetting and giving up is a luxury to me and it's not because I'm a hero . . . I wish my family [member] was not detained . . . I wish sometimes that I would be hit by a car and lose my memory because this is the only way that I'll be able to stop.'

I admittedly had little awareness of what was happening in Syria for the first few years of the war. That was until early 2014, when I was a freshly graduated intern on Christiane

Amanpour's CNN International show *Amanpour* in London, as she broke the story of the Caesar photographs. These were a trove of images of tortured and emaciated Syrian detainees, taken by a former military photographer turned defector who had risked his life to smuggle this shattering evidence out of the country, by means that included hiding flash drives in a sock or between bundled loaves of bread. Caesar, of course, was a codename. At least 6,786 detainees who had died in detention or military hospital were pictured in tens of thousands of images.

The photographs were analysed by war crimes prosecutors and forensic experts before being shared with us. I remember the unusual hush that came over my seasoned colleagues as they crowded around a laptop screen to look at the graphic evidence, not yet censored for broadcast. Later, live on air, Christiane called the photographs 'reminiscent of the most horrific . . . crimes that we've seen in history'. She showed one corpse, its face blacked out, with marks of strangulation around its neck; another with thick, parallel welts in lines all down its torso and onto its pelvis. By the time the live show ended, our report was trending worldwide. A feeling of deep, visceral disquiet lasted long after I left the office that night. I had never seen anything like that before – so gruesome and so clearly systematic. There was a lot I still did not understand, like why were the photographs taken in the first place, and how was it possible that a regime – even one known for such barbarity – had no qualms about meticulously documenting its crimes? How could those responsible have such certainty that they would get away with it?

At an event in the US Holocaust Memorial Museum, Yahoo News chief investigative correspondent Michael Isikoff compared the photographs to 'images we've seen from Nazi concentration camps'. The *Guardian* newspaper described them as 'evidence of the existence of the Syrian death machine'.[11] Syrian president Bashar al-Assad, predictably, disputed their veracity – and his hold on power continued.

In countries across the world, the relatives of disappeared Syrians began scouring the same photographs, looking for their missing loved ones. Some found them.

Nearly a decade later, I would meet a woman who discovered proof of the death of her child through the Caesar revelations.

Mariam al-Hallak's fourth-floor apartment, in Berlin's suburbs, was humble but cared for. There was a single bed, separated by a curtain from the grey couches we sat on. Mandarins grew in a little pot. On the walls were pictures of her family members – alive and dead.

I was there to hear about her youngest son, Ayham Mustafa Ghazzoul. Mariam already had two boys, the younger aged thirteen, when Ayham was born in 1987. There was no ultrasound at that time, Mariam explained. She'd longed for a girl – that's why she tried for another baby in the first place. Yet looking into Ayham's face, she felt no disappointment. 'He was just very pretty,' she recalled.

By then, Mariam and her husband had a 'settled' life. 'It's different when you decide to have a kid later on. I was really happy. Everybody was really happy.' Ayham's childhood felt easy. 'He studied hard. He never needed guidance. He was a good boy, polite.' In ninth grade, he ranked as one of the best students in Syria, she said with pride. They bought him a computer as a reward.

Aged fifteen, Ayham became a regular in internet cafés, where he downloaded books, and other material that intrigued him, onto floppy disks. This was where he first came across information about the darker sides of the Syrian regime.

The first influential book he read was a novel by Syrian writer and former detainee Mustafa Khalifa, titled *The Shell: Memoirs of a Hidden Observer*. I have read it too. It unfolds like a diary, beginning with Khalifa's protagonist Musa boarding a plane home from France with a scheme to become a film director, rather than remaining as 'any old refugee' abroad. Instead, Musa ends up in the 'Desert Prison', where he witnesses abuses, executions and describes prisoners communicating between cells through taps, similar to Morse code. The prison was based on Tadmur – where the author himself was locked up for twelve years. It is an astonishing and devastating piece of literature.

Mariam was a longtime member of the ruling Ba'ath party. This was a tool of control and many posts in the public sector were reserved for its members. First, Mariam was a teacher, then a headmistress. This meant she had responsibility for ensuring children learnt anthems and recited slogans, such as 'unity, freedom, socialism' and 'one Arab nation with an eternal message'. Syrian children were indoctrinated from a young age.

Caged birds do not know what it feels like to soar. In a dictatorship, people keep their heads down. They impose restraints on themselves, and not always consciously. Mariam's faith in Syria's leadership was never particularly challenged until Ayham came along. 'He was the first one to put this political knowledge to me, despite me being older and smarter,' she recalled.

After secondary school, Ayham studied dentistry and volunteered with charities. His master's degree involved supervising

Mariam al-Hallak, in her apartment in Berlin's suburbs, in June 2023.

other students. When Syria's uprising began, 'like everybody, he started going along to the protests,' Mariam said. 'I was very happy seeing him doing this, because the feeling of freedom that he and his peers felt is something that I wanted to feel and never did.' She could picture her son's face as he walked through the door after returning from demonstrations, his cheeks red and his eyes 'very happy'. He diligently described the scenes for her: the music played; the dances young men did on the streets.

Ayham looked for safe ways to involve his young nephews in what he was convinced was a movement towards a brighter future. The trio made paper planes, writing revolutionary words like 'freedom' on the sides, and threw them from Mount Qasioun, a mountain with panoramic views of Damascus. (Biblical and Qur'anic traditions suggest that Mount Qasioun is where Cain killed Abel, with Abel's blood subsequently turning the bottom half of the mountain red.) Back in the safety of their home, the children staged fake demonstrations, which Ayham filmed 'to make them feel like it was a real protest'.

As the state's reaction to the public demonstrations turned increasingly violent, Ayham began documenting the number of people being killed. He was detained for three months. When he was released, Mariam said he had an internal haemorrhage in his kidneys, but he seemed to recover quickly.

Within six months, Ayham travelled to the Lebanese capital, Beirut, for a workshop. He spent his final night there singing with friends by Beirut's famous Raouché Rocks – two spectacular formations that rise from the sea by the city's corniche. The next morning, Ayham returned to Damascus, telling his mother that he'd had a wonderful time and would fill her in on everything later, as usual.

Mariam paused here, her eyes scanning my face. 'Before we continue, what do you really want to drink? Arabic coffee?' she asked. The juxtaposition felt jarring but I accepted, not wanting to interrupt her but also realising this might be Mariam's effort at taking a pause – hospitality as a punctuation mark. She poured water into a pot on a small gas stove and lit the flame.

'He went to university in the morning and he never came back,' Mariam then said. Ayham was arrested for the second time on 5 November 2012, right as he completed his daily student supervision. An office inside the university's medicine department had been turned into a torture chamber, she said, and that was where her son was taken.

Mariam stopped again here and asked me whether she should list the specifics of the torture. I said it was not necessary if she did not want to, I had already sourced accounts online. Mariam said there was no hesitation from her side, and then continued. 'They tied his hands, took his toenails from his feet, put holes in his ears. There were fifteen people . . . They tied them and started beating him. One of them hit him with a steel pipe, a metal pipe on his head, he blacked out. Then they poured hot water on him.'

This ordeal was recounted to Mariam by another detainee captured with Ayham, who survived and was released three months later. Ayham was not so lucky. As he was dragged to a car to be transported to a location known as Branch 215, his students, still outside, observed the trail of blood left behind him. 'People called his brother and said they didn't think he was going to make it,' Mariam recalled. He was just twenty-five.

For the first three months after Ayham was taken away, Mariam searched for him. This was despite the fact that, five days in, she had a vision of Ayham's body being thrown into his bedroom by four people, which she interpreted as ominous.

When Ayham's fellow detainee, Mohamed, was released, he said Ayham had died days after their arrest. 'Mohamed told me the details: how he was hit, how when he first arrived into the detention centre his body started to go blue. Mohamed opened the hatch on the prison door telling the security Ayham needed immediate medical attention and the security replied: "Just let us know when he dies." '

Mariam had come to another halt. She poured the coffee – 'Would you like sugar?' She took a deep breath in and out, and then proceeded.

While Mariam registered this detailed account of her son's death, she began hearing other, conflicting reports, to the extent that she started doubting which one was true. 'There is a proverb that the drowning would hold onto any straw,' she explained. 'I didn't know what to do, but I had hope and I had to cling to it.'

She began visiting locations where she might find answers. 'All the detention centres, all the hidden security offices everywhere in Syria every day. I never had a break. And I asked them one question: "Is he alive or dead?"' In the morning, she first went to the military court, where she paid bribes of up to 250 Syrian lira for a piece of paper listing who she was searching for. Next, she took that to the military police.

This went on for a year and five months. 'It was impossible. They humiliated me, they threatened me. In one of the detention centres, called 248, I asked one of the officers "Where did you bury my son?" He responded: "If you weren't an older woman, I would have put you inside and you would have never have left this place".'

Mariam was far from alone. 'Of course it wasn't the same people every day, but there was repetition,' she recalled. 'There were some fathers, but the majority were women.' Daily, she estimated that she met fifty other mothers doing parallel circuits and seeking comparable answers: as they encountered each other 'we didn't speak, we literally only whispered and cried.' When, discreetly, she suggested some form of protest, she perceived their fear. Those families were already facing attacks and extortion. Security forces came to the home of one woman whose son had been detained, throwing her husband from a balcony and raping her daughter, Mariam said. And yet, even then, 'that woman didn't want to protest because she had hope, she wanted to protect the son she believed was still alive in detention.'

On what turned out to be her final day doing the usual rounds, Mariam was summoned to 'Room 11'. 'I knew that with this room specifically, anyone who enters had a relative who is already dead.' Inside, others were handed ID cards, sometimes accompanied by a phone or other cheap belongings (the expensive ones always seemed to disappear). Mariam was only given an instruction to go to the Tishreen Military Hospital, the same site where the defector codenamed Caesar was summoned to take his first photographs of corpses. Standing outside, she saw a car pull up. 'I saw them dumping bodies from that car. They were naked, wrapped in transparent plastic. There were fifteen corpses that they dumped and conscripts, soldiers, were putting the corpses next to each other. On the other side there were five young men blindfolded. Their hands were tied and they were being hit by a stick ... Until that point, [the soldiers] didn't notice that I was there, then they yelled at me.'

The hospital issued a death certificate for Ayham. It said he had suffered from a heart attack, though this was commonly understood to be one false explanation used when a Syrian prisoner died from torture or other abuses. Mariam wanted to know where Ayham was buried, where his belongings were, but she received no further information. 'I was being discouraged from pursuing answers for my questions. People were saying "your son is not the only one who died, hundreds of people are being killed every day".' Her voice was shot through with longing. 'I was his mother,' she said. 'I was his friend. I told him everything, he told me everything. I just want a grave to go there to tell him stuff and maybe he will tell me stuff. It is symbolic. In a grave, he would be human, but now he is just a number.'

Mariam's efforts at uncovering the truth were pushing her further away from it. Less than three weeks after she identified the security branch Ayham had been held in, intelligence forces drove her out of her brother's house. Her family fled to neighbouring Lebanon. It was Mariam's first time ever leaving Syria.

Mariam was in Lebanon when the Caesar photographs were published on Facebook. Because of the dates they covered – May 2011 to August 2013 – she felt certain Ayham would be among them. She tried to look herself. 'The pictures were extremely painful, I couldn't,' she said. A contact of hers found Ayham, and Mariam's sister made a second identification in May 2015 – almost exactly one year after Mariam received Ayham's death certificate.

I have seen the photo in question. It shows Ayham, dead, on his back. 'Number 2129' is written on paper placed on his chest. On his forehead is a sticker reading: 'a body for company 215 No. 320'. What look like latex gloves lie on the ground beside him.[12]

When Mariam arrived in Lebanon, she was ready to talk publicly. It felt like a chance to represent all of the mothers inside Syria who were on perpetual, anguished quests, shuttling between detention centres, intelligence sites and the military court. She participated in a documentary film and provided evidence to the respected organisation Human Rights Watch.[13] She heard about a legal attempt to prosecute some of the heads of the Syrian security forces, and was accepted as a witness.

That case was how Mariam got permission to travel to Germany, where she claimed asylum. It was in Germany that Mariam started meeting other Syrians who had also recognised their relatives in the Caesar photographs. Seven of them came together to found the Caesar Families Association. By the time we met, seventy-five families were involved.

Their efforts included the introduction of facial recognition software, an innovation which saved the bereaved from having to scroll through each image themselves. With another organisation, the Truth and Justice Charter, Mariam added to the pressure on the UN and international organisations to push for information about the fates of the missing. 'We go everywhere,' Mariam told me. 'I went to the UN many times, I went to the Security Council in New York. I met lots of UN delegates from lots of countries.' She was scheduled to go to Paris the following week.

Birds sang outside her window as the sun sank towards the horizon, another day over. This small apartment was her refuge now, but it must be a lonely one, I thought. Mariam's husband had died more than a decade before, when they were still in Syria. Despite all of her courageous activism, I was reminded that Mariam was also an older woman, turning seventy the next week. The responsibilities she had taken on meant she was constantly reminded of all she had lost. The memories must sometimes feel crowded together, omnipresent, leaving no respite.

Journalism often compels you to ask seemingly insensitive questions. One very common one is 'How do you feel?' I have asked it of Eritrean teenagers right after they escaped a dictatorship, and of Somalis watching their communities starve as a result of climate change-related drought. I have asked it of the widow of a man poisoned to death in London by Russian assassins and of Cubans in Panama, risking their lives on the treacherous journey towards the United States. We are asking someone to describe their feelings, so that others – usually with better luck and more privilege – might imagine what it is like to be them; to consider their emotions even though they probably expend a lot of energy shutting them off, so they maintain the capacity to move forward. We ask even though the answer is usually obvious, because we want to hear it in their own words. Now, I was asking this again of a mother who had lost her son in one of the most terrible ways possible.

Mariam was willing to answer this kind of question. She knew there was a purpose to it, that enabling people to imagine what it was like to be her might make political action more likely. 'People always ask me why at this age I do all this work and I never relax: it's because of this look in those mothers' eyes. I feel like it's my duty to carry their voices.' She was referring, again, to the many women with similar stories whom she met in Syria. In a way, my interview with her was a practice session. One day, Mariam hoped she would give the same testimony all over again, but this time in court.

After her husband and son disappeared, Fadwa also travelled to Lebanon, where she received word that a warrant for her arrest had been issued in Syria. Prejudice and hostility towards Syrians was increasing throughout its much smaller neighbour, where the Syrian refugee influx was soon equal to around one quarter of the population. Fadwa's other son was already in Germany, and in 2015, Fadwa flew to join him, with help from a connection in Beirut's German embassy.

There, her campaigning began 'right away, I never stopped'. The so-called families' movement started in 2016, she said. In 2017, they travelled around Europe on a double-decker bus they named the 'Freedom Bus', covered with photographs of the missing. Fadwa even took part in a theatre production which raised awareness of the plight of detainees. It was performed in Italy and France.

The number of collectives of relatives and victims working for justice kept expanding. Fadwa said she felt propelled forward constantly, though not by anger. 'If you're angry you cannot achieve anything. What motivates me is my belief that we all have an equal right to lead a good life.'

Her husband, Abdulaziz, and son Maher were always in her mind. 'I've actually devoted my whole life to the cause of my husband and my son. That's what I do twenty-four seven,' Fadwa told me. As I had with Mariam, I apologised for making Fadwa relive her past. She brushed it away. 'You didn't cause me any extra pain because that story never leaves my mind. I'm thinking about them and waiting for the day for them to come back.'

When I first spoke to Fadwa in September 2022, she had already experienced a breakthrough. UN Secretary General António Guterres had come out to publicly support the setting up of an independent institution, which would focus on finding out what had happened to Syria's missing. His twenty-page report specifically credited the wives and mothers of the disappeared for pushing forward the quest for justice, noting 'the leadership, strength and courage of the families whose right to know and struggle to learn the fate and whereabouts of their loved ones remain the driving force behind this initiative'.[14] The next step would be trying to pass a resolution in the UN General Assembly, where all 193 member countries would vote. Fadwa spent nine months campaigning.

On 29 June 2023, I watched an online livestream of the UN General Assembly in New York. I was on my laptop in Freetown, the capital of Sierra Leone, where I was covering an election. At the last minute came an announcement that nine other countries, including the UK, had been added to the resolution as co-sponsors. It was a good sign.

Luxembourg's representative offered an introduction, saying the resolution had 'a humanitarian goal . . . We owe it to these

families to act decisively and to act now.' Next came a representative of the Syrian regime. A balding man with a small grey
moustache, grey suit, and wine-coloured tie, he called the resolution 'politicised', saying it 'reflected flagrant interference in
[Syria's] internal affairs' and provided 'new evidence of the hostile approach being pursued by certain Western states against
Syria'.

Syria had support from other sources, perhaps worried
about their own human rights records. Venezuela's representative said the resolution would cause 'suffering and pain'.
North Korea called it part of a 'politicised agenda pushed by
Western countries'. China and Nicaragua agreed. Russia's
representative listed times people had died or gone missing as
a result of US actions in Syria, saying the body would not be
'independent nor impartial . . . Their goal is not helping
people.'

Then came the vote and an almost instantaneous decision.
Green pluses, yellow Xs or red lines appeared on the screen
beside each country's name. Eighty-three countries were in
favour and eleven against, with sixty-two abstentions. 'The
draft resolution . . . is adopted,' announced Csaba Kőrösi,
president of the General Assembly, using a wooden gavel to hit
the table in front of him.[15]

The aftermath saw other representatives, whose countries
had gone through crises involving their own missing people,
make further statements – a reminder that while Syria's experience might be distinctive, in the way that all human rights
crises are, such abuses are far from unknown.

'Our work is still ongoing, even though thirty years have
passed,' said Chile's representative, referring to the more than
1,000 people missing since the Pinochet regime. A speaker for
Lebanon, who raised what she saw as problems with specific details

of the resolution, also wanted to extend warm greetings to the relatives of Lebanon's missing from the civil war, saying 'this issue remains a bleeding wound in the collective memory of our country.'

Colombia's representative said 'the scourge of missing persons' was a wound which Colombia 'has attempted to cleanse . . . Truth is a key component for reconciliation and reparations in society and for peace.' Official estimates put the number of missing there as high as 210,000.[16]

'We have lived through the tragedy of massive violations of human rights and we know what that means,' said Argentina's spokeswoman. In her country, the 'Mothers of the Plaza Mayo' had become famous for banding together in the 1970s and 1980s, protesting publicly after their children were taken by the military government.

That day was a notable success for Fadwa, who described it as the 'crown jewel of the past two years' work'.

This is where I thought this chapter ended.

And then, in the closing weeks of 2024, the unthinkable happened.

Beginning in late November, a rebel coalition launched a shock assault and advanced across Syria. From Lebanon, I followed online as maps changed colour and videos emerged showing triumphant fighters gaining ground. As the opposition took territory, the regime's security forces sometimes fought back but often put down arms and shed their uniforms, leaving the sites they had guarded with such zeal; the rebels entered prisons hours later, opening the doors and locks and beckoning inmates out to freedom. Activists on social media began counting down the miles left until they reached Sednaya Prison, the most notorious of Assad's detention facilities, known as *al-Maslakh al-Basharia* or 'the human slaughterhouse'. The Association of Detainees and Missing Persons of Sednaya Prison estimated that more than thirty thousand people had been executed there or died of torture, starvation or a lack of medical care between the beginning of the war and 2018. Survivors said victims were often beaten before being killed in pre-dawn hangings.[17]

In Beirut, I fell into a fitful sleep and wakened in the early hours of Sunday, 8 December. Videos from Sednaya were being posted online now: people being ushered outside, their shadows barely visible on dark streets. It felt emblematic that shortly afterwards came the news everyone was waiting for: dictator Bashar al-Assad had fled the country. The regime was over. More than half a century of brutal rule, an exercise in ultimate domination, had crumbled with barely a whimper.

The following day, I drove to Syria. The road to Damascus

A man sets fire to a portrait of ousted dictator Bashar al-Assad.

was covered in torn-up posters of Assad and his father, Hafez. During my only visit to regime-held Syria in 2017, those portraits had been ubiquitous, an ever-present reminder of whom to be frightened of; which person exerted absolute control. Now, I saw Syrians burning them, shooting at them; an elderly man with weathered skin carefully and repeatedly stamping on their faces. This had been unimaginable even days before. It was symbolism brought to life.

The border posts had been a series of intimidating checkpoints, where civilians who were 'listed' could be pulled away and disappeared. Now they were blackened shells, burnt and abandoned. I met men in khaki outfits, wielding guns, but they introduced themselves as local villagers who had come to stop the looting, claiming the regime forces' weapons and keeping watch until the arrival of their new leaders – the rebels themselves. The men were jovial, posing for photographs. There had been a lot of robberies the previous day, even car batteries had been extracted from parked vehicles, they explained. Later, I would hear from Syrians who had stolen things then: they were actually 'reclaiming' what belonged to the people, they said (though others complained that they could at least have left fuel in the generators powering the phone lines).

I passed into Syria without even showing my passport.

The days after the fall of a regime were something I had never experienced before and will likely never experience again. There was euphoria and disbelief. There were jubilant civilians waving flags and blaring pro-revolution songs from cars, almost in a test of whether this reality was real. The three-starred revolutionary flag quickly replaced the two-star regime standard, with its stripe of red, which civilians told me they used to interpret as blood. In a typical display of clever entrepreneurship, flags of cheap material were already on sale at stands in Damascus's famous Al-Hamidiyeh Souq, alongside keyrings with the design painted on them with nail varnish: later, more carefully produced dresses, hats, jumpers and other memorabilia would join them.

In the nearby Umayyad Mosque, a key landmark of the city, I saw rebels handing around their rifles and helping fans wrap scarves around their heads to imitate rebel garb for photographs. I even happened upon a journalist I knew wearing full khaki: 'That's the style now,' he quipped.

Former security services and military buildings were easy to spot because of their blackened façades – they had been stormed, ransacked, and sometimes set on fire, either by those absconding from them or the crowds who moved in afterwards. I walked through one abandoned military base, in Eastern Ghouta. It contained anti-aircraft missiles lined up in rows; a machine gun on a roof; instructions for maintaining weaponry lying on the ground. The office chairs had been stolen, the beds. Uninterested in missiles, locals were chopping down the trees in the base instead, for wood, and removing machine-gun bullets for their copper. The soldiers here used to 'step on us', one local told me, calmly and with a proprietorial air, as he led me on a tour of this base he had never been able to enter until a few days before.

Exuberance was accompanied by the sudden unveiling of what had previously been only whispered about, a seeping abhorrence. That first afternoon in Syria, with other journalists, I drove to Sednaya Prison, which was located on a remote hill outside Damascus. The route was dotted with the discarded uniforms of regime soldiers: trousers, a jacket, patches with stars conveying rank. Kilometres away, it became impossible to drive further because the road was so packed with people and vehicles. We parked our car and joined the throngs.

As the regime fell, tens of thousands of Syrians had fix-ated on this place. They travelled from near and far, motivated by an urgent desire to finally find their loved ones. Though prisoners had been released the previous morning, online rumours were still spreading, saying there were hidden under-ground rooms, possibly protected by electronic systems that no one had cracked into yet. There must still be people alive there, everyone thought. There must still be a prospect of deliverance.

The sun was setting as we completed the final stretch, trek-king a hill up to this loathsome complex, the sky now shimmering purple. We picked our steps carefully, following the snaking lines of new arrivals, who took turns to warn each other that the ground away from the trodden path might be mined with explosives. Closer to the entrance, we came upon a crowd.

They were sharing around handwritten documents, which they pulled from woven rice sacks. A young man, whose friend had gone missing in 2012, scanned one: but it related to deten-tions decades ago. In the chaos, other papers were being trodden into the ground.

Spotting foreign journalists, a lawyer approached to express his worry: crucial evidence was being destroyed. It was clear what he meant. People sitting on the grass closer to the prison had even lit fires to keep warm, pieces of paper burning between them.

In the darkness, searchers walked in every direction, using phone torches to hunt for clues. They opened manholes, dug dirt and wielded sledgehammers to break down walls. In the murk of this disturbing setting, they passed a prosthetic leg; a stretcher; medications scattered across the dirty ground. In one cell, I watched a man hammering at a wall. His quest

Families search for missing loved ones in Sednaya Prison, the day after the fall of the Assad regime.

seemed to epitomise the desperation permeating this place: even when others called out that there could be nothing between the walls he was focused on – there was barely any thickness at all between them – he kept hammering, and others kept watching, their expressions still hopeful.

Ibrahim Sawuan's worn face emerged from the darkness. He wanted to find his son. In 2013, the twenty-year-old had been serving in the Syrian army but was detained for planning to run away. Sawuan himself was imprisoned three years later, spending four years and eight months locked up, including eighty days underground. The reason, he said, was that the regime had decided he had too much money. 'They confiscated all my properties. They called me a terrorist but I'm a farmer.'

Another man, twenty-nine-year-old Mohammad Nawras Zewani, said his mother and two sisters had been taken from the Zahra neighbourhood of Homs. 'I don't know anything,' he sighed. Nadia Saadsaad's sixteen-year-old son Mouiad

Fawzi Harfoush was detained in August 2013, after stepping out to buy phone credit. With Mouiad's stepbrother, Iyad, she stayed in Sednaya from 7 a.m. until 8 p.m. on Sunday, and again on Monday. They were planning to return on Tuesday too, despite having no means of transport (we ended up giving them a lift home). 'People say there are seventeen floors underground,' Iyad said, hope distorting his voice. Later, I would think back to what Mariam, in Berlin, had told me about her own quest, how 'the drowning would hold onto any straw'.

A man smoking on the steps of the prison said he was looking for his uncle, who was arrested in 2016. 'They said he died here. I came to the prison [before] and they gave me his ID,' he said. As he spoke, warplanes flew overhead and an airstrike sounded in the distance. Smoke mushroomed outwards. It was Israeli forces hitting military targets. Israel would launch hundreds of airstrikes that week, saying they did not trust the new leadership in Syria and did not want the regime's arsenal of weapons to fall into their hands.

A second airstrike caused the sky to glow from secondary explosions as the searching continued. These attacks would continue all night, though my mind seemed keen to ignore the persistent sounds of bombing in the distance. After months of war in Lebanon, I was surrounded by Israeli bombardment in yet another country, a development that felt too surreal to comprehend.

Back in the desperate turbulence of Sednaya, there was some commotion when a recent inmate passed by, encircled by a crowd clamouring for his attention. The scrawny man had been incarcerated in the 'white prison' for two months, he said, but he also worked in the prison kitchen. In that job, he said he had seen a thick door with a hinge that led to a tunnel. He seemed confused, repeating and physically acting out parts of his story multiple times. He was frail too, at one point stumbling to the ground. It took four people to open that door, the man said, and inside were prisoners held behind metal wire or mesh. But he had no idea where the door was located.

Those around me questioned how reliable these memories could be. The sad reality was that many prisoners – even when they had spent years in one facility – had no idea what the broader complex looked like: their horizon might not extend beyond their own cell. They were likely blindfolded when they arrived and forced to keep their eyes down every time they were moved around; they were obliged to jump and face windowless walls when guards approached. They might not even know whether they were being held under or above ground.

Despite the yearning and rumours, in a statement in the early hours of the following morning, Syrian civil defence organisation the White Helmets said it had finished search operations. Its rescuers discovered no hidden or secret cells, and found no evidence that they had ever existed. 'We share the profound disappointment of the families of the thousands who remain missing and whose fates remain unknown,' the organisation's statement read. 'We stand in solidarity . . . fully understanding their anguish and their longing for answers.'

I was inside Sednaya Prison when my grandmother, Sheila de Courcy, died. Weeks before, she had turned ninety-eight surrounded by family: all of these generations who owed their existence to her and my grandfather, like many branches extending from the trunk of a single tree. Her wise presence was interlaced with my life and my memories. Though I moved away from Ireland when I graduated from university, I was back in 2021, finishing my first book, and again, from

2022, when it was published. I stayed in her house after she moved to a nursing home down the road, meaning I could regularly visit her. She had dementia, so our conversations were often the same, but she almost always remembered me, asking where I was travelling to next and telling me how brave she thought I was.

I had no phone connection in Sednaya and received the sad news while driving away afterwards, crammed together in the car with three other journalists and two Syrians who had been searching for a missing child. I pictured my grandmother's elegant poise; the smile that lit up her face when she saw her grandchildren; how she always walked me out and waved at the end of a visit, originally standing beside my grandfather, and then alone, on the porch of her house, and later from behind the glass in the dementia unit of her nursing home.

A strange and potentially selfish aspect of being an international reporter is missing important moments with family and close friends. We customarily fail to offer support to those closest to us in their times of need, even as we dispense it to strangers. I thought about my love for my grandmother, my loss, and all of these other losses around me in that moment that towered over it, grief on grief, sorrow on sorrow, love on love. I did not yet tell anyone with me in Syria what had happened.

I stayed in Syria and kept reporting. Over the following days, hundreds of missing person posters went up on the walls of central Damascus. Dozens of mutilated or emaciated corpses were discovered, and photographs of their faces and identifying marks on their bodies were printed out, lining the wall of a central hospital, as Syrians jostled each other trying to identify them. Some searchers moved on to the morgue, cramming inside in an effort to spot their loved ones.

One mother recognised her son by his chest tattoo. Another body was identified as the famous activist Mazen Hamada, who had somehow been lured back to Syria from the Netherlands in 2020 and disappeared, his fate unknown until then. Mazen received a proper funeral, with devastated mourners marching through the streets.

In hospitals around Damascus, searchers crowded around prison survivors too damaged to speak or to explain who they were. In some cases, this led to fights as an impossible number of people claimed a single inarticulate patient as their own long-lost relative. They debated how much someone's physical appearance could change after a decade or more in prison. They submitted that it was possible their missing loved one would no longer recognise or remember them. Relatives scoured writings and marks on the walls of detention sites, which sometimes included names and phone numbers for those loved by the incarcerated.

'Don't be sad, mother. This is my fate,' read one scrawl, in the notorious Palestine Branch detention facility in Damascus.

'God, fill me with me patience and don't let me despair,' said one another.

And there was *'ashtaqtilak'*, Arabic for 'I miss you'.

Though more information trickled out, it was far from a comprehensive picture. Recovered execution reports and death certificates meant social media timelines filled with tributes. A friend of mine found the name of his father – missing for a decade – on a list of prisoners held in Sednaya on a particular date years earlier, though it came with no further information about his subsequent fate. Mass graves, long an open secret in certain areas, were now visited freely by journalists. In Tadamon, a neighbourhood of Damascus, children played football beside human bones: they even offered to dig up more of them for me in return for payment (I obviously declined).

I spoke to an experienced forensic specialist who visited Syria in the months after the regime's fall. He told me that the country did not have the capacity to deal with this legacy in its entirety – the equipment and resources; the political will. 'In terms of looking at war crimes and collections of evidence, the number of graves will have been heavily compromised at this stage.' But even if every individual was unlikely to be identified, he suggested, you can still attempt to 'tell a broader story and try to give the dead some dignity'.

Lingering unknowns ranged from the basics of survival and murder – why, when, where? – to conundrums touching the heart of what it means to be human. How to understand death without a body? How can you move forward when it feels like high treachery? How could one country, one people, process this grief? How could anyone bear it?

Through their lengthy and continuing ordeals, the love shown by the families of Syria's missing had been overwhelming; their endurance stunned me. I envisaged each missing person as the centre of a web. Lines stretched outwards: their close relatives; extended family; friends; neighbours; acquaintances. Every person was affected by every void. There would be no closure.

On 15 December 2024, Wafa posted an update on Instagram:
It's been a week since Assad fled, leaving Syria in ruins. Every day since I've been:

1. Search[ing] for my father through videos, images, lists, and groups – a deeply painful process.
2. Coordinating with people on the ground to visit hospitals, mosques, detention centres and morgues to look for those released but unrecognisable, or to identify bodies.
3. Trying to return to Syria, despite having only a German travel document that limits where I can go and risks my asylum status if I enter Syria.
   No news about my dad yet. My family is in Damascus searching for him.
   Soon, Syria will fade from your feeds, but our pain remains. Assad is gone, but his legacy endures. For detainees' families, the struggle is far from over – it's just beginning.

In her apartment in Berlin, Fadwa stayed wide awake the entire night the Syrian regime fell. She had spent her life dreaming of this moment, the end of 'the whole regime, the whole system'. Yet the 'joy of liberation' felt missing for her and many others. Months later, she described this anticlimax on a WhatsApp call to me – improbably, I was now connecting from a rented room in Damascus. Fadwa was still not able to return to Syria: she did not feel psychologically prepared, but also, like Wafa, she worried about losing the legal protection Germany offered her.

Fadwa was frustrated. The Assad regime was gone but there were still logistical challenges, she pointed out. There continued to be no comprehensive list containing the names of everyone who was missing. The UN mechanism that she campaigned so hard for had not started work inside Syria, because the new government had not yet granted permission, she said. Nor had the new authorities set up their own committee to investigate the fates of Syria's missing people, despite promising to do so (they finally announced one in May 2025). After years of being pitted against a clear enemy, a 'different type of struggle' was presenting itself, Fadwa determined.

'Look,' she said, making it clear that her mind was plotting the next steps forward, as it had so many times before. 'As long as I'm alive I will not give up on my campaign and I will continue my insistence to know the destiny of my beloved ones and the disappeared people. We will not, will never, give up looking and seeking justice. Neither with the old regime nor with a new regime, nor any regime that is coming and trying to put obstacles or barriers in front of the path of justice. We need justice. Justice is the only solution.'

Chapter 9

Japan: Love after death

> 'A world of grief and pain,
> Flowers bloom,
> Even then.'
>
> – Japanese poet Kobayashi Issa (1763–1828)[1]

> 'We have only a little time to please the living. But all
> eternity to love the dead.'
>
> – Sophocles, *Antigone*[2]

It is called the drifting post, he explained, because the letters drift between heaven and earth. Set within a stretch of coastal woodland, in rural Japan, this post box receives letters written to the dead. Yuji Akagawa, a grandfather in his seventies, was the proprietor and key administrator.

'Yesterday was the tenth anniversary,' he told me in March 2024, the first day we met, about the drifting post's founding. Akagawa was smaller than me, I guessed less than five feet. He was wearing sandals with blue socks, a bowl haircut and a big smile, when I first saw him standing outside Mizusawa-Esashi Station in Iwate Prefecture, almost 500 kilometres north of Tokyo. Akagawa lived some of the time nearby, with his wife and their fifteen-year-old dog. Snowy peaks were visible in the distance, providing a contrast to the flat urban landscapes through which the car moved smoothly. This area felt more remote than most places I have been. We deposited ourselves in a booth at a coffee franchise famed for its desserts.

The spot of land by Rikuzentakata, a coastal town an hour's drive away, was supposed to be Akagawa's refuge. He'd longed for an isolated life in the countryside, far from the cities where he had earned his money. He was born in Yokohama, in Tokyo Bay, and built his career in the capital. It is unusual for Japanese people to move to rural communities without direct connections, he told me, and he was worried he would be excluded as a stranger. But at the same time, though he could not explain why, he had always felt a deep and yearning longing for solitude. After he and his wife first relocated to Mizusawa-Esashi, he decided he needed a retreat somewhere even more remote. He named his second home, in Rikuzentakata, *Mori no Koya*, or 'the small house in the forest'.

Akagawa retired two years before the Great East Japan Earthquake struck in 2011. He was in his second home, alone, when its violent shaking decreed that suddenly 'everything was foreign.' He walked outside, only to realise that his small house – his refuge – was swaying from side to side. 'I gave up the house in my heart. I decided to accept that the house would be destroyed.' He waited a while longer, and the building was still standing. Going inside, he saw splintered objects on the ground and considered vacuuming them up, but the electricity had been cut. His wife sent a worried message saying she, at least, was fine, but he did not immediately reply. Later, he would regret that, after the communications networks were completely cut off.

His home's isolation meant Akagawa was not immediately aware of the tsunami risk that followed the earthquake. An older woman arrived through the trees and invited him to move over to her house, so he would not be alone any more. There, passing fishermen began referring to the frightening state of the nearby sea.

Rikuzentakata had twenty-four thousand residents when the earthquake and tsunami struck. The waves that hit it reached thirteen metres – higher than many three-storey buildings. 'It's not a town, not anymore,' emphasised Al Jazeera reporter Harry Fawcett in the following days.[3] 'The everyday permanent fixtures of life have just gone in an instant, along with countless lives,' he said, standing in front of brown debris, which included shattered walls and what appeared to be a roof attached to the top floor of a house. 'The disaster didn't discriminate . . . An iron railway bridge, twisted and broken like wire. Cars tossed and smashed.' The final death toll there was around 1,700.

A letter writer says this year will mark the thirteenth anniversary of the death of the person they are writing to, and they have begun to think of them again. They have not accepted the death yet and still reflect on the memories the two created together, including driving without any purpose, watching baseball games and playing soccer.

They wonder if it was the addressee's serious side that made them try to complete their work, even after the tsunami warning was issued. The writer attempted to phone them the next day, before finding out about the body . . .

The day of the disaster is known as '3.11' in Japan, or *San-ten-ichi-ichi*. At 2:46 p.m. local time, on 11 March 2011, there was a magnitude 9.1 earthquake, the most powerful the country had experienced since records began. Shaking lasted around six minutes. The subsequent tsunami, which hit Japan at 3.20 p.m., peaked at a height above 130 feet.

Survivors described watching buildings being consumed by the wave. A cloud of dust and debris rose above it, before that, too, was swallowed by the water. The wave broke through sea walls which were supposed to protect people. It destroyed everything in its path: roads, properties, family photo albums, laptops, phones, shrines to ancestors. Around 2,000 kilometres of Japan's coastline was affected, and more than 400 square kilometres of land covered in water.[4] The reactors at the Fukushima nuclear power plant were flooded, triggering a nuclear disaster which forced more than 150,000 people to evacuate. Some areas would remain deserted for over a decade, because of the risk of radiation poisoning.

More than twenty-two thousand people were declared dead or missing in the aftermath of the earthquake and tsunami, according to government figures.[5] Over one million homes were fully or partially destroyed.

Some survivors described an uncannily quiet moment, an other-worldly pause, when the sea drew back from the shore before the big wave came. The sound of water, which normally underlay everyday life, had been momentarily eradicated. In videos showing the tsunami's arrival there is a strange slowness, which can make it difficult to imagine the terror and jeopardy of impact. Victims were not only drowned, they were hit by trees, cars, pieces of buildings. They were submerged, sucked under, tossed and propelled in divergent directions, according to which currents they fell to the mercy of.

Some people remember seeing fires starting above the water, with no idea how this clash of elements was even scientifically possible. Despite any flames, the weather was bitterly cold. Survivors who fled to higher ground struggled as a result of the temperature, with some dying later on from exposure to the elements.

When crisis hits, the factors that result in the difference between a life extinguished and one with decades more on this earth can be arbitrary and yet so permanent. Like in a bombing, a tsunami or earthquake also makes the private suddenly, almost indecently, public. The insides of people's homes were exposed, personal belongings floating in the water or spread out on the ground as it receded. Prized possessions were laid bare.

It took time to figure out who had lived and who had died. One sixty-year-old from Fukushima was discovered two days later, ten miles out at sea, floating on a piece of the roof of his home.[6] His wife, who had been with him when the tsunami struck, was still missing. It would be months or even years before some bodies were recovered. Thousands never were.

A writer says they feel lonely and sad. They ask if their intended recipient felt pain in the water and wonder why he did not listen to what the writer told him. The writer says they tried to follow after him but were saved by a precious grandchild, who is now five years old. They will live the rest of their life among their children and grandchildren, though they expect to cry many times until the pair are reunited. They will write again.

Three days after the tsunami, when Akagawa decided to return home to his wife, he found that the road which led to her no longer existed. He began driving anyway, though he struggled to surmount the *gareki* – the rubble or debris left by the tsunami. Maps had become useless; streets and landmarks washed away or hidden. At one point, he climbed a hill to scrutinise the area around him. 'The city was all black, there was something moving like ants: that was the self-defence army's helmets,' he realised.

Akagawa passed by lines of his countryfolk, now homeless, and he began to cry. He drove and drove, making it to the outskirts of the town where his wife lived. His phone began to buzz and ping with messages from worried friends and relatives – it was the first time he'd had phone reception in three days. When Akagawa finally saw his wife again, she was convinced he was a ghost. She slapped his legs, checking for a solid body and some proof that he was real.

Over the coming months, Akagawa experimented with ways to help the people affected. He negotiated with the owner of a hot spring, and began to drive the so-called 'evacuees' to the spring so they could bathe. He realised that people living in the new evacuation centres – which were noisy, with little privacy – needed somewhere to relax. 'The places were so crowded that you couldn't take steps. People didn't laugh at all, they just had torment in their hearts.' He invited them to visit his second home 'to refresh their mind'.

When the initial shock wore off, 'a certain period later', he said, 'people's worlds changed. People began to say "please listen to me", they wanted to talk about the emotions that had been kept inside them since the earthquake. I tried. They talked about people who died or were still missing, the times when the bodies were found, that kind of thing. I asked people: "Why are you talking to me, we only met today".' For some reason, Akagawa realised, that made it easier. Talking to those close to them was hard; often the other person would shut conversation down – they too had problems. 'I listened to people speaking for one and a half years,' Akagawa said.

'The people who talked felt release, but I was tortured by listening.'

It was Akagawa's struggle with how to cope with this responsibility that sparked the creation of the 'drifting post'.

A writer notes that September is almost over, though the late summer heat continues. The passage of time has been a form of medicine for them, though they continue to write these missives and believe each one is being received. The writer also asks the letter recipient to thank Mr Akagawa for providing delicious food during their visit.

The next time I met Akagawa, it was in Rikuzentakata itself. Around us were rolling hills flecked with houses, dappled by the sun shining through the clouds.

Old tourist guides reference pine trees – there reportedly used to be seventy thousand of them along two kilometres of coast. Just one survived the tsunami: a two-hundred-year-old that locals call the 'miracle pine'. The road we were driving along had only reopened a year before: a huge concrete wall was first erected on the right, protecting it from the sea and blocking the water from our sight. It reminded Akagawa of Fuchū, one of Japan's largest prisons, he said. Along our left flank was a line of bamboos.

The road wound upwards, past a sloping graveyard and cedar trees. We passed another hamlet of houses, and I started to spot various signs pointing towards the drifting post. Through a final flurry of trees, it at last became visible. There was a rectangular yellow post box – the 'real' one, Akagawa said, and another upstanding coral-coloured 'ornamental' one. There were bicycles and benches, a big wooden house, and more trees all around. Further back from the structure of the main building was a DIY room – 'my treasure box,' Akagawa smiled.

Yuji Akagawa who established the 'drifting post', pictured in his second home in March 2024.

At the very end of the garden was another room, like a cabin, built by Akagawa himself. It housed sixteen binders of letters, six chairs and a desk, where people could relax or take a moment if they were 'trying not to cry'. Sometimes multiple visitors turned up at once. Occasionally, they made friends with each other. Unless writers specified that they wanted their letter to remain private, Akagawa would place them in his binders so they could be read by other mourners; it might help them assemble their own thoughts. The writers were willing for their letters to be made public, he said: this made the mourning more collective. 'Finding out that you are not alone is the most important thing, finding out that you are not the only person who is grieving.' As I leafed through the binders, the wind outside was so strong that it sounded like heavy rain.

In front of the cabin was a low wooden chair, where visitors could lean back and look at the sky; it was bright that day, despite the wind. 'People think the dead person is in the sky above this building,' Akagawa explained. He built the room on naturally elevated ground, to honour the belief that the higher you are, the closer you are to heaven.

'I read all the letters,' he added, talking through his role. 'People send the letters to be read.' There are common threads between them. 'Many people assume that heaven exists, they ask "How's the life there?" And they say they know it's hard, but they'd like to get a reply.'

Some people came in person to deliver letters; others simply wrote 'The Drifting Post, Iwate Prefecture' on the envelope. 'The first six months were the most torturous because all the letters were so sad,' Akagawa remembered. 'I saw the aftermath of 3.11 so I could clearly imagine the situation, I thought about quitting many times.'

A writer pens many letters over many months. She writes about a trip to an island in southern Japan where she danced to live music; it was so hot that she had to use an air conditioner and fan from early morning, for the first time in her life. She details the weather getting cooler and a cloudy sky. She notes the passing of their fifty-fourth wedding anniversary, and the transition into a new year: her seventh being alone. She says she knows he is most likely with both of their parents now. She does not want to worry him but she hopes to join them as soon as possible.

The wind whooshed, whistled and sometimes wailed through the yellow fluttering flags on the outside of the Iwaki 3.11 Memorial and Revitalisation Museum, which had messages from schoolchildren written all over them. 'Our train is going slowly because of strong winds,' came an announcement as we chugged gradually towards the train station in Iwaki – a city nearly 300 kilometres south of the drifting post, and 200 kilometres north of Tokyo, on Japan's eastern coast. From there, I boarded a bus to take me towards the sea again. Quickly, the landscape began to feel desolate – there was an emptiness, a sense that something notable was lacking. But others were making the bus journey to the museum too.

More than a dozen people sat in plastic chairs that Saturday afternoon, watching Ohtani Keiichi animatedly point at an image of tsunami damage displayed on a big projector. Keiichi came from the local area, Usuiso, a place where 'one hundred and sixteen people died out of seven hundred and eighty,' he said. Waves would have been visible through the window to his left, if not for the high embankment, planted at its top with pine trees. The sand on the nearby beach has historically been called *nakisuna*, or 'weeping sand', because of the noise it makes when someone walks on it.

Keiichi – a seventy-five-year-old, wearing a green flat cap and azure blue jacket – launched into his story. He was at home when the earthquake occurred. The roof on his neighbour's house collapsed, but his survived, though two-metre cracks appeared in his walls. 'I still thought it's OK because I had insurance and I thought I can cover that.'

Panic makes people act in erratic ways. He went outside to assess the scene. Elementary school students were walking along the road; one was crying. He told them to stay in the centre of the tarmac, not to walk at its edges. 'The students went home but now I think that if I had told the students to go back to school then they could have survived,' he said. Two of them would die.

Keiichi's TV would not turn on, so he tried the radio.

'They were saying to evacuate the area and they also announced about the tsunami. At first, its estimation was about three metres high, then six, then ten,' he recalled. The announcer said the tsunami was twelve kilometres away, it would hit at 3.10 p.m. 'I checked my watch but still there was no tsunami so I thought maybe the tsunami will not come. I somehow got angry that they were giving false information.' He headed towards the sea, 'to check the condition'.

That was a remarkably stupid thing to do, he admitted to the assembled audience. The water, when he got there, seemed highly unusual. He turned around, to clear his vision, then looked again. 'I saw the black sea bottom and the waves directed out towards the ocean rather than land. It was not the usual scenery, so I instinctively knew the tsunami would come.' Keiichi's memory cuts out there until he arrived back at home. He found his wife trying to help a ninety-two-year-old woman who was unable to walk alone, along with a seventy-seven-year-old who could. Keiichi hoisted the older woman onto his back and began to run towards higher ground, but she fell from him. He swung around to look for her, but instead saw a cloud of dark dust rising in the air. Houses were being covered by rushing water. He left the woman behind. Three days later, they would discover her body.

'I prioritised my life,' Keiichi recounted. 'I cannot forget the eye colour of the old woman. It took eighteen months until I could talk about the experience, before that when I slept I sweated so much that my pillow would be drenched. The first time I talked about my experience I was crying so much, but I felt my shoulders becoming lighter. Sadness or heavy feelings should be talked about with other people. It's better to show those kinds of emotions.'

Keiichi's home was at the entrance to a Shinto shrine. He

remembers running through the torii gate, which marks the beginning of sacred ground, and climbing ten steps. Behind him, the gate disappeared under water. 'In the background, there were houses floating. I couldn't recognise my house, but I instinctively knew the shrine entrance was gone.'

When survivors describe this day – how they felt, what they did – their accounts can veer between sounding mechanical and improbable, though those who spoke to me emphasised that there were many inconceivable tales of endurance under such circumstances. Keiichi jumped ahead in his story to the point when he realised the surge had passed. He walked down to the debris, stretched out over where their homes had been, and saw the head and neck of the seventy-seven-year-old woman his wife had helped earlier poking through it. Keiichi pulled her out and brought her to the shrine, where they gave her dry clothes. 'The fact that I could save one person made my mental situation stable after the disaster.'

In the years afterwards, Keiichi – a former 'salaryman', or office worker – became a *kataribe*, or 'storyteller'. The tradition of Japanese *kataribes* subsisted for more than a millennium before 3.11: they travel around giving talks aimed at conveying the experience of living through a disaster, with the goal of passing on lessons. *Kataribes* spoke in Japan after the atomic bombings of Hiroshima and Nagasaki, warning of the dangers of nuclear weapons. They spoke after other earthquakes, such as the 1923 Great Kanto Earthquake and the 1995 Hanshin-Awaji Earthquake. Keiichi estimated that he gives one hundred and forty paid talks each year about what he witnessed, testifying in schools, community halls, museums, on bus tours and anywhere else he is invited. Talking about the experience relieves his mental burden, he said. 'I will present you that burden as a souvenir,' he told the crowd, who laughed.

Ohtani Keiichi became a kataribe, or storyteller, to warn others of the danger of tsunamis.

Despite his detailed storytelling, Keiichi alluded to missing fragments, his memory like a spliced recording if interrogated too far. 'Both types of people exist, those who want to forget and those who don't want to forget,' he told me, sitting in the now emptied lecture room. 'Even within me, I both want to remember and want to forget. The parts that I don't want to remember are what my brain eliminates for my mental safety . . . I think having some parts that you don't want to remember is not a bad thing.'

That was the reason he was hesitant to get psychological help, something that is 'not normal' in Japan. Instead, Keiichi said he channels his energy into preparing others in case a similar crisis occurs again. 'Disaster can happen everywhere and what makes the difference here is whether you can think at the time as fast as possible. The instinctive decision is very important.'

In the museum behind him, display cabinets included a clock, stopped at 3.27 p.m., and a school blackboard, bearing chalk marks from the day of the tragedy, made before lessons were interrupted.

A writer asks where the addressee is now. He says their mother has lost all energy waiting for the person to return. He requests that they come back quickly to make everyone relieved.

I landed in Tokyo in March 2024.

Sakura, or cherry blossom, season was approaching. In shops around the city, I found cherry blossom-flavoured coffee and commemorative beer. There were pink roof hangings and tea lights. My hotel served complimentary cherry blossom-flavoured liqueur, which they recommended drinking with soda water. Sakura are Japan's national flower. They are meant to symbolise new life and renewal, but they are also a reminder of transience. It was at this time of the year that the tsunami struck.

When a foreigner visits Japan, they are warned about the many, sometimes unspoken, rules. Do not eat or drink while walking the streets. Do not speak on the phone on trains. Do not jaywalk. Punctuality and politeness are key. I would learn that changing an interview location after a plan was made, or even asking to slightly alter its start time, was frowned upon. I was told not to be too loud. Traditionally, stillness and *chinmoku*, which translates as silence, have been highly prized.

While planning my trip, I came across a book, published in 1986, called *Japanese Death Poems*. It contained hundreds of *jisei*, poems sometimes written in the last moments of the writer's life. There were poems by Zen monks alongside poets of varied backgrounds. Scholar and editor Yoel Hoffmann, who compiled the collection, said they offered evidence that, before death, Japanese writers tended to break the usual restraints of culturally appropriate politeness which may have held them back while alive.[7]

One of Tokyo's major landmarks emerged from a story about grief, death and loyalty, set a century before I landed there. It is a statue of a dog called Hachiko, who used to wait at Shibuya Station each day to meet his owner, Hidesaburō Ueno, after work. When the professor died in 1925, Hachiko is said to have continued making the trip every day for nearly a decade, until his own demise. A statue of Hachiko now serves as an assembly point; when I passed, groups of friends were taking selfies with it.

A writer addresses their older brother, asking if he is happy in heaven with their parents, and if he gave their mother a carnation on Mother's Day. The writer imagines him on a tiled roof, cold, lonely and in pain during the earthquake. Even after that, the writer notes, their brother continued to work as a tile craftsman, in the rain, wind or scorching heat, while taking care of his siblings. The writer is sorry that they could not save him, this brother who died of acute heart failure while still in his fifties. The writer harvested and boiled bamboo shoots recently and offered them to his grave. They are trying to live each day by finding some hope.

Japanese people have various words for social isolation and death.

A *kodokushi* is a 'lonely death', where an old person dies alone at home. A *hikikomori* is someone – usually young and male – who socially isolates from everyone, often staying inside one room. A culture where people are typically reserved leaves many on the sidelines, more than one Japanese person told me. It can be hard to make friends or build up a social circle.

The 2011 disaster destroyed social networks that had taken generations to establish. Many people were left alone, without ways to express or even acknowledge the depth of their grief.

I read more about bereavement. I read an academic study on the 'grief tech industry', and particularly a programme that allowed bereaved people to feed old text messages, emails, voice notes and videos into an app, so the dead person could be recreated as a digital avatar or chatbot, which they called 'grief-bots'. Two of the academics were in Japan. Their interviewees included a man simulating his deceased fiancée, and another simulating his dead father. The study concluded that this technology could be helpful, particularly in cases where the death was unexpected or left mourners with regret or anger. Men, in particular, seemed willing to accept and use 'griefbots', it noted.

'Social support has been known to be critical in helping mourners cope with grief. Moreover, meaningful social connection has also been proven to be associated with mental well-being and better quality of life,' the study said.[8] 'While the research team did initially have concerns regarding mourners' potential social withdrawal due to developing emotional attachment to the chatbot, to our surprise, many mourners emphasised that they still value their real-life social connections and, if anything, their connections with the chatbot further complemented their real-life social activities.'

I wondered at what point someone should be compelled to move on from their memories. Does our sense of the deceased's continuing presence in our world need to be challenged?

When lives are extinguished, it is often at an arbitrary point and there are questions that we cannot ask the dead, but might like to. Is there an afterlife? Do they approve of the choices we have made since they left us? Would they have grown with or apart from us, had they lived longer? Did we fail them in any way? Was there a chance we could have prevented what happened to them? Was the depth of our love known to them, despite the obvious human shortcomings at expression?

How do you love a person after they are gone? The longer each of us lives, the more we will have to develop our own answer.

A writer misses the disappeared person who loved them like a little sister. They have moved and say they are happy, but on the eleventh day of each month they face the direction of the city where the pair spent so much time together and speak to them, their words projected into the air.

Japan's 2011 tragedy drew dividing lines, even between victims. Those who had lost property felt their sorrow did not compare with those who had lost relatives. Those who had lost one family member felt a separation from those who had lost several. Sometimes that made interactions and open communication difficult. But they were all grieving, even if they did not feel they had the right to do so. 'Most people lost their friends or neighbours,' said Buddhist monk Yozo Tanikawa, a professor of practical religious studies at Tohoku University. 'There are people who calm down much earlier and those who take much longer.'

We were in Sendai, the largest city in Tohoku, the northeast region of more than eight million people which the tsunami hit. Tanikawa's office was packed with shelves of books on grief, death and trauma, but there were also packets of biscuits, trinkets and religious objects. It seemed like a room that had welcomed a lot of visitors. Outside, the sky, buildings and concrete walkways were all in shades of grey, interspersed only with brown conifer trees, protruding from rotting leaves and green moss. Yellow signs in the area warned students to 'be aware of wild boars'.

Though many Japanese people will say that they are not religious, culturally their traditions are usually Shinto or Buddhist, or a mixture of the two. Repeatedly, Japanese people told me that their culture is not a place where psychological help is appreciated or understood. That is why religion played a key role. Tanikawa said chaplains of different faiths had come together in Sendai, after the 3.11 earthquake and tsunami, to talk about how to help people. 'Disaster chaplains' were deployed, many of whom had previously worked in hospitals, prisons or schools. They chanted prayers for the missing and said Sutras at funerals. On the eleventh of each month, they prayed over the bones of unidentified victims.

Buddhist monk Yozo Tanikawa, a professor of practical religious studies at Tohoku University.

This happened even as traditional mourning processes were interrupted: crematoriums could not operate because of a lack of electricity; some religious ceremonies were performed without bodies. 'When a person is just missing, the decision whether to have a funeral or not is very difficult. If they hold a funeral then they have to accept that the person is dead,' Tanikawa said. Some families felt pressured into declaring a missing loved one dead in order to receive government compensation, even when they did not want to believe it themselves.

Tanikawa referred to the work of American professor Pauline Boss, who spent decades studying 'ambiguous loss' and concluded that people need to go on living without being pressured into finding 'closure'. Boss says that those who are grieving can find some meaning, even in the absence of facts. 'The important thing is to continue with life as usual, as before, when the person was alive and with them,' Tanikawa said. From what Tanikawa knew, he said suicide rates had actually dropped in this region in the years after 2011, 'because people realised the importance of their lives'.

Tohoku University had trained three hundred new chaplains since 2012. The certificate took two years to earn, but in truth, Tanikawa had concluded, dealing with grieving people came down to something very simple. 'If the person needs information about religion, chaplains can provide it, but it's not proselytisation,' he said. Most importantly, he told chaplains: 'just listen to them.'

A writer says they would search for their missing classmate if the person was alive, but they also need to restart their life.

'You are wearing face masks so it's not apparent, but you are definitely getting older. We all get old and die,' Buddhist monk

Taio Kaneta told the assembled crowd. He said he had over-heard them 'boasting' about their medical problems. 'You may have experienced illnesses, but it's good if you can change the mood towards laughter . . . You can talk anything you want, even about your boyfriend,' he continued. 'But please be ser-ious at 2.46 p.m. and give a moment of silence.'

We were in a community centre in Ishinomaki, a port city with a small-town feeling. Its streets were dotted with statues of manga characters. In one area, Frank Sinatra songs played from street speakers. There were also blue markers, noting the height the tsunami reached in 2011, reminding residents that death can come quickly. In the sushi restaurant I ate in on my first night there, the water had risen above my height. It had destroyed part of the *ryokan*, or traditional Japanese inn, that I slept in. One-fifth of those who died in total on 3.11 died in Ishinomaki.

Now it was the tragedy's thirteenth anniversary, and I was at Café de Monk, Kaneta's creation. Present were dozens of tsunami survivors, as well as Buddhist monks and associated volunteers. This was one of two or more similar events each month: one took place in Kaneta's temple and another on the road, in different parts of Japan. The name is a play on words. As well as being a reference to the monks themselves, *monku* means complaint. Kaneta is also a dedicated fan of American jazz musician Thelonious Monk. He mentioned jazz when we spoke, saying it inspired him to come up with new ideas, solu-tions and means of expression.

New arrivals took off their shoes upon entry, and sat on cushions on top of tatami mats or on plastic chairs placed around tables. There were drinks and an assortment of cakes. One corner had been commandeered by a masseuse offering back massages. A short woman in a multicoloured sweater dress and green hooped earrings laughed and clapped together her hands, topped with spiky pink nails, when Kaneta pointed her out: she was standing in front of trays with arrays of different-coloured nail varnish, ready to give manicures. He chatted with a wizened man who had worked on the disaster response in 2011: together they recalled the sadness that hung over the evacuation centres.

I caught another attendee's eye. Sayuri told me she had spent three cold months in evacuation housing with her elderly mother. Their former neighbours went elsewhere, destroying their long-standing community networks, and when her mother died, eleven years later, grief hit Sayuri all over again. 'I don't have anyone else,' she said.

Sayuri didn't want her real name or her age included because she used to work for a Christian organisation and 'this is a Buddhist event.' It was her first time attending Café de Monk, so she remained a little tentative, but she was enjoying it: 'it's comfortable here.' She felt relaxed enough to explain that she was a rock and roll fan, listing her favourites: the Bay City Rollers; Duran Duran. She once saw Kate Bush play at a festival, she said, her eyes lighting up. 'After 3.11 there was no space to listen to music but now I'm reminded of it.'

Sayuri's hair was in a ponytail; she wore round gold glasses and a beige coat that matched her bag. She had the type of face that is visibly welcoming from across a room, though she said she felt like a bit of an outsider because, unlike many others there, she had her own home again.

Two of her friends died on 3.11. They had been close since elementary school; she knotted her fingers as she thought about it. 'Human relationships are most important after a disaster. Stuff – money, belongings, furniture can be replaced but family and friends cannot,' she said. She still thought about her friends at night; felt a jolt of memory when she passed schools and parks they'd spent time in together. News programmes around the anniversary certainly reminded her of them, though when I asked her if it would be better for everyone to stop talking about the tragedy she said: 'I cannot forget even if I try.'

At another table sat sixty-seven-year-old Eiko Abe and Junko Segawa, who was thirteen years her senior. The pair had just met for the first time, but they chatted and joked like their camaraderie stretched back decades. 'We shared the experience of the earthquake so we can get to know each other so quickly,' said Junko. Both nodded when I asked if it is easier to talk to other survivors than anyone else.

'We don't talk about the experience with others who didn't go through it, they don't understand. We lost family, we lost friends, we lost fortunes. It's very different to people who have normal lives,' said Eiko. She had copper hair and was wearing a grey sweater with Mickey Mouse on the front.

'This is a special space,' said Junko, in a yellow cardigan. Her advice to anyone going through a disaster was to 'open the mind. Socialising is so important. If you close your mind, you cannot make any friends. And don't keep your sadness inside your heart. Show it to people. Just wait, sometimes time can solve the problem.'

'Time is medicine,' said Eiko, who had been to at least five other Café de Monk events. 'When I first came the atmosphere was very dark. No one laughed. But after time passed the atmosphere changed.'

A volunteer was distributing beaded keyring decorations. Both women stuck their hands out for one. 'Bright days: laugh every day. It always makes you happy' was written on the packet. Around them, others were eating slices of sweet potato.

'The important thing is to live every day taking care of others and smiling. That's my motto,' said Eiko.

'Hardship will end,' added Junko, and the two women grinned at each other.

Kaneta spent time in affected coastal areas in the wake of the earthquake and tsunami. On the forty-ninth day afterwards, acting on a Buddhist tradition, he led a religious procession. That experience forced him to acknowledge that there were limits to what religion could achieve. 'I saw that everything was destroyed and I couldn't say anything,' he said. 'I thought I had to throw away the religious frame and language, to confront the severity.' He started collecting donations to provide hot meals. This was not enough either. 'I seriously thought about what I can do for people when I returned to the temple.'

Japanese society was already not in a 'good condition' before 3.11, Kaneta believed. He called the previous decade 'the lost ten years', when more than 300,000 people were recorded as dying from suicide.[9] (In a stand-up comedy performance in Tokyo, I heard one comedian joke that suicide was a 'national sport'.) After the tsunami, Kaneta studied the faces of survivors he met: they appeared blank to him. 'First, they have to retrieve their expressions,' he thought to himself. And so, 'I decided to have a movable café. It's not that I came up with the idea, the inspiration came from the sky or from the earth. I decided to name it Café de Monk because it means in the café the monk will listen to your complaints or grief . . . Having tea, the monk will also suffer with you.'

Kaneta experimented with how to create the right ambience at Café de Monk. Minor touches became meaningful, such as presenting those who came with choices about which cakes and flowers they wanted – choice was notably lacking in the evacuation centres, he said. He knew Japanese people are loath to access mental health support. 'We're not counsellors or therapists, not doing interviews,' Kaneta made clear. He advertised in the centres, on the TV and radio, and patrons came. Those early days weighed heavily: Kaneta remembers vacating the room multiple times, venturing outside to train his eyes on the sky and regulate his breath. 'I think I was being tested by something higher,' he said. 'There were so many tragic stories.' He felt overwhelmed.

'There was people's spiritual pain that me or other religious people couldn't respond to, for example questioning why they lived and others died, or why they couldn't help someone who died, or why they still existed though their granddaughter died. They had to face those kinds of questions.' He began abandoning religious vocabulary and even the concept of heaven, 'since I have never been'. To those who were struggling he began to say: 'I cannot answer your questions but we both survived so together we will be able to find the answer. We will work together, even though this is a bad time.' In the meantime, he suggested that they try to limit worrying and not be too serious. 'I also told that to myself and continued my activity,' he said.

One year after the disaster, Kaneta led another procession along the coast. He felt the difference immediately. 'In the wind, from the sea, there was a smell of sea salt. Standing in the same place as the previous year I could see a fisherman harvesting seaweed. So the people, including me, thought that the sea was recovering.'

The 'wind of recovery' came with an understanding that there was a power superior to both life and death, he said. If the sea could restore itself, 'I was also convinced that people can recover from the tragedy because people have the resilience to stand again. That's why human beings can survive on this earth.'

While many people at the 2024 café told me that the mood felt lighter there compared to the years before, interpreting this as a sign of recovery 'doesn't catch the reality', Kaneta underlined. 'Even the people laughing still have sadness or grief behind the laughter. The knowledge of how much they lost, or the importance of that to them, does not change, even though time has passed, but human beings have to live.'

One expression of that spiritual pain had been sightings of ghosts, or people saying they had been possessed by spirits. This phenomenon, in that part of Japan, has even been studied by academics.[10] 'It's not a supernatural story' but more an expression of 'internal hurt', Kaneta said. 'It's so difficult to explain to foreign people because we don't share base beliefs with each other.' He said someone who can 'scientifically' dispute the presence of ghosts or spirits is probably forming that judgement from 'a safe position', unlike the individuals who made reports. The sightings continued, he added.

Whether someone believes in spirits is totally dependent on the person themselves, Kaneta said. 'For example, I lost my father three years ago but I feel like my father is there and I sometimes think he became a blackbird and can see me.'

Café de Monk gives the grieving an alternative way to deal with what they have lost, an 'expression of living together and sharing the dead people,' he said.

When asked how long the cafés would keep operating for, Kaneta – by then sixty-seven – said the answer is in the wind. One predictable characteristic of wind, he added, is that it always 'passes', but 'there will be a leftover smell.'

A writer says this will be their final love letter. They apologise for leaving: they married someone else, had babies and their life is busy, yet every day for the past ten years they have thought of the individual they are writing to. That person had a deep sense of humanity and wanted to be cared for, even if relationships could be a struggle for them. So much regret means that it was the wrong choice to give up, the writer says: the two of them should have stayed together.

In the summer, Akagawa lives full time at his second home in the woods by Rikuzentakata, the drifting post visible from his windows. During winter, when snow is thick on the ground, Akagawa stays with his wife and visits the post box just once every ten days. She has little to do with his drifting post activities, he told me. 'We have our own ways so we don't interfere so much with each other.'

Akagawa imagined that the ten-year anniversary of the tsunami would mark 'a kind of separation' from this work for him. But the letters never stopped arriving. Each year, the frequency increases around 11 March. Letters or cards also turn up on dead people's birthdays; birthday flowers have even been delivered. Some of the people writing have no connection to 3.11 at all; they lost loved ones due to health problems or other causes.

'The saddest letters are from mothers who lost their children, those are the hardest for me to read,' Akagawa said, as we sat in his cosy cabin, surrounded by artwork and photos given to him by supporters. 'As time passed, the people who write these letters became so important to me, I realised that I could communicate with people at the lowest point in their life.' Sometimes, people who write to the drifting post include an extra letter for him. Only then will he reply. ('People in Tohoku are very patient, but I think having a place where they can express their suffering and sadness reassures them a lot,' read one letter addressed to Akagawa, from a person who had learned about the drifting post from a newspaper. 'My feelings

The cabin where letters written to the 'drifting post' are stored.

were moved by you,' wrote another, sent from Sasebo city in southwest Japan.)

Akagawa has begun to talk about quitting, though he shook his head even as he expressed his desire to. 'I communicated with the people who wrote the letters and they haven't allowed me to quit,' he said. 'I want to be released from this activity but I think it was so good starting this drifting post. I received a great gift from people who are grieving a lot. I've realised the relationship between people is much more than family connection. A relationship can exist when people are at the bottom.'

Once a year, Akagawa takes the letters to a nearby Buddhist temple, where a monk prays over them. Akagawa taught me about the Buddhist term *kuyou*, a ceremony held 'to pray for people after death, to send the people to heaven'. The letters, he explained, now go through a similar process, transmitted 'to heaven by the power of Buddha'. Following the annual ceremony, he packs them up and brings them home again, to his cabin in the woods.

Akagawa has never written a letter himself, 'but I asked my wife to write to the drifting post after my death', he told me. 'The letter will go to heaven, so it doesn't matter that I'm not there to read it in person. One of my consolations is, if I die, people will write these letters to me.'

Epilogue

*'But, did you bring the essentials bag? Yes, we filled it with
childhood memories, items from adventure trips, gifts from
friends, our little dreams, and unending hope.'*

– An Instagram post by Fadwa Anwar Farhat, one of more than
one million people displaced by the Israeli bombardment of
Lebanon in 2024

*'I feel like there is nothing more truly artistic than to love
people.'*

– Vincent Van Gogh[1]

A ceasefire happens slowly and then all at once. An escalation
in attacks, counterintuitively, might be the surest sign a cessation is coming. Pronouncements appear, first materialising in
the media through anonymous sources, before more official
voices add foundation. At the hard end of political decisions
are bewildered civilians: they crowd around televisions, radios
and smartphones; they whisper, shout, murmur and pray, as it
dawns on them that their fates may have shifted.

I was in the darkness of central Beirut's Martyrs' Square,
in late November 2024, when we began to understand that the
ceasefire was a real possibility. Whole families had gathered
around makeshift bonfires for warmth. Elder relatives snoozed

inside cars, the only sheltered area available to them. Mothers held babies and small children protectively close. Some had been displaced multiple times, yet they had to evacuate again that very night, as an unprecedented new wave of airstrikes hit the city.

Back home, I stayed awake into the early hours, almost drifting away before being jolted by a final warning, posted by an Israeli army spokesman after one o'clock in the morning, about an airstrike expected to hit hundreds of metres from my apartment.[2] Quick calculations showed that I was just outside of the likely danger range, and I finally fell asleep shortly before the ceasefire was due to come into force, at 4 a.m. When I was roused into consciousness some hours later, our fortunes had been rewritten.

War plays tricks on your mind, and even though I heard the news that a ceasefire had begun, I did not believe it. Searching for visual proof, I went onto the streets, joining the throng of vehicles packed with displaced people already heading back towards their homes in heavily affected southern Lebanon or south Beirut, mattresses loaded onto car roofs.

Their arrival would be bittersweet, as returnees were confronted with the full extent of what they had lost. I spotted one woman wailing out the window of a car, her face contorted in grief. 'My son, we are going home without you,' she called. Tears streamed down the faces of a young girl and boy in the seat in front of her.

In Beirut's devastated southern suburbs, residents handed out sweets. A man on a motorbike, directly ahead of me, raised his pistol to the sky, letting out a volley of celebratory gunfire. There was cheering and beeping. Some people were still waving Hezbollah flags, though large numbers had lost trust in the militant group by then; others had never had it in the first place. I approached a family standing on top of what remained of the ten-floor building where their apartment had been, searching for their belongings. 'It's our memories,' explained a twenty-nine-year-old woman, her nephew in her arms. She was beseeching me to understand.

Living through a war is very different to parachuting into one and reporting for a week or two, as I had done in many countries, many times before. The reality is not that normality disappears, it is that the abnormal becomes normal. Monitoring evacuation warnings and waiting for the subsequent boom, smoke and dust pillar of an airstrike, hearing the omnipresent buzz of Israeli surveillance drones – it all happens alongside sending emails and sipping coffee and shopping for groceries. But it becomes impossible to think long term, to have any certainty. Your immediate surroundings, that distinct period in time and space, and the people close to you are all you can be sure of.

Despite more than a decade working as a journalist, that experience gave me a whole new education in the fragility of the human body. Between September and November 2024, I reported across Lebanon as Israel carried out its mass aerial offensive on what it said were Hezbollah-linked targets, often using US-made munitions. The civilian toll was unimaginable. More than one million people were displaced, more than two hundred children killed and over twelve hundred children wounded, some losing limbs. Although the bombing became repetitive, it was impossible to settle into any routine of covering it.

In the first week, I reported on grassroots initiatives. Civilians mobilised en masse to provide necessities for some of the hundreds of thousands of people who had fled their homes. Volunteers distributed vast quantities of food. Chef Mehyo el Jawhary, a curly-haired man in his early thirties, told me one hundred people offered to help out at the Beirut kitchen he was coordinating. 'It's still day two,' he said, the choreography of numerous cooks in motion behind him. 'We don't know what's happening tomorrow so we're taking it day by day.'

A Catholic church a short walk from my home was shelter-ing fifty displaced migrant workers and their families, with more expected to arrive shortly. Children overcame their shyness to play together, while their exhausted parents were simply relieved to reach a location which was not being bombed. Though they were making the best they could out of everything, ' "How are you?" is not really a good question to ask people right now,' Jesuit priest-in-training Michael Petro warned me.

Over the following weeks, I met many others whose first reaction to this crisis had been to offer assistance. In Nabatieh, a Lebanese city under Israeli evacuation orders, I interviewed medics who risked everything to save lives. Explosions sounded from outside the hospital entrance as a doctor cited the Hippo-cratic oath, his colleague explaining that they were obligated to stay put because the poorest civilians – with no means to leave or anywhere else to go to – were the ones getting injured. 'The hospital is still working, treating every person: men, women, children,' said Dr Mukhtar Mroue. 'We are here to help civilian people, we can't leave this area. It's our duty, of course. So many wounded.'

At the same time, I was practising how to stay calm when the rush and thunder of missiles woke me up, and to fall back asleep as the ambulance sirens followed soon afterwards. I learned to ignore the rumble of warplanes, and to scrub my memories after seeing fragments of human flesh removed from airstrike sites in plastic bags – body parts which medics would attempt to piece together later, so that mourning family members could carry out a burial and procure a death certificate. I picked my way through rubble, spotting children's toys, playing cards, university notes and family photographs. 'Love is just a word, until someone comes along and gives it a meaning,' was written below one picture of a couple posing, their bodies pressed together, in front of a scenic backdrop of mountains and trees. A full rescue operation had faced significant challenges, and the abiding smell betrayed the fact that not all of the victims at that site had been recovered.

These scattered belongings brought to mind once again how amid every war, economic collapse and natural disaster is a tangle of personal relationships. That should be obvious to people outside the catastrophe, but all too often it is overlooked. During a speech I gave in the European Parliament in late 2023 about human rights abuses being carried out against refugees and migrants at Europe's borders, I projected a definition of dehumanisation on a screen behind me:

- to deprive (someone or something) of human qualities, personality, or dignity: such as
  a: to subject (someone, such as a prisoner) to inhuman or degrading conditions or treatment
  b: to address or portray (someone) in a way that obscures or demeans that person's humanity or individuality

Dehumanisation happens when we deliberately or negligently fail to appreciate the elaborate beauty of other people's existence, including the loves that drive and bind them. Violence, exploitation, torture or disregard increase in contexts where dehumanisation is taking place. The more we fail to acknowledge that other people are the same as us, the easier it is for us to hurt them.

I have come away from my work over the past decade with the sense that there is a specific kind of detachment crisis going on. We are witnessing rapidly growing inequality and a lack of care for the vulnerable. Systems, structures and algorithms are being strengthened that separate humans from each other, keeping us in our own bubbles. It has become ever easier for the elite to reside at a remove, to avoid seeing the consequences of what they are responsible for.

The more this is enabled, the more remorseless subsequent actions taken by the powerful will be. Empathy and compassion feel dangerously lacking today. And what is empathy or compassion but love turned towards humanity itself?

While humankind is interdependent, the more privileged a society is, the easier it is for people to withdraw into solitude.

In 2023, the World Health Organization declared loneliness a 'global health concern', launching a new 'commission on social connection'. 'Anyone, anywhere, can be lonely or socially isolated. Across all ages and regions, loneliness and social isolation have serious impacts on our physical and mental health, and the well-being of our communities and society,' the commission's website read.[3]

This is the 'anti-social century', wrote American journalist Derek Thompson in a 2025 cover story for *The Atlantic*. Developments in technology – first cars and televisions, then smartphones and AI bots – have encouraged people to withdraw, he said – and never so much as now. 'The village is our best arena for practicing productive disagreement and compromise,' wrote Thompson, determining that 'it's no surprise that the erosion of the village has coincided with the emergence of a grotesque style of politics'.[4] A 2023 study found that lonely people appear more likely to display a desire to 'incite chaos' by circulating hostile political information, including conspiracy theories and what has become known as 'fake news'.[5] The health risks related to loneliness can be as bad as smoking fifteen cigarettes a day, said US surgeon general Dr Vivek Murthy that same year. Older people who are lonely may have a 50 per cent greater risk of developing dementia. Their risk of having a stroke or suffering from coronary artery disease can be 30 per cent higher.

Murthy released an eighty-two-page advisory document on the 'epidemic of loneliness and social isolation', saying that his recognition of loneliness as an 'urgent public health concern' had come after travelling across the US on a listening tour.[6] His advisory defined belonging as 'a fundamental human need', and empathy as 'the capability to understand and feel the emotional states of others, resulting in compassionate behaviour'. In 2018, it noted, only 16 per cent of Americans reported feeling very attached to their local community. 'Throughout history, our ability to rely on one another has been crucial to survival,' Murthy wrote. 'We have an opportunity, and an obligation, to make the same investments in addressing social connection that we have made in addressing tobacco use, obesity, and the addiction crisis . . . If we fail to do so, we will pay an ever-increasing price in the form of our individual and collective health and well-being . . . Instead of coming together to take on the great challenges before us, we will further retreat to our corners – angry, sick, and alone.'

In the Irish language, there is no direct translation for 'I love you'. Instead, someone can say *is tú mo ghrá*, meaning 'you are my love'; *tá grá agam duit*, translating as 'I have love for you', or *táim i ngrá leat*, which is 'I am in love with you'. When I reflect on this linguistic quirk of my ancestors, I consider how else language might limit the way we connect with each other, express ourselves and vocalise our experiences, and how it may affect what we honour and celebrate in our societies.

Love is about more than having others care about you. It is about the human capacity for trust, hope and connection, and the ability to give, when you might not receive anything back. Those capabilities can be shattered by trauma or hindered by fear. Instability and abuse reshape humans in ways that can be invisible externally but challenging to overcome. Refugees who have fled dictatorships, for example, have told me that they completely lost their ability to trust anyone. It is a muscle that needs to be exercised and slowly built up; one that may never have been able to fully develop in the first place.

I have wondered, how could the world be reshaped to provide us all with a better home? We are thrown into the pains of existence, forced to make our way; and, while some adapt better than others, we all have moments of struggle. I have lost many friends and people I admire to suicide, or to behaviours that arise from wrestling with a life they never asked for.

It is impossible to pinpoint when exactly idealism disappears. Heady conviction gets steadily blunted through grinding disappointment and exposure to realpolitik. Illusions are shredded. Many of us starting out – not just as journalists, but as humans – have the sense that anyone can fight for what is right and have impact. I once believed that journalists could change the world. At some point, that certainty left me.

I did not realise that in many of the situations I would arrive into there would be no definite recovery, no heroes capable of swooping in and rescuing people when whole structures and systems had been constructed to hold them down. I did not reckon on the scale of corruption, profiteering and apathy. I did not recognise that journalists could be part of the problem, compounding pain as we expose it.

These days, I often struggle to find motivation. I find myself unable to comprehend the agony that is being caused in places from which I have reported; the damage carried out or endorsed by some of the world's most powerful countries. I speak to those directly affected and can give them no reassurance that anything would change if the broader public were better informed. I scroll through news updates in horror and worry that my own sense of morality has been affected; that, in part, this relentless assault is aimed at grinding us down and making everyone accept the unacceptable.

But there are reasons to stay committed. I know with confidence now that if you look for goodness, care or kindness amid any crisis you will find it. I know that local heroes are always present too, even if their good deeds go unseen or unappreciated, and their actions only improve the situation on a micro level as opposed to transforming it completely. I gathered this reportage partially as my atonement for more than a decade in the journalistic world, which can strip detail, remove agency and flatten emotion, in comparison to the real world, which is brimming with all of those things. But I also hope it stands as an entreaty to the reader to always remember that people exist at the centre of geopolitics.

It was late afternoon. The ceasefire had been in place for two months, though drones still buzzed overhead and Israel continued to bomb Lebanon periodically. I was back in an apartment I evacuated from during the war, on a morning when an airstrike warning came through while I was making pancakes. From the balcony now, I watched a brown and

tabby cat scuttle across the road below. A van selling vegetables rolled up, its wares announced through a loudspeaker.
People on the street collided and drew apart: a woman in a
hijab pulled a small child by the hand; a group of men chatted, their ease together evident in their stances; a trader called
out a greeting; a boy on a bicycle failed in his attempt at a
wheelie; an elderly couple seemed nonplussed by the possibility of traffic as they strolled down the street's middle, the man
using a cane. A grey-haired lady in a thick black coat, fanned
out at the bottom like a tutu, gripped a younger woman's arm
for support and the two trod gracefully, their dainty steps
befitting the plimsolls the younger woman was wearing.
Across from me, stripy jumpers in blue and red were pegged
to a washing line; the plants on the balconies around them
were so carefully tended. I could see the beauty in humanity,
I thought then.

The people I saw below me, and anyone who survives a
crisis, could be described as resilient, though I have long had
an aversion to that word. While a few embrace it, I notice
many interviewees cringe when resilience is mentioned. They
rightly question why they should be forced to keep restoring
and rebuilding, ever at risk of being pummelled down once
again by unequal systems from which others profit.

As I sat on that balcony in Beirut, I gazed at the shades of
blue, purple, mauve and green on the mountains in the distance,
and wondered how such a beautiful world could be so cruel. As
the sun sank lower the clouds seemed to mushroom out, their
shape and light making me think of fantastical stories I had
read, as a child, about the Greek gods in Mount Olympus.
Somehow, in our tangible, material world, everything coexists:
the smoke rising from the airstrikes, the dust-coated destruction, and these tinted streaky clouds, like oil paint brushed

across the sky. Somehow, humans manage to lay laughter over trauma and love over inhumanity.

I considered the improbability of it all. How we suddenly appear here, blobs of consciousness, hurtling along for a limited bout of space and time, expected to reside together amid chaos and brutality. We may be born and die alone but our lives can still be measured in the love we bear and the connections we form; the ways people support each other. That is at least one wonderful truth, I told myself then.

Acknowledgements

Thank you to everyone I met and interviewed for this book, some of whom are not in the final pages but all of whom have informed it.

It could not exist without my agent Patrick Walsh, who has supported me from the beginning, as well as Margaret Halton, Cora MacGregor, Dorcas Rogers, Rebecca Sandell, John Ash, Alex Chernova, and all at PEW.

Thank you to my editors: Jo Thompson, the first champion of the book at Fourth Estate; and Kishani Widyaratna, who saw it through; as well as Chris Richards, at Scribner, who has been kind and considerate throughout. Thanks also to the ever patient Alex Gingell, Patrick Hargadon, and Aoife Inman at Fourth Estate, and Madison Than, Addie Gilligan and John Mark Boling at Scribner (sorry if I missed others).

My first reader (again) for everything was Sheila de Courcy. Catherine de Courcy gave brilliant advice on structuring (and everything else). Others who read the proposal, various chapters, or early drafts of the manuscript, include Jessie Hayden, Karen Alvey, Gemma Shine, Brigie de Courcy, Niamh Ni Ruairc, Phoebe Hurst, Maddy Crosti, Keith Finn, and Anna de Courcy. Kevin McGee advised me on appropriate translations of ancient Greek. My wonderful late godmother and aunt Mary (Mer) de Courcy forensically read my first book before publication, and her support over the past few years has meant so much.

A major thank you to my *Irish Times* editors, Chris Dooley, Martin Clancy, Ruadhán Mac Cormaic, Conor Goodman and Carl O'Brien. I appreciate their support when I told them

268   *Acknowledgements*

I had another book to write, and for allowing me to balance that with my other work.

To the women I met in Ukraine, including Viktoria Papushyna, Viktoriia Savelieva, and Iryna Srebrodolska, I'm very sorry that I couldn't fit in everyone's story, but I am so grateful to you for sharing what you have been through. I'm also grateful to Amy Dawson, who spoke to me about her daughter Emily and her My Wind Phone project.

In Lebanon, Nader Chams helped with some interviews and translation. In Berlin, Sabry Abouamiry helped with translation, and Ola Suliman helped with a remote translation. In Ukraine, Oleg Malakhovskyi helped with contacts and translation. Oleksandra Korotkova, during her brief visit to Dublin, inspired me to go to Ukraine in the first place.

In Mosul, Younes Qays and Noor Al-Attar helped with contacts and translation, and Ali Al-Baroodi showed me around the Old City. In Japan, Rina Motomiya was incredibly competent and patient as we travelled in the north together. Abou Fatty worked with me in the Gambia and Salifu Bai Kamara helped me ask people about love in Sierra Leone: that sadly did not make the final version of this book, but I am grateful for his assistance and friendship. Otim Alpha introduced me to northern Uganda.

Kind people who gave me accommodation at various points included Ryan Bailey, John Sweeney, Anne Doyle, Will Pollard, Phoebe Hurst, Will Dobson and Maria Jabbour. Dearbhla Walsh lent me warm clothes for a Ukrainian winter, and the Rory Peck Trust gave me a bursary for hostile environment training before I went. The Irish Arts Council gave me a literature bursary to take time off work. Dublin's libraries gave me a nice working space at an early stage to puzzle through chapter structures and transcribe interviews, and the UCD

Sutherland School of Law gave me an office to do a full read through. My first trip to Rwanda was funded by the Simon Cumbers Media Fund.

Paul Starkey very generously sent me a copy of *The Shell: Memoirs of a Hidden Observer* (which he translated), when I couldn't find one for sale. It is referenced in the Syria chapter.

I got advice and recommendations from many different people along my travels: they included George Henton, Jake Hanrahan, Johnny O'Reilly, Dan McLaughlin, Sara Cantillon, Emiko Jozuka, George Azar, and Alice McCool. Heidi Pett helped with brainstorming titles. A lot of people advised on different parts of the writing process, responded to sudden fact-checking questions, or listened to me talk extensively about the book, including Bill Hayden, Leon McCarron, Christina Lamb, Cosette Molijn, Edwin Hage, Gabriel Cooney, Matthieu Karam and Alex Perry. Kroo gave their opinion on everything from the cover to specific quotes.

Maria Talar Telfeyan and Roo (the cat) lived through the 2024 war in Lebanon with me. My reporting companions there included Fawzi Ibrahim Kleit, Ed Ram, and Raghed Waked.

I wrote much of the original proposal in John Wearing's flat in Freetown. John was a close friend and a wonderful person. I was devastated by his loss in 2024 and will continue to cherish memories of the adventures we had together. The world feels emptier without him.

Another friend, Conor Gallagher, once tried to convince me to write about the underrated beauty of platonic love. He is quoted in the chapter which references Ireland's same-sex marriage referendum – it was a joy to celebrate with him on that day. Conor sadly passed away in 2019 and we miss him still.

While researching this book, I thought often of my grandparents, who taught me so much about the importance of appreciating those close to you. I was lucky and blessed to have them in my life for so long.

Hani Alagbar both lived the 2024 war in Lebanon with me and brought me with him to Syria the day after the regime fell. His lovely family were so generous to welcome us there at such a momentous time. I am thankful for his support throughout all of this.

I dedicated this book to my family, who have supported me in immeasurable and uncountable ways throughout my life and my career. That has meant more than I could ever articulate, but I hope they know I am grateful.

Notes

Epigraph

1 Oscar Wilde, 'An Ideal Husband', 1895

Prologue

1 Albert Camus, *The Complete Notebooks*, P484, Chicago University Press, 2025
2 Elon Musk on 'The Joe Rogan Experience', 28 February 2025.
3 'Israeli strikes in Lebanon have been most intense and deadly in decades', *Washington Post*, 2 October 2024 (last accessed 8 October 2025), https://www.washingtonpost.com/world/2024/10/02/israeli-strikes-lebanon-deadliest/
4 'Overview and key findings of the 2024 Digital News Report', 17 June 2024 (last accessed 8 October 2025), https://reutersinstitute.politics.ox.ac.uk/digital-news-report/2024/dnr-executive-summary

1 Ukraine: A wartime Christmas

1 'Conflict in Ukraine's Donbas: A Visual Explainer', Crisis Group (last accessed 26 September 2025), https://www.crisisgroup.org/visual-explainers/conflict-ukraines-donbas-visual-explainer; 'MRS No. 77 – Internally displaced and immobile people in Ukraine between 2014 and 2022: Older age and disabilities as factors of vulnerability', IOM, 7 September 2023 (last accessed 26 September 2025), https://reliefweb.int/report/ukraine/mrs-no-77-internally-displaced-and-immobile-people-ukraine-between-2014-and-2022-older-age-and-disabilities-factors-vulnerability
2 'Where Ukraine is counter-attacking and the Russian's 2,000km fortification line', Reuters, 16 June 2023 (last accessed 26 September 2025), https://www.reuters.com/graphics/UKRAINE-CRISIS/MAPS/klvygwawavg/#where-ukraine-is-counter-attacking-and-the-russians-2000-km-fortification-line
3 'Seizing the Initiative in Ukraine: Waging War in a Defense Dominant World', CSIS, 12 October 2023 (last accessed 26 September 2025), https://www.csis.org/analysis/seizing-initiative-ukraine-waging-war-defense-dominant-world

4 'Ukraine Support Tracker: New aid drops to lowest level since January 2022', Kiel Institute, 7 December 2023 (last accessed 26 September 2025), https://www.kielinstitut.de/publications/news/ukraine-support-tracker-new-aid-drops-to-lowest-level-since-january-2022/

5 'As Russia Gains Confidence, a New Urgency Grips Ukraine', *New York Times*, 13 December 2023 (last accessed 26 September 2025), https://www.nytimes.com/2023/12/13/world/europe/ukraine-under-pressure-russia.html

6 'Zelenskyy issues plea for support during Washington visit as Ukraine funding stalls in Congress', Associated Press, 12 December 2023 (last accessed 26 September 2025), https://apnews.com/article/ukraine-zelenskyy-us-military-russia-8663f4d1e1b8b05828fde1c0be05686d

7 'Ukraine says 53, including 6 children, hurt in Russian missile strikes on Kyiv', Reuters, 14 December 2023 (last accessed 26 September 2025), https://www.reuters.com/world/europe/dozens-injured-kyiv-russias-second-missile-assault-this-week-ukraine-2023-12-13/

8 'Klitschko: Kyiv's population returns to pre-war level', *Kyiv Independent*, 30 December 2022 (last accessed 26 September 2025), https://kyivindependent.com/klitschko-kyivs-population-returns-to-pre-war-level/

9 *Ukraine: Enemy in the Woods*, BBC, broadcast 2 April 2025, https://www.bbc.co.uk/programmes/m001xr50

10 'Mother and Child's Desperate Run for Cover in Kyiv Ends Outside Locked Shelter', *New York Times*, 1 June 2023 (last accessed 26 September 2025), https://www.nytimes.com/2023/06/01/world/europe/russia-missiles-mother-daughter-kyiv.html

11 'U.S. intelligence assesses Ukraine war has cost Russia 315,000 casualties – source', Jonathan Landay, Reuters, 12 December 2023 (last accessed 26 September 2025), https://www.reuters.com/world/us-intelligence-assesses-ukraine-war-has-cost-russia-315000-casualties-source-2023-12-12/

12 'The Journey of the Warrior's Beloved: 2024 results', Veteran Hub (last accessed 26 September 2025), https://veteranhub.com.ua/wp-content/uploads/2025/07/the-journey-of-the-warriors-beloved.pdf

13 'Ukraine's average soldier is 43. How can they keep Putin at bay?', *The Times*, 20 January 24 (last accessed 26 September 2025), https://www.thetimes.com/world/article/ukraines-average-soldier-is-43-how-can-they-keep-putin-at-bay-zf5bqb26m?srsltid=AfmBOorIPYP-2ShhlxxPwV7XPsr229NKodQrYiUo5v-9CZtJunk-YRnm

14 '"This War Made Him a Monster." Ukrainian Women Fear the Return of Their Partners', *TIME*, 13 March 2023 (last accessed 26 September 2025), https://time.com/6261977/ukraine-women-domestic-violence/

15 Viktor 'Frenchman' Pylypenko (last accessed 26 September 2025), https://qua.community/virtual-pride/viktor-pylypenko/

16 'Lawmaker: Over 1,000 Ukrainian combat veterans commit suicide since 2014', *Kyiv Post*, 24 April 2018 (last accessed 26 September 2025) https://archive.kyivpost.com/ukraine-politics/1000-ukrainian-combat-veterans-commit-suicide-since-2014.html

2 Rwanda: Forming new families

1 Julius O. Adekunle, *Culture and Customs of Rwanda*, p.54, Greenwood Press, 2007).

2 From *Maxims and Counsels of St. Francis de Sales For Every Day of the Year*, translated by Ella McMahon, M. H. Gill & Son, 1884.

3 'Bodies Clog Rwandan River: Officials Count Hundreds of Corpses Per Day Floating Into Tanzania', *Washington Post*, 1 May 1994 (last accessed 04 October 25), https://www.washingtonpost.com/archive/politics/1994/05/02/bodies-clog-rwandan-river-officials-count-hundreds-of-corpses-per-day-floating-into-tanzania/7fd1d9a8-5d89-4b79-b0ed-1ba52be6b0be/

4 'Kwibuka20 – Amaharo Stadium – Kigali, 07 April 2014' (last accessed 4 October 2025), https://www.youtube.com/watch?v=GDamCuodDiY

5 E.g. Jeffrey Gettleman, 'The Global Elite's Favorite Strongman', *New York Times*, 4 September 2013 (last accessed 4 October 2025), https://www.nytimes.com/2013/09/08/magazine/paul-kagame-rwanda.html; Michela Wrong, *Do Not Disturb: The Story of a Political Murder and an African Regime Gone Bad*, Fourth Estate, 2021

3 Iraq: Secret weddings

1 See 'Love in Displacement', IOM, 7 November 2018 (last accessed 29 September 2025), https://iraq.iom.int/stories/love-displacement; Jenan Moussa tweet, 'Great AFP pics of mass wedding in Erbil of couples who fled Mosul', 8 April 2017 (last accessed 29 September 2025), https://x.com/jenanmoussa/status/850765832015810560

2 'Unsanctioned Suffering: A Human Rights Assessment Of United Nations Sanctions On Iraq', Center for Economic and Social Rights, May 1996 (last accessed 29 September 2025); https://www.cesr.org/sites/default/files/Unsanctioned%20Suffering%201996.pdf; 'Iraq sanctions lead to half a million child deaths', *BMJ*, 9 December 1995 (last accessed 29 September 2025), https://

www.bmj.com/content/311/7019/1523.1.full; 'Iraq's legacy of UN sanctions', 9 December 2008 (last accessed 29 September 2025), https://www.aljazeera.com/news/2008/12/9/iraqs-legacy-of-un-sanctions

3 '*New York Times:* we were wrong on Iraq', 26 May 2004 (last accessed 30 September 2025), https://www.theguardian.com/media/2004/may/26/pressandpublishing.usnews

4 'Creating Refugees: Displacement Caused by the United States' Post-9/11 Wars', Costs of War, Brown University, 21 September 2020, p.14 (last accessed 30 September 2025), https://watson.brown.edu/costsofwar/files/cow/imce/papers/2020/Displacement_Vine%20et%20al_Costs%20of%20War%202020%2009%2008.pdf; 'The Iraq war – by the numbers', NBC News, 20 March 2023 (last accessed 30 September 2025), https://www.nbcnews.com/meet-the-press/meetthepress-blog/iraq-war-numbers-rcna75762; 'Human Cost of Post-9/11 Wars: Direct War Deaths in Major War Zones', Brown University, 1 September 2021 (last accessed 30 September 2025), https://costsofwar.watson.brown.edu/paper/human-cost-post-911-wars-direct-war-deaths-major-war-zones

5 'Mosul', Arab Digest podcasts, 23 April 2021 (last accessed 8 October 25), https://podcasts.apple.com/gb/podcast/arab-digest-podcasts/id1502904460?i=1000518377902

6 https://www.rand.org/content/dam/rand/pubs/research_reports/RR1900/RR1970/RAND_RR1970.pdf

7 'Islamic State guide for female jihadists says women can marry from age nine', *Washington Post*, 5 February 2015 (last accessed 11 Feb 26) https://www.washingtonpost.com/news/worldviews/wp/2015/02/05/islamic-state-guide-for-female-jihadis-says-women-can-marry-from-age-nine/

8 'More than three million Iraqis displaced by fighting', AP via Al Jazeera, 23 June 2015 (last accessed 30 September 2025), https://www.aljazeera.com/news/2015/6/23/more-than-three-million-iraqis-displaced-by-fighting

9 'Inherent Resolve Commander Addresses Reports of Mosul Civilian Casualties', 28 March 2017 (last accessed 8 October 2025), https://www.war.gov/News/News-Stories/Article/Article/1133019/inherent-resolve-commander-addresses-reports-of-mosul-civilian-casualties/source/inherent-resolve-commander-addresses-reports-of-mosul-civilian-casualties/

10 Azmat Khan and Anand Gopal, 'The Uncounted', *New York Times*, 16 November 2017 (last accessed 30 September 2025), https://www.nytimes.com/interactive/2017/11/16/magazine/uncounted-civilian-casualties-iraq-airstrikes.html; 'Mosul is a graveyard: Final IS battle kills 9,000 civilians', AP, 21 December 2017 (last accessed 30 Sep 25), https://apnews.com/article/middle-east-only-on-ap-islamic-state-group-bbea7094fb954838a2fdc11278d65460

11 'International airstrikes and civilian casualty claims in Iraq and Syria: March 2017', 13 April 2017 (last accessed 30 September 2025), https://airwars. org/research/international-airstrikes-and-civilian-casualty-claims-in-iraq- and-syria-march-2017/

12 'Romance returns to Iraq's war-torn Mosul', AFP via France24, 14 February 2018 (last accessed 30 September 2025), https://www.france24.com/en/ 20180214-romance-returns-iraqs-war-torn-mosul

13 https://www.rferl.org/a/every-man-in-mosul-ordered-to-grow-a-beard/ 26985105.html

4 Uganda: Radical forgiveness

1 bell hooks, 'All About Love: New Visions', Harper, 1999.

2 'Joseph Kony's first exclusive interview (clip)', Vimeo (last accessed 28 Sep- tember 2025), https://vimeo.com/8617828

3 'Witnessing *Ongwen*: A Betrayal of Expectations?', *Journal of International Criminal Justice*, 4 September 2024 (last accessed 28 September 2025), https://academic.oup.com/jicj/advance-article/doi/10.1093/jicj/mqae029/ 7749304

4 'Uganda: UK government is neglecting the victims of Africa's longest run- ning war', Oxfam, 30 November 2005 (last accessed 28 September 2025), https://reliefweb.int/report/uganda/uganda-uk-government-neglecting- victims-africas-longest-running-war

5 Patrick Wegner, *A Genocide in Northern Uganda? – The 'Protected Camps' Policy of 1999 to 2006* (last accessed 28 September 2025), https://justiceincon- flict.org/2012/04/09/a-genocide-in-northern-uganda-the-protected- camps-policy-of-1999-to-2006/

6 'UN urges end to Ugandan "horror"', BBC, 22 October 2004 (last accessed 28 September 2025), http://news.bbc.co.uk/2/hi/africa/3943677.stm

7 The Bitter Root', Chad Clendinen, 2021, https://www.imdb.com/title/tt15089136/

8 David also told his story in the short film 'The Bitter Root' (last accessed 28 September 2025), https://vimeo.com/678489138

9 'The Amnesty Act, 2000' (last accessed 28 September 2025), https://mia. go.ug/sites/default/files/resources/The%20Amnesty%20Act%2C%202000. pdf; Kasper Agger, 'The End of Amnesty in Uganda: Implications for LRA Defections', Enough Project, August 2012 (last accessed 9 Oct 25), https:// www.enoughproject.org/files/GuluDispatch.pdf

10 'Whose Justice? Perceptions of Uganda's Amnesty Act 2000: The Potential for Conflict Resolution and Long-Term Reconciliation', Refugee Law

Project Working Paper No. 15 (last accessed 28 September 2025), https://au.int/sites/default/files/documents/39191-doc-146._whose_justice_perceptions_of_ugandas_amnesty_act_2000._the_potential_for_conflict_resolution_and_long-term_reconciliation.pdf

11 'The Government of Uganda, the ICC Arrest Warrants for the LRA Leaders and the Juba Peace Talks: 2006–2008', 5 December 2013 (last accessed 28 September 2025), https://papers.ssrn.com/sol3/papers.cfm?abstract_id=2363595

5 Ghana: Love under siege

1 For a timeline of legal developments, see the Human Dignity Trust page for Ghana (last accessed 3 October 2025), https://www.humandignitytrust.org/country-profile/ghana/

2 'No Choice but to Deny Who I Am: Violence and Discrimination against LGBT people in Ghana', Human Rights Watch, 2018, p. 23 (last accessed October 3, 2025), https://www.hrw.org/sites/default/files/report_pdf/ghana0118_web.pdf

3 See 'How a US group with links to the far-right may have influenced a crackdown on Ghana's LGBTQ community', CNN, 8 October 2021 (last accessed October 2, 3035), https://edition.cnn.com/2021/10/08/africa/ghana-lgbtq-crackdown-intl-cmd/index.html; 'Homophobia in Africa: The American far-right's footprint', *Deutsche Welle*, 15 March 2024 (last accessed 3 October 2025), https://www.dw.com/en/lgbtq-in-africa-how-the-us-far-right-whips-up-homophobia/a-68562333; Haley McEwen, *The U.S. Christian Right and Pro-Family Politics in 21st Century Africa*, Palgrave Macmillan, 2023

4 'Top Ghanaian doctors use misinformation to train nurses in "conversion therapy"', openDemocracy, 28 July 2022 (last accessed October 3, 2025), https://www.opendemocracy.net/en/5050/ghana-anti-lgbtiq-bill-conversion-therapy-training-doctors/

5 'Promotion of Proper Human Sexual Rights and Ghanaian Family Values Bill, 2021', Duty to report, 5(1) and 5(2) (last accessed 3 October 2025), https://cdn.modernghana.com/files/722202192224-0h830n4ayt-lgbt-bill.pdf

6 Some have been lightly edited for length and clarity.

7 'Ghana's homophobia problem | The Listening Post', Al Jazeera, 28 July 2022 (last accessed 3 October 2025), https://www.youtube.com/watch?v=mwehMvElwRs

8 'Exclusive: US Christian Right pours more than $50m into Africa', openDemocracy, 29 October 2020 (last accessed October 3, 2025), https://www.opendemocracy.net/en/5050/africa-us-christian-right-50m/

9 'US Christian right group hosts anti-LGBT training for African politicians', 27 October 2020 (last accessed 3 October 2025), https://www.

opendemocracy.net/en/5050/us-christian-right-group-hosts-anti-lgbt-training-african-politicians/

10 'Ghana Should Resist World Congress of Families' Anti-LGBT Message', Human Rights Watch, 31 October 2019 (last accessed 3 October 2025), https://www.hrw.org/news/2019/10/31/ghana-should-resist-world-congress-families-anti-lgbt-message

11 Stephen O. Murray and Will Roscoe, eds., *Boy Wives and Female Husbands: Studies in African Homosexualities*, 1998, p. 268, https://soar.suny.edu/bitstream/handle/20.500.12648/1714/9781438484099.pdf; 'Same-sex relationships and recriminalisation of homosexuality in Ghana: A historical analysis', *Sociolinguistic Studies*, August 2023, p. 50 (last accessed 3 October 2025), https://www.researchgate.net/publication/372983360_Same-sex_relationships_and_recriminalisation_of_homosexuality_in_Ghana_A_historical_analysis

12 'Eric Gyamfi presents "Just like Us"', Magnum Foundation (last accessed 3 October 2025), https://vimeo.com/205078188?fl=pl&fe=ti

13 'Just Made a Queer Memory? Drop a Pin', *New York Times*, 25 June 2023 (last accessed 3 October 2025), https://www.nytimes.com/2023/06/25/style/queering-the-map-lucas-larochelle.html

14 'LGBTQI Ghana: LGBTQ+ #Ghanagetsbetter campaign launch as police arrest 22 lesbian wedding suspects', BBC, 31 March 2021 (last accessed 3 October 2025), https://www.bbc.com/pidgin/world-56586865

6 Nigeria: motherly love and acts of bravery

1 'Global Terrorism Index 2015: Measuring and Understanding the Impact of Terrorism', Institute for Economics & Peace, 17 November 2015 (last accessed 26 September 2025), https://reliefweb.int/report/world/global-terrorism-index-2015-measuring-and-understanding-impact-terrorism

2 'Our job is to shoot, slaughter and kill: Boko Haram's reign of terror in northeast Nigeria', Amnesty International, 2015, pp. 4, 48–9 (last accessed 26 September 2025), https://www.amnesty.org/fr/wp-content/uploads/2021/05/AFR4413602015ENGLISH.pdf

3 'Nigeria regional conflict: ten-fold increase in number of children used in "suicide" attacks', Unicef, 12 April 2016 (last accessed 26 September 2025), https://www.unicefusa.org/press/nigeria-regional-conflict-ten-fold-increase-number-children-used-suicide-attacks

4 'Nigeria: huge displacement and humanitarian crisis require urgent life-saving and protection measures', OHCHR, 29 August 2016 (last accessed 26

September 2025), https://www.ohchr.org/en/press-releases/2016/08/nigeria-huge-displacement-and-humanitarian-crisis-require-urgent-life-saving
5 'International Day of the Disappeared: Whereabouts of almost 14,000 children in Nigeria remain unknown', ICRC, 30 August 2022, https://www.icrc.org/en/document/international-day-disappeared-whereabouts-almost-14000-children-nigeria-remain-unknown
6 'They Didn't Know if I Was Alive or Dead', Human Rights Watch, 10 September 2019 (last accessed 26 September 2025), https://www.hrw.org/report/2019/09/10/they-didnt-know-if-i-was-alive-or-dead/military-detention-children-suspected-boko
7 'Nigeria: Babies and children dying in military detention', 11 May 2016 (last accessed 26 September 2025), https://www.amnesty.org/en/latest/news/2016/05/nigeria-babies-and-children-dying-in-military-detention/; ' "If you see it, you will cry": Life and death in Giwa Barracks', Amnesty International, 2016 (last accessed 26 September 2025), https://www.amnesty.org.uk/files/if_you_see_it_you_will_cry_0.pdf
8 'Finding Nigeria's Forgotten Mass Graves Through Satellite Data', HumAngle, 18 September 2023 (last accessed 26 September 2025), https://humanglemedia.com/finding-mass-graves/
9 Andrew Walker, 'Join us or die: the birth of Boko Haram', *Guardian*, 4 February 2016 (last accessed 26 September 2025), https://www.theguardian.com/world/2016/feb/04/join-us-or-die-birth-of-boko-haram
10 Hilary Matfess, 'Boko Haram: History and Context', 26 October 2017 (last accessed 26 September 2025), https://oxfordre.com/africanhistory/display/10.1093/acrefore/9780190277734.001.0001/acrefore-9780190277734-e-119?p=emailAEafCb1xfGcIY&d=/10.1093/acrefore/9780190277734.001.0001/acrefore-9780190277734-e-119
11 'VOA Interview: Mother of Boko Haram Leader Speaks Out', 14 June 2018 (last accessed 26 September 2025), https://www.voanews.com/a/voa-interview-mother-of-boko-haram-leader/4438375.html
12 Vincent Foucher, 'Last Words of Abubakar Shekau: A Testament in the Politics of Jihadi Extraversion', *Materials & Fieldwork in African Studies*, 2021 (last accessed 26 September 2025), https://shs.hal.science/halshs-03447170v2/document

7 Lebanon: Crimes in the name of love

1 'Israel/Lebanon Out of all proportion – civilians bear the brunt of the war', Amnesty International, 2006 (last accessed 9 October 2025), http://news.bbc.co.uk/2/shared/bsp/hi/pdfs/21_11_06_amnesty.pdf; 'Israel's lessons in Lebanon:

Two invasions failed to defeat Hezbollah and Palestinian militias', *El Pais*, 31 October 2023 (last accessed 9 October 2025), https://english.elpais.com/international/2023-10-31/israels-lessons-in-lebanon-two-invasions-failed-to-defeat-hezbollah-and-palestinian-militias.html

2 'Lebanon Public Finance Review', World Bank Group, July 2022 (last accessed 27 September 2025), https://thedocs.worldbank.org/en/doc/1f10124 70cef4e4e5d3080dc5ceda3c4-0280012022/original/mena-lebanon-Public-Finance-Report-Ponzi.pdf

3 'Mapping the Damage From the Beirut Explosion', *New York Times*, 4 August 2020 (last accessed 27 September 2025), https://www.nytimes.com/interactive/2020/08/04/world/middleeast/beirut-explosion-damage.html; 'They Killed Us from the Inside': An Investigation into the August 4 Beirut Blast', Human Rights Watch, 3 August 2021 (last accessed 27 September 2025), https://www.hrw.org/report/2021/08/03/they-killed-us-inside/investigation-august-4-beirut-blast

4 'Lebanon split into two time zones in row over daylight saving', 26 March 2023, Associated Press, via the *Guardian* (last accessed 27 September 2025), https://www.theguardian.com/world/2023/mar/26/lebanon-split-into-two-time-zones-in-row-over-daylight-saving

5 'Armed man takes hostages at Beirut bank demanding return of frozen funds', CNN (last accessed 27 September 2025), https://edition.cnn.com/2022/08/11/middleeast/lebanon-bank-hostages-beirut-intl; 'Robin Hood in Hamra? Bank hostage taker leaves in custody after hours-long standoff', 11 August 2022 (last accessed 27 September 2025), https://today.lorientlejour.com/article/1308257/armed-man-holding-employees-and-citizens-hostage-in-hamras-federal-bank.html

6 'A man took hostages at a bank in Lebanon. People came to support him', *Washington Post*, 11 August 2022 (last accessed 27 September 2025), https://www.washingtonpost.com/world/2022/08/11/man-took-hostages-bank-lebanon-crowds-came-support-him/

7 'Man who took hostages demanding his own money becomes public hero in Lebanon', *Guardian*, 11 August 2022 (last accessed 27 September 2025), https://www.theguardian.com/world/2022/aug/11/gunman-takes-hostages-at-beirut-bank-to-try-to-free-his-trapped-savings

8 'Joint statement by Dr Tedros Adhanom Ghebreyesus, WHO Director General, and Dr Ahmed Al Mandhari, Regional Director for the Eastern Mediterranean, on Lebanon', WHO, 19 September 2021 (last accessed 27 September 2025), https://www.emro.who.int/media/news/joint-statement-by-dr-tedros-adhanom-ghebreyesus-who-director-general-and-dr-ahmed-al-mandhari-regional-director-for-the-eastern-mediterranean-on-lebanon.html

9   'Man "Robs" Bank to Withdraw His Own Money', VICE, 26 January 2022 (last accessed 27 September 2025), https://www.vice.com/en/article/5dg59n/lebanon-man-robs-bank-to-withdraw-his-own-money

10 'On the run, Lebanese woman who stole own savings says she's not the criminal', Reuters, 22 September 2022 (last accessed 27 September 2025), https://www.reuters.com/world/middle-east/run-lebanese-woman-who-stole-own-savings-says-shes-not-criminal-2022-09-21/; 'Lebanon's "Wonder Woman" in hiding after bank heist', Al Jazeera, 21 September 2022 (last accessed 27 September 2025), https://www.aljazeera.com/features/2022/9/21/lebanons-wonder-woman-in-hiding-after-bank-heist

11 Tweet on 14 September 2022 (last accessed 27 September 2025), https://twitter.com/GeorgesHSiam/status/1569979919278477313

12 'Lebanese banks declare three-day closure over security concerns', Arab News, 16 September 2022 (last accessed 27 September 2025), https://www.arabnews.com/node/2163721/%7B%7B

13 'Former Lebanese ambassador holds sit-in at Beirut bank amid new wave of heists', 4 October 2022 (last accessed 27 September 2025), https://edition.cnn.com/2022/10/04/middleeast/lebanon-ambassador-beirut-bank-heists-intl/index.html

14 'Israel warns can send Lebanon "back to Stone Age" as UN seeks de-escalation', Al Jazeera, 27 June 2024 (last accessed 27 September 2025), https://www.aljazeera.com/news/2024/6/27/israel-warns-can-send-lebanon-back-to-stone-age-as-un-seeks-de-escalation

15 'Lebanon says Israeli GPS jamming confounding ground, air traffic', AFP via France24 (last accessed 27 September 2025), https://www.france24.com/en/live-news/20240702-lebanon-says-israeli-gps-jamming-confounding-ground-air-traffic

8 Syria: A quest for justice

1   'Former Syrian prisoners detail horrific conditions', MSF, December 13 2024 (last accessed February 13 2026), https://www.doctorswithoutborders.org/latest/former-syrian-prisoners-detail-horrific-conditions

2   'SNHR's 12th Annual Report on Enforced Disappearance in Syria on the International Day of the Disappeared: Enforced Disappearance is an Ongoing Crime in Syria', 30 August 2023 (last accessed 27 September 2025), https://snhr.org/blog/2023/08/30/snhrs-12th-annual-report-on-enforced-disappearance-in-syria-on-the-international-day-of-the-disappeared-enforced-disappearance-is-an-ongoing-crime-in-syria/

3 'The Arabic Word Thakla Speaks to Gaza's Grief. There's No English Equivalent', *TIME*, 1 November 2023 (last accessed 27 September 2025), https://time.com/6330481/thakla-grief-gaza-israeli-airstrikes/

4 'Files from Aleppo intelligence facility show extent of Assad repression', *Washington Post*, 14 December 2024 (last accessed 27 September 2025), https://www.washingtonpost.com/world/2024/12/14/aleppo-prisoners-syria-assad/

5 Sam Dagher, *Assad or We Burn the Country: How One Family's Lust for Power Destroyed Syria*, Little, Brown, 2019

6 'Civilian Death Toll', SNHR, 30 August 2024 (last accessed 27 September 2025), https://snhr.org/blog/2024/08/30/civilian-death-toll/

7 'Syrian detainees' families forced to pay huge bribes to corrupt officials – report', *Guardian*, 4 January 2021 (last accessed 27 September 2025), https://www.theguardian.com/world/2021/jan/04/how-syria-uses-prison-to-extort-money-report-arrest-funding-assad-regime

8 'Syria: Index condemns murder of Raqqa is Being Slaughtered Silently journalist', Index on Censorship, 1,7 December 2015 (last accessed 27 September 2025), https://www.indexoncensorship.org/2015/12/index-condemns-murder-of-rbss-journalist/

9 'Briefing to the UN Security Council by Wafa Mustafa', Syria Campaign, 23 July 2020 (last accessed 9 October 2025), https://diary.thesyriacampaign.org/briefing-un-security-council-wafa-mustafa/

10 'Closing statement for witness and plaintiff Hussein Gherir before Koblenz Court', 10 January 2022 (last accessed 27 September 2025), https://dlockyer.wordpress.com/2022/01/10/koblenz_trial-closing-argument-for-witness-and-plaintiff-hussein-gherir-i-fled-out-of-fear-of-disappearing-again-syria-enforced_disappearance-part-25/

11 '"They were torturing to kill": inside Syria's death machine', *Guardian*, 1 October 2015 (last accessed 27 September 2025), https://www.theguardian.com/world/2015/oct/01/they-were-torturing-to-kill-inside-syrias-death-machine-caesar

12 'Documentation of 72 Torture Methods the Syrian Regime Continues to Practice in its Detention Centres and Military Hospitals', SNHR, 21 October 2019 (last accessed 27 September 2025), https://snhr.org/wp-content/pdf/english/Documentation_of_72_Torture_Methods_the_Syrian_Regime_Continues_to_Practice_in_Its_Detention_Centers_and_Military_Hospitals_en.pdf

13 See 'Syria's Disappeared: The Case Against Assad' (last accessed 27 September 2025), https://www.youtube.com/watch?v=zkpeKOGv2Wg; 'If the

Dead Could Speak', 16 September 2015 (last accessed 27 September 2025), https://www.hrw.org/report/2015/12/16/if-dead-could-speak/mass-deaths-and-torture-syrias-detention-facilities

14 'Missing people in the Syrian Arab Republic: Report of the Secretary-General', 2 August 2022 (last accessed 27 September 2025), https://documents-dds-ny.un.org/doc/UNDOC/GEN/N22/447/69/PDF/N2244769.pdf?OpenElement)

15 'General Assembly Adopts Resolution Establishing Independent Institution on Missing Persons in Syria, as Speakers Debate Text's Merit', 29 June 2023 (last accessed 27 September 2025), https://press.un.org/en/2023/ga12514.doc.htm

16 'Colombia: UN Committee releases visit report with roadmap to combat enforced disappearances', April 30 2025 (last accessed February 13 2026), https://www.ohchr.org/en/press-releases/2025/04/colombia-un-committee-releases-visit-report-roadmap-combat-enforced#:~:text=A%20critical%20structural%20issue%20highlighted,providing%20reparation%20to%20the%20families.

17 See 'Chain of command behind atrocities at Syria's most notorious prison Sednaya revealed', report by the Association of Detainees and the Missing of Sednaya Prison, 3 October 2022 (last accessed 27 September 2025), https://www.admsp.org/en/chain-of-command-behind-atrocities-at-syrias-most-notorious-prison-sednaya-revealed/; 'Syria: Human slaughterhouse: Mass hangings and extermination at Saydnaya Prison, Syria', 7 February 2017 (last accessed 27 September 2025), https://www.amnesty.org/en/documents/mde24/5415/2017/en/

9 Japan: Love after death

1 *Haiku: Eastern culture*, Reginald Horace Blyth, p177, 1949, The Hokuseido Press.

2 From *Sophocles: The Theban Plays*, translated by E. Watling, Penguin, 1947

3 'Rikuzentakata destroyed by tsunami', Al Jazeera English, 14 March 2011 (last accessed 29 September 2025), https://www.youtube.com/watch?v=dT3pAXYMTC4

4 'Ten Years After the Tsunami', NASA Earth Observatory (last acccessed 29 September 2025), https://earthobservatory.nasa.gov/images/148036/ten-years-after-the-tsunami

5 Great East Japan Earthquake, Japan Reconstruction Agency (last accessed 29 September 2025), https://www.reconstruction.go.jp/english/topics/GEJE/

6 Justin McCurry, 'Japan tsunami survivor Hiromitsu Shinkawa found 10 miles out at sea', *Guardian*, 13 March 2011 (last accessed 29 September 2025), https://www.theguardian.com/world/2011/mar/13/japan-tsunami-survivor-shinkawa-rescued-fukushima

7 *Japanese Death Poems*, compiled by Yoel Hoffmann, 1986, p. 28

8 Anna Xygkou, Panote Siriaraya, Alexandra Covaci, Holly G. Prigerson, Robert Neimeyer, Chee Siang Ang, and Wan Jou She, 'The "Conversation" about Loss: Understanding How Chatbot Technology was Used in Supporting People in Grief', in CHI'23: ACM CHI Conference on Human Factors in Computing System, 23–28 April 2023, DOI:10.1145/3544548.3581154

9 'Suicide prevention strategies in Japan: A 15-year review (1998–2013)', *Journal of Public Health Policy*, October 2014 (last accessed 29 September 2025), https://www.researchgate.net/publication/267735217_Suicide_prevention_strategies_in_Japan_A_15-year_review_1998-2013

10 T. Hara, 'The Ghosts of Tsunami Dead and Kokoro no kea in Japan's Religious Landscape', *Journal of Religion in Japan* 5(2), January 2016, pp, 176–98, DOI:10.1163/22118349-00502002

Epilogue

1 Letter from Vincent van Gogh to Theo van Gogh, Arles, *c.* 17 September 201888 (last accessed 3 October 2025), https://www.webexhibits.org/vangogh/letter/18/538.htm#:~:text=You%20are%20kind%20to%20painters,do%20without%20art%20and%20artists

2 Evacuation warning posted by an IDF spokesman, 27 November 2024 (last accessed 26 September 2025), https://x.com/AvichayAdraee/status/1861548368188633440

3 'WHO declares loneliness a "global public health concern"', *Guardian*, 16 November 2023 (last accessed 26 September 2025), https://www.theguardian.com/global-development/2023/nov/16/who-declares-loneliness-a-global-public-health-concern; WHO Commission on Social Connection description on website (last accessed 26 September 2025), https://www.who.int/groups/commission-on-social-connection

4 'The Anti-Social Century', *The Atlantic*, 8 January 2025 (last accessed 26 September 2025), https://www.theatlantic.com/magazine/archive/2025/02/american-loneliness-personality-politics/681091/

5 'The "Need for Chaos" and Motivations to Share Hostile Political Rumours', *American Political Science Review*, 17 February 2023 (last accessed 26 Feb 25),

https://www.cambridge.org/core/journals/american-political-science-review/article/need-for-chaos-and-motivations-to-share-hostile-political-rumors/7E50529B41998816383F5790B6E0545A

6 'Our Epidemic of Loneliness and Isolation: The U.S. Surgeon General's Advisory on the Healing Effects of Social Connection and Community', 2023 (last accessed 26 September 2025), https://www.hhs.gov/sites/default/files/surgeon-general-social-connection-advisory.pdf